W0246728

PUFFIN BOOKS

A CHILDREN'S HISTORY OF INDIA IN 100 OBJECTS

Devika Cariapa trained as an archaeologist but found her calling uncovering stories from stones, making the world of archaeology accessible for children.

An award-winning author, her first book *India through Archaeology: Excavating History* was awarded the Sahitya Akademi's Bal Sahitya Puraskar 2019 and the Hindu Young World-Goodbooks Award 2018. Her subsequent works have been awarded the Neev Book Award for Distinguished Children's Literature 2021 and have been shortlisted for the *Times of India* AutHer Awards 2022 and the Neev Book Award 2022.

When she's not writing, Devika enjoys exploring the art of calligraphy. She is a professional loiterer, often found wandering around monuments or between the shelves of Bangalore's marvellous independent bookstores.

Priyanka Tampi is an illustrator, animator, storyteller, and an amateur poet. All her years of creative work have involved everything from commissioned illustrations to music videos and animated reels, and it's been a thrilling ride!

To all those long-gone creative souls whose work remains
an eternal testament to human ingenuity and skill.

A CHILDREN'S HISTORY OF INDIA IN 100 OBJECTS

DEVIKA CARIAPA

Illustrations by Priyanka Tampi

PUFFIN BOOKS

An imprint of Penguin Random House

PUFFIN BOOKS

USA | Canada | UK | Ireland | Australia
New Zealand | India | South Africa | China | Singapore

Puffin Books is part of the Penguin Random House group of companies
whose addresses can be found at global.penguinrandomhouse.com

Published by Penguin Random House India Pvt. Ltd
4th Floor, Capital Tower 1, MG Road,
Gurugram 122 002, Haryana, India

First published in Puffin Books by Penguin Random House India 2023

Text copyright © Devika Cariapa 2023
Illustrations copyright © Priyanka Tampi 2023

All rights reserved

10 9 8 7 6 5 4

The statements and views expressed in this book are the author's own. Every effort has
been made to make this book as accurate as possible. However, this book should serve
only as a general guide and not as an ultimate source of the subject information. The
author and publisher bear no liability or responsibility towards any loss or damage
incurred, or alleged to have been incurred, directly or indirectly, on account of the
information contained in this book. All maps and sketches in the book have been created
solely for explaining the author's views in this book, and must be viewed as such. The
boundaries, topographical and geographical features depicted therein, whether historical
and contemporary, are neither purported to be correct nor authentic by Survey of India
directives. No part of this book intends to hurt or cause offence to any individual,
community, region, linguistic identity, caste, religion, or gender.

ISBN 9780143452423

Book design and layout by Isha Nagar and Samar Bansal
Typeset in Futura Round by Manipal Technologies Limited, Manipal

Printed in India at Acme Print O Pac. Pvt. Ltd. Noida

This book is sold subject to the condition that it shall not, by way of
trade or otherwise, be lent, resold, hired out, or otherwise circulated
without the publisher's prior consent in any form of binding or cover
other than that in which it is published and without a similar condition including this
condition being imposed on the subsequent purchaser.

www.penguin.co.in

❧ Contents ❧

CONTENTS

CONTENTS

❧ Introduction ☙

Our ancestors certainly knew how to leave a mark! The trail of objects and treasures they left behind are testament to their creativity and resourcefulness. Today, we can see some of their handiwork enduring in ancient stone tools, fragments of pottery, fine sculpture, or in lustrous art painted on dark cave walls centuries ago. However, often these objects seem mysterious and inaccessible. Every now and then we get a glimpse of them, possibly displayed behind the locked glass cases of a museum, but they seem silent, their stories unknown.

Why, then, are they considered so significant?

Archaeologists and historians call these treasures 'material remains'. Smaller, movable remains are known as artefacts. Immovable remains, such as structures, are known as features. Since these material remains belong to a time and place far removed from our own, it is not always easy to figure out their original purpose. So, scholars have to study them carefully to find clues to what they were made for or how they were used. In doing this, they are able to use these objects from the past to reveal unique, often untold, stories about people of the time and how they lived.

There are different ways of getting information from an object.

One way is to ask questions about the object itself. Who made it, when, and for what purpose? Where was it found? Has it travelled away from its place of origin? Was it always used for the same purpose for which it was made? Tiny seals from the Harappan civilization of the third millennium BCE, for example, were found in faraway Mesopotamia, speaking of contact between the two peoples and of merchants and sailors who braved the long journey from the Indian subcontinent to establish trade and cultural connections.

Another way is to look at objects as time capsules that reflect the period in which they were made. The same Harappan seals capture a moment in time, revealing information about the craft skills, literacy, beliefs, and the everyday lives of the people of a civilization going back more than 4000 years!

Whatever the method used, the study of objects offers a richer understanding of history through all the various contexts they present.

In this book, we will discover stories from Indian history traced through 100 objects, charting a roughly chronological course from prehistoric times to our present, modern nation. The objects are wide-ranging, from moveable artefacts to immovable features, but what they have in common is that they have been conceived by the human imagination and shaped by the human hand. Each carries an account of how people on the Indian subcontinent lived, interacted, and transformed. Each embodies the values and choices of a specific time in our history. They have been chosen from all parts of our huge subcontinent, reflecting, as much as possible, our diverse people and their varied cultures.

I hope these stories will spark your imagination and help you discover a whole new way of looking at the past. Once you have read them, perhaps your next trip to a museum or an ancient monument will take on an exciting dimension in which you will be able to explore and question our rich material culture. And, in doing so, you may become aware that history is not distant, but is, in fact, all around us.

Time: A Rough Guide

When you see the letters BP placed after a date, it refers to years 'Before Present'. The present in question is not the year we live in but the fixed reference year—1950. This year was chosen because it was around this time that radiocarbon dating was invented. The term BP is generally used to refer to dates in the very distant past.

For more recent times, there is BCE and CE.

BCE or Before Common Era was formerly known as BC or Before Christ. It goes backward from the assumed year of the birth of Jesus Christ.

CE or Common Era is the term formerly known as AD or Anno Domini, which is Latin for 'the Year of Our Lord'. It goes forward from the assumed year of the birth of Jesus Christ.

The new terms came about as the world decided not to reference one particular religious figure but have a more neutral dating system.

A small c. before a date is short for circa, which means approximately. This is used when historians are not quite sure of the exact date.

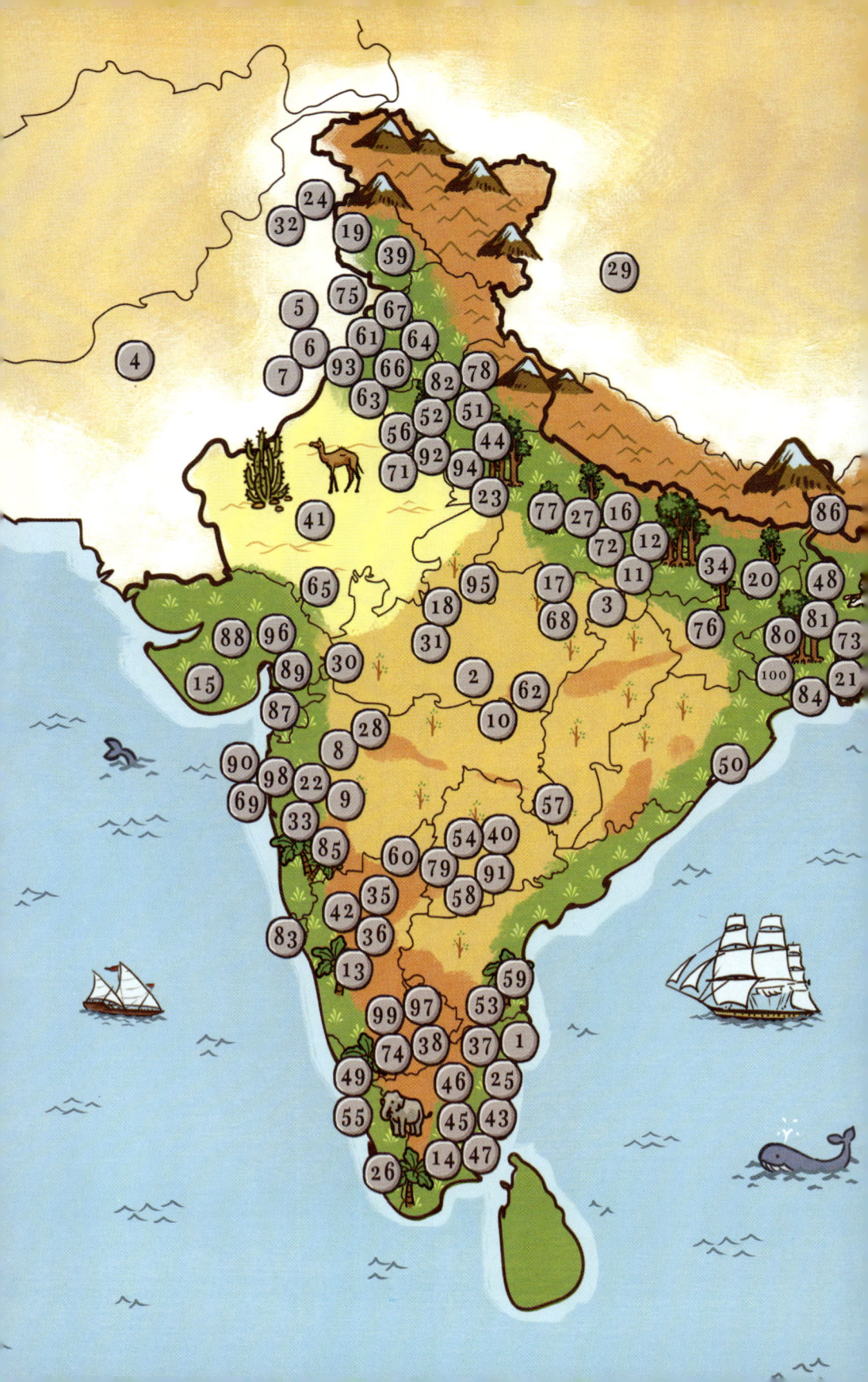

LOCATING THE 100 OBJECTS

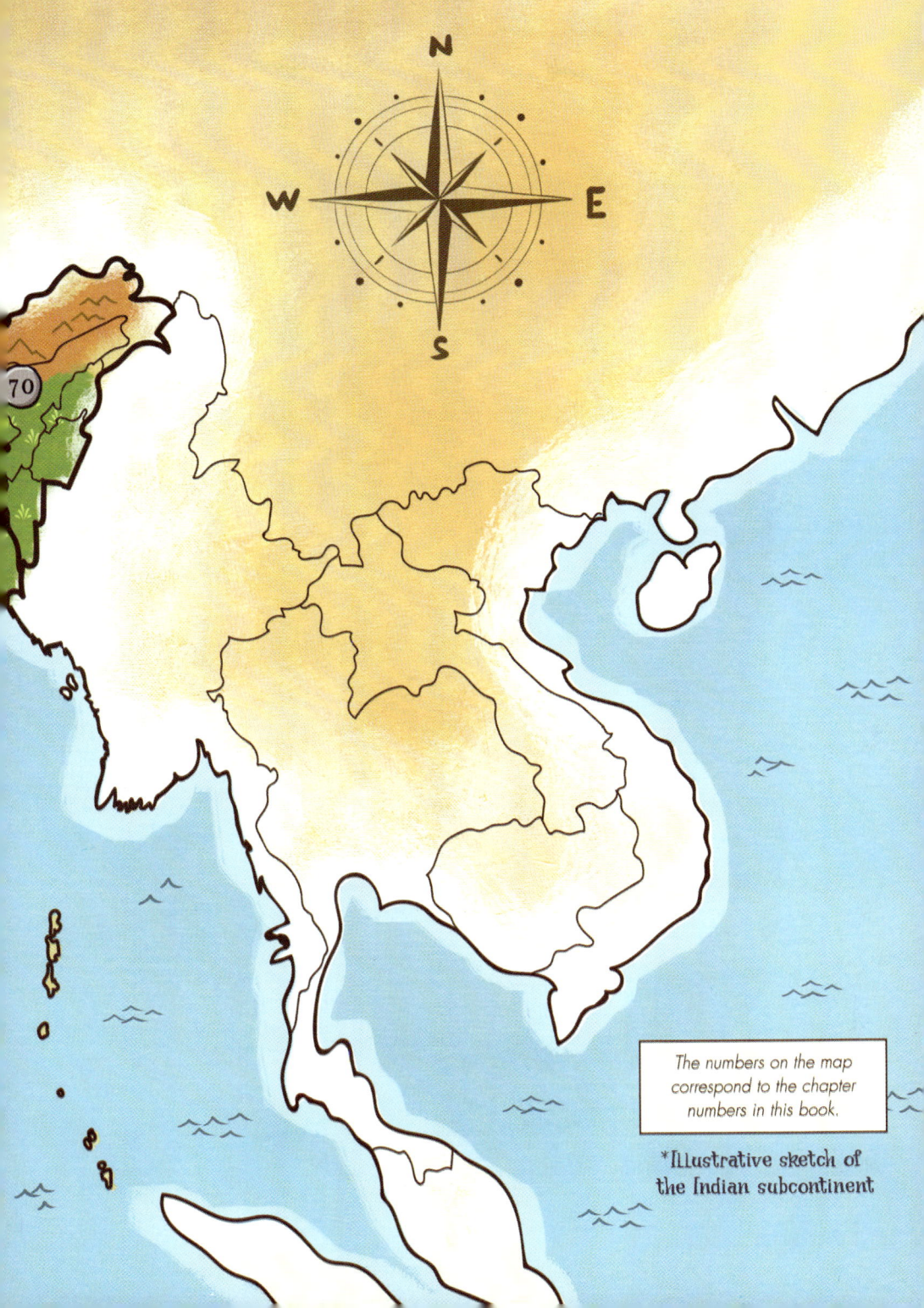

70

The numbers on the map correspond to the chapter numbers in this book.

*Illustrative sketch of the Indian subcontinent

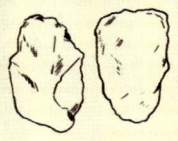

1

Tools from the Stone Age

Stone Hand axe, Pallavaram, Tamil Nadu, c. half a million years BP
Stone Cleaver, Attirampakkam, Tamil Nadu, c. one and a half million years BP

When you visit the museum where they are displayed, it is very likely you may not even notice these two chunks of stone. They are quite small, probably no bigger than your palm, and look rather uninteresting. And yet, archaeologists consider these to be key artefacts in reconstructing the story of human life in India.

In the illustration on the next page, the piece on the left once lay at the bottom of a gravel pit in Pallavaram, near Chennai. It would have gone unseen, probably lost forever, if not for an extraordinary man named Robert Bruce Foote. In 1863, the young officer of the Geological Survey of India was working in the area when some irregularly shaped stones in the gravel pit attracted his attention. He began to sift through the soil in the pit when he found this piece. And right away, he knew that this was no ordinary stone.

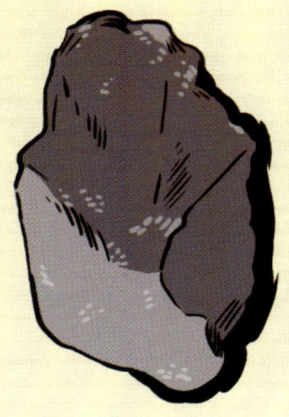 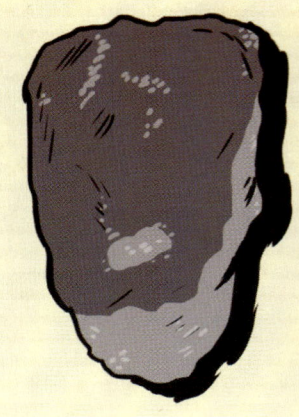

Stone Hand Axe, Pallavaram   *Stone Cleaver, Attirampakkam*

It was roughly flaked on either side and had a broad, rounded bottom at one end and a sharpened edge tapering to a point at the other. Foote was a keen student of the newly emerging subjects of human prehistory and evolution. He had studied similar pieces that had recently emerged from sites in Europe and Britain which were thought to be hundreds of thousands of years old, based on the geological deposits in which they were found. Foote realized that the object he held in his hand was, in fact, a prehistoric hand axe, crafted by early humans!

A few months later, Foote and a fellow geologist were walking along a dried-up river bed near Attirampakkam village, not far from Chennai, when they spotted a whole heap of the same kind of carefully worked stone tools. These included the piece on the right in the illustration—a cleaver. They belonged to what archaeologists called the Palaeolithic, or Old Stone, age (Palaeo means old and lithos means stone), the part of history before writing existed.

Everything we know today about prehistoric people comes from the objects they made and used that have survived to this day. Archaeologists call them artefacts. We know they had to survive by hunting animals, fishing, and gathering plants, roots, seeds, and tubers. To help with these rather difficult tasks, they fashioned stone tools that would enable them to dig, scrape, cut, and pierce. They started out with basic chopping tools made with single pebbles and then gradually learnt how to make finer, more efficient tools out of small flakes and blades, which were probably mounted on wooden or bone handles or spear shafts. Since bone and wood are perishable, only the remains of their stone tools have survived the test of time.

Enthused by these finds, Foote went on to discover more than 450 prehistoric stone-age sites in south India. The stone tools he found and documented were the first recorded evidence of early human life in the Indian subcontinent. Modern-day dating methods had still not been invented in 1863. So, in order to estimate the approximate age of these tools, Foote used the principle of stratigraphy (that is, the deeper a tool is buried, the older it is). Bone fossils of ancient or extinct animals that were found along with the stone tools also provided a clue to their age.

The site of Attirampakkam is still being excavated today and has thrown up many important discoveries. Recently, archaeologists found a set of animal hoof prints and the fossilized teeth of horses and water buffaloes, suggesting this arid place was once a lush lake environment where groups of people would have gathered to make tools and to hunt. They made smaller and more sophisticated tools that have now been dated using state-of-the-art techniques. Based on all this work, archaeologists have now come to the exciting conclusion that Foote's hand axe could be about half a million years old and the cleaver an astonishing one and a half million years old!

2

The Early Human of Hathnora

Prehistoric fossil skull, Hathnora, Madhya Pradesh, c. 250,000 BP

On a winter's day in 1982, Arun Sonakia of the Geological Survey of India walked along the banks of the Narmada river, near Hathnora village in the Indian state of Madhya Pradesh. For weeks, Sonakia and his team had been scouring the pebbly gravel layers of the riverbank for evidence of prehistoric human activity. So far, they had only found a number of stone tools in the area. These were mainly flake tools chipped off large stones and pebbles which were then deliberately fashioned into oval or pear-shaped hand axes with sharp cutting edges.

Based on shape and size, archaeologists concluded that they belonged to the late Acheulian style. This style of toolmaking was believed to have begun as far back as one and a half million years ago in Africa. The style was first associated with *Homo erectus*, an ancestor of the modern human species of *Homo sapiens*, generally thought to have inhabited the earth from around 1.8 million to 200,000 years ago. These human ancestors would have used such tools to chop and dig, cut bone, scrape skin or bark, and make spears for hunting.

Also embedded along these gravel layers, they found fragments of fossil bones of long extinct animal species. Among them were the *Stegodon*, a giant cousin of the modern elephant, wild dog, boar, hippopotamus, and ostrich eggshells. These were wild creatures that early humans once shared the land with and possibly hunted for food.

But there were other questions that palaeontologists—or experts that study fossils—in India were asking. Who were the creators of these tools? Were they the first inhabitants of the Indian subcontinent? Where did these early humans come from? How had they come here? What did they look like? These questions could be answered only if human fossils, that is, the remains of ancient human skeletons, could be uncovered. Till 1982, despite their best efforts, palaeontologists had found none.

According to genetic evidence, it appears that humans today are descended from waves of *Homo sapiens* that migrated from Africa nearly 125,000 years ago and fanned out to Europe, Asia, and the Indian subcontinent, finally reaching the Americas about 18,000 years ago. Puzzlingly, stone tools that are almost one million years old have also been found in India. Had ancient human species been here before the *Homo sapiens* migrations from Africa? The absence of human fossils meant that palaeontologists could not accurately identify the toolmakers themselves.

But that day, as Sonakia's eyes swept carefully over the river beds, he saw an amazing sight. Embedded in the gravel was a fossilized piece of a human skull. Sonakia had made the discovery of the century. This piece, as illustrated on the next page, was a part of the skull of a short-statured woman, about thirty years old. Finally, a glimpse of the earliest inhabitants of the Indian subcontinent! Sonakia named her *Homo erectus narmadiensis* and believed her to be about 500,000 years old. However, scholars now believe the Hathnora skull is a very early form of *Homo sapiens*, might even be male and possibly dates back to around 250,000 years ago. A few years later, the fossilized rib and collar bones of another ancient human were found in the same layer of gravel.

Technically, a skull is not an object. An object or artefact is typically something that is shaped by the human hand. But the Hathnora skull was the first prehistoric fossil of a human ancestor found in South Asia and occupies a very important place in the study of Indian history. It represents the people who mark the beginning of that history. And its discovery has encouraged palaeontologists to keep exploring, hopeful of finding more human fossils, which will enable them to reconstruct the story of the people who first occupied the Indian subcontinent.

The Hathnora Skull

3

Sacred Stones

Triangular stone in the middle of
a rubble circle, Baghor, Madhya Pradesh,
c. 9000 BCE

Discovering stone tools was a big step in helping archaeologists understand how prehistoric people lived. A closer examination of these tools gave them insights into how early humans were able to hunt and gather food; the implements they invented to make their tasks easier; how far they travelled to get suitable raw materials for these tools; the places they chose to live in; and how they constantly moved from place to place in search of food and water sources.

It appears they also shared their ideas and information with each other to help survive an environment which could often be harsh or dangerous. And even though it seems like they had no time for anything other than survival, now there are clues that show us otherwise!

On the walls of some of the caves and rock shelters that these early people occupied, archaeologists discovered remarkable paintings. Galleries of them filled with vibrant groups of stick figures hunting animals, fishing, gathering honey and fruit, cooking, looking after children, and even dancing. Prehistoric rock paintings, some dating back as far as 10,000 years, have been found all over India, with the largest concentration at Bhimbetka, Madhya Pradesh. These detailed scenes from the lives of people who lived long ago are evidence that ancient people did not just survive, but, in fact, they laughed, shared, and celebrated. So, it looks as if survival was not their only concern.

Then, archaeologists excavating the palaeolithic site of Baghor at the foot of the Kaimur hills in Madhya Pradesh unearthed something very unusual. They found the remains of a circular rubble platform. In the centre was a small piece of natural stone with a peculiar pattern of concentric triangles in varying shades of red and yellow. Looking around, they discovered nine more stone fragments with the same distinctive pattern. Much to their delight, the pieces fitted together perfectly like a jigsaw puzzle to form the triangular stone illustrated on the facing page. These archaeologists believed that the unique, colourful stone had been deliberately placed in the middle of this stone circle around 9000 BCE by a group of palaeolithic hunter gatherers.

Circular Rubble Platform

What did this mean?

When they began to explore the areas surrounding Baghor, the archaeologists found to their surprise that the people of the Kol and Baiga tribes who live in the area today make similar circular rubble platforms! They even look out for the same colourful stones with concentric triangular patterns to place in the centre, which they then worship as a symbol of a mother goddess. Numerous other present-day local shrines had similar patterned stones on rubble platforms which were worshipped as a form of a goddess. It seemed that they were following a tradition practised thousands of years ago by groups of early people who first occupied these lands.

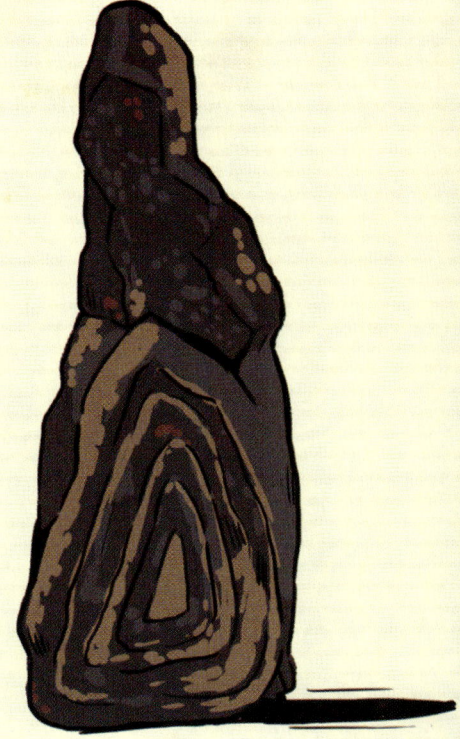

The Triangular Stone of Baghor

Based on this evidence, scholars now believe the triangular stone of Baghor is one of the earliest objects with a divine or spiritual significance that has been discovered on the Indian subcontinent. It is also a sign that these groups of early people were not just concerned about physical survival but were able to reflect and wonder about the world around them.

4

Sickles for the Harvest

Flint blades set in bitumen, Mehrgarh, Balochistan, c. 8000 BCE

In the late 1970s, some tiny flint blades were found in Mehrgarh, an archaeological site of the Indian subcontinent situated in the Bolan valley of Baluchistan, in what is now Pakistan. The site, occupied from around 7000 BCE to around 2000 BCE, is located on an important route connecting Iran and the mountainous valleys of Afghanistan with the Indus valley. This route is believed to have been used by traders, nomadic tribes, and migratory animals for thousands of years.

These flint blades, many of them just a few centimetres long as you can see in the illustration on the facing page, were set slantwise in bitumen or natural tar, and would once have been attached to a wooden handle, forming a sickle. Sickles are curved tools used to harvest tall grain crops or to cut grass.

The sickle fragments were excavated from the lowest and, hence, earliest, level of the Mehrgarh dig and are thought to be about 8000 years old. Archaeologists were excited to find them because they were evidence of probably the first farmers in South Asia.

We know that humans had occupied the Indian subcontinent from almost one and a half million years ago. They were nomadic hunter-gatherers, always moving either in search of water sources or following animal migrations or seasonal plants for food. Around 12,000 years ago, changing weather patterns around the world led to a warmer climate and the formation of more grasslands. There was a sudden increase in the number of grass-eating animals like deer, goats, sheep, and cattle. At the same time, grain-bearing grasses like rice, wheat, and barley sprung up in plenty. Early humans began to consider new ways of finding food.

These groups of people began to think about growing wild, grain-bearing plants for themselves. They observed the behaviour of animals, looking out for those they could tame and herd. Hunter-gatherers were gradually turning into farmers. Leading a farming way of life meant that people had to stay in one place and watch over their animals and their crops. Since they could not wander around as much as they did previously, they began to live in small village settlements.

Mehrgarh was one such settlement—one of the earliest villages on the subcontinent. Archaeologists have found evidence of barley and wheat grains in the lower layers of the site, millets in the upper layers, and even the earliest evidence of cotton cultivation in South Asia! The sickles would have been used for harvesting these crops, very much like farmers still do in many parts of India.

The lower layers of the site also had boar and antelope bones while the upper levels had large numbers of goat, sheep, and cattle bones. This meant that while they still hunted wild animals, over time, they had managed to tame and herd domesticated ones as well. The people of Mehrgarh lived in rectangular, multi-room mudbrick houses and buried their dead near their habitations. They made beautiful crafts, beads, pots, and clay human figurines. Some of the materials they used, such as shell and turquoise, were sourced from faraway places. They made mortar and pestle sets to grind grain and constructed granaries to store their excess grains. There is even evidence that they practised an early form of dentistry, using drills to deal with cavities! In the later phases, they discovered the use of copper and began to make copper implements.

Scholars had once wondered how the sophisticated cities of the Harappan civilization had sprung up quite suddenly in the Indus valley, beginning around 3000 BCE. They now see the developments at Mehrgarh as a sort of link between the early wandering hunter-gatherers and the evolution of the earliest cities of the subcontinent.

Recent excavations have uncovered evidence of early rice cultivation along the Ganga basin in central India as well. In Lahuradewa, Uttar Pradesh, the charred grains of a domesticated variety of rice have been dated to over 7000 years ago.

The Mehrgarh sickle tells us that early humans were transitioning to a whole new way of life, from nomadic hunter-gatherers to the more settled existence of food producers.

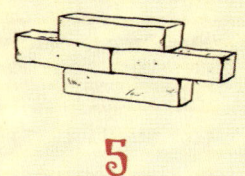

5

The Beguiling Brick

Baked brick, Harappa, Indus Valley, c. 3200 BCE onwards

How did a humble mud brick change the telling of Indian history?

It all started in 1856, when railway engineers of the British Raj were laying down a railway track between Lahore and Multan, two cities in the Punjab province of current-day Pakistan. As the workers dug high earthen mounds near a village named Harappa, they began to unearth hundreds of baked bricks. They were beautifully made and, surprisingly, all of uniform size. Delighted with their find, the contractors hauled off cartloads of them. Little did they know the bricks they were so freely using for ballast on the newly laid railway tracks were thousands of years old and dated back to one of the most ancient civilizations in the world!

There had been signs earlier hinting that Harappa was probably a very ancient city. From its earthen mounds, early nineteenth-century adventurers and explorers had reported the discovery of tools, ancient pottery, and seals with pictures of animals and strange writing on them. Archaeologists had not paid much attention to these artefacts. At the time,

historians relied mostly on religious texts like the Vedas and Puranas and the accounts of foreign travellers to piece together the history of India. Based on these writings, they believed Indian history could be traced back to around 1200 BCE with the arrival of groups of people from Eurasia. These people spoke an Indo-Aryan language and proceeded to settle down in the areas around the River Ganga.

The discovery of the Harappan bricks was the first sign that underneath lay something much more ancient than was previously believed.

Meanwhile, at around the same time as the railway engineers made off with their ready-made bricks in Harappa, almost 600 kilometres away, at the Mohenjodaro site, located in the Sind district, archaeologists began to dig up heaps of the same material. The bricks were identical to those found at Harappa, as skillfully made, moisture proof, and, puzzlingly, all sized in length, width, and height in the perfect ratio of 4:2:1! This was definitely something that required more investigation. Serious excavations then began at both sites.

What emerged, stunned the archaeologists. Beneath the rubble mounds were the remains of ancient human occupation. But these were no makeshift villages. These were planned cities with perfectly laid-out roads, neatly built mud-brick houses and public buildings and probably the first urban sanitation system ever. There was evidence that the people of these settlements carried out overland and coastal trade with Mesopotamia which is in present-day Iraq and with other places that are now in Oman and the Persian Gulf. And most interestingly, they also had a written script.

As for the bricks, they were obviously made by skilled hands at first. Later, they began using moulds to shape them, an astonishingly advanced technology for the time. The brick buildings, massive walls, dockyards, and huge fortifications were built solidly, with bricks laid in alternating rows of long and short sides. This is a technique that gives the maximum load-bearing strength to the wall and is still used in modern construction. The surprisingly consistent proportions of each individual mud brick led scholars to believe they were manufactured under the supervision of a central authority which made sure all bricks were made to a standard size and were of a certain quality. All of which meant that these cities were once inhabited by very sophisticated people.

In 1924, when John Marshall, the Director General of the Archaeological Survey of India, made the dramatic announcement of the discovery of the Indus Valley Civilization (later called the Harappan Civilization, after the first city that was discovered), the world was astounded. Harappa and Mohenjodaro were more than 4500 years old, with their earliest settlements dating back as far as 3200 BCE, making these Indus settlements contemporaries of the ancient civilizations of Egypt and Mesopotamia.

This ordinary-looking baked mud brick was the clue that pushed back the beginning of Indian history by more than 2500 years!

6

Travelling Seals

Inscribed steatite, a Harappan site, Indus Valley, c. 2600 BCE

A tiny square stone, this Harappan seal is not more than a few centimetres big. But it certainly reveals an amazing amount of information. In the early years of the twentieth century, when archaeologists started excavating the sites of Harappa and Mohenjodaro along the River Indus, seals were among the first objects that they found.

However, the first of these seals was found way back in 1872, long before Harappa and Mohenjodaro had been discovered. A seal, almost exactly like this one, was found near the village of Harappa, in the Punjab province of what is now Pakistan. It was handed over to Alexander Cunningham, the then Director General of the Archaeological Survey of India. He was quite mystified and declared, 'The most curious object discovered at Harappa is a seal . . . The seal is a smooth black stone without polish. On it is engraved very deeply a bull, without a hump, looking to the right, with two stars under the neck. Above the bull there is an inscription in six characters, which are quite unknown to me. They are certainly not Indian letters; and as the bull which accompanies them is without a hump, I conclude that the seal is foreign to India.'

He was wrong about it being foreign, of course, and later excavations revealed one of the greatest river valley civilizations in the world.

Since then, thousands of these stone seals have appeared at Harappan sites. Most of them are about the size of a postage stamp, made of soapstone, and then heated to give them a shiny surface. They are skilfully carved in intaglio or sunken engraving. Which means that when the seals were pressed into wet clay, they left a raised impression of the carved images on the clay.

Most of the seals feature a single large animal in profile—bulls, antelopes, tigers, elephants, crocodiles, rhinoceros, and even a mysterious one-horned creature described as a unicorn that you can see in the seal illustrated below. Many animal seals even feature a thoughtfully placed feeding trough. Other seals depict human figures and plants that may have carried some spiritual meaning.

Above the picture motif is usually a line of symbols or pictograms which scholars are still trying to decipher. It is an exciting thought that not only could this turn out to be one of the earliest scripts in the world, but also that many of the Harappan people could have been literate.

A Harappan Seal and Its Clay Impression, Featuring the Mysterious Unicorn

The important question is, what were these seals used for? They seem to have had multiple uses, most of them linked to trade. Merchants used them as personal brand tags, pressing them onto moist clay tags called sealings. The imprinted tags were used to seal ropes that held together sacks of grain or clay jars full of oil before they were loaded onto trading boats. The motifs and symbols were probably the names of the merchants or workshops that created them. Intact seals ensured the goods were not tampered with. Some seals have rounded projections at the rear through which a thread could have been strung. They may have been worn as amulets or necklaces by well-to-do merchants, priests or other important people, almost like identity cards. Some may have been used as currency.

More than three thousand seals have been found across Harappan sites, ranging from Pakistan to northern and western India. Some have even been found in the ancient cities of Mesopotamia (present-day Iraq), Central Asia and the Persian Gulf, proving that the Harappans were part of a network of long-distance trade.

This tiny seal speaks about art, writing, trade, beliefs, and language, as well as the rich, artistic, and adventurous lives of the Harappans. Today, it is probably the most distinctive artefact from the Harappan civilization.

7

A Sliding Monkey Toy

Hand-modelled terracotta figurine, Mohenjodaro, Indus Valley, c. 2500 BCE

The little terracotta monkey that you see on the next page was once a toy. It was designed to slide up and down a small wooden stick to entertain a little Harappan child more than 4000 years ago! And it tells us something very interesting about the Harappan people.

After the discovery of Harappa and Mohenjodaro in the 1920s, archaeologists went on to discover a wealth of information on the Harappan people. All the way from Afghanistan, across Pakistan, to Jammu, Gujarat, and Maharashtra in India, they recorded the remains of numerous towns and cities that belonged to a once great 4000-year-old river valley civilization. At its height, the Harappan Civilization would have covered more than a million square kilometres with a population estimated at over five million. Suddenly, an ancient civilization to match those of Egypt and Mesopotamia had been unearthed!

What did these archaeologists find?

What stood out the most from these finds was an extremely sophisticated form of city planning. The Harappan cities were methodically planned

with rows of neat, brick houses featuring attached bathrooms and indoor plumbing, broad streets and well-made public buildings, such as large baths, granaries, and dockyards. They found evidence of a rich and varied diet, flourishing agriculture, great artistic skill with crafts like pottery and bead-making, thriving inland and overseas trade in a network that covered places in Central Asia and the Middle East and a formal writing system. The Harappans made implements of bronze and copper and loved to dress up in stylish jewellery and clothes.

Despite being scattered across a huge area, archaeologists were fascinated that the Harappan pottery, beads, seals, weights, and bricks were all almost identically made. This would have required a whole lot of control and coordination. Scholars wondered who had made the rules. Since there was no evidence of grand palaces and royal tombs akin to those in Egypt, it was unlikely they were ruled by kings and queens. Some believe the Harappans were probably controlled by a central authority of some kind, maybe a group of wealthy merchants or priests, who decided how things were to be done.

So, we know quite a lot about how the Harappa people lived.

But what were these people *really* like?

The climbing monkey toy helps us understand a little bit more about the Harappans.

This object is one of thousands of toys excavated from Harappan sites. Other toys found include pull-along clay carts, terracotta tops and balls, marbles, bird-shaped whistles, board games, and rattles. There are a variety of tiny clay animals, like bulls with nodding heads, squirrels, and cheerful-looking dogs with collars. There are miniature kitchen sets and furniture, ivory and terracotta board-game counters, clay marble mazes, and a remarkably modern-looking six-sided dice. A number of small clay discs have also been found which are believed to have been used to play *pithu* or *lagori*, a game that is still widely played in India today but with flat stones, where clay discs are piled up and hit with a ball.

It appears that amidst their busy lives of building, trading, producing food, and making beautiful crafts, the Harappans also remembered to enjoy themselves. Keep in mind that, unlike the mass-produced toys of today, each of these pieces must have been carefully handcrafted by an artist or potter, possibly with their children helping them. The attention to detail and the beauty of the sliding monkey show not only great imagination and artistic skill but also reveals an expression of affection for the child for whom it was made. The object suggests that the Harappans were perhaps light-hearted and fun-loving. After all, they cared enough for their children to spend the time and effort involved in making these beautiful toys.

Scholars believe many more Harappan sites are yet to be discovered. Hopefully, more such objects will appear, giving us a deeper insight into the lives of the Harappans.

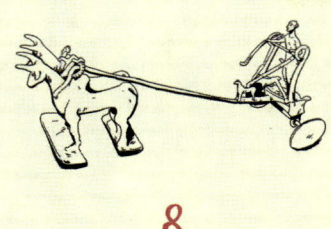

8

The Bronze Charioteer

Bronze figure, Daimabad, Maharashtra, c. 1800 BCE

The man in the object you see on the next page looks like he's having fun. He is no bigger than a toothbrush, standing on a two-wheeled chariot, yoked to two bulls. In one hand, he holds the bar of the chariot tightly, while, in the other, he clutches a long, curving whip. Eyes wide open, hair neatly tied back in a bun, chin jutting, and knees bent, he is accompanied by his faithful dog, perched on the bar in front of him. Both seem set for a joyride.

This rather remarkable figure was one of a small stash of bronze objects found by a Bhil farmer in Daimabad village, Maharashtra, while he was digging up the base of a shrub. He found three other objects—an elephant, a rhinoceros, and a water buffalo—all of them standing on four-wheeled platforms. They were heavy, weighing almost sixty kilograms in all, and beautifully cast. Although they did not come out of an archaeological site, later excavations in the area led archaeologists to believe that these bronze objects dated back to a time when the Harappan cities were slowly going into decline.

Who made these figures and what were they for? Were they deliberately buried or naturally covered by centuries of soil and dust?

To answer these questions, we have to go back a bit, to 1870. Two young shepherds watching over their herd in the village of Gungeria, Madhya Pradesh, chanced upon a curious metal object sticking out of the earth. While digging it out, they were astounded to discover a huge hoard of copper and silver objects. There were over four hundred pieces, together weighing over 300 kilograms, buried in the earth! Soon, more such hoards began to appear all over the Ganga–Yamuna doab—the rich, fertile land between the two rivers. More than a hundred hoards, groups of copper articles ranging from a few pieces to over forty, were dug up subsequently. There were harpoons, spearheads, axes, swords, and strange, flat figures that seemed to represent humans. Some of these copper hoards, as they were called, were found in present-day West Bengal, Odisha, and Haryana.

Mysteriously, none of the hoards were found at an actual archaeological site. They seem to have been buried independently, almost as if the owners wished to hide them. Based on the quality of the metal, the style of the artefacts and the type of pottery sometimes found along with the hoards, archaeologists generally agreed they could be dated to around 1500 BCE. But since they were never associated with the remains of settlements, scholars could not agree on who had made these artefacts or who had buried them, or even if these could have been two different sets of people.

Some insist these hoards were buried by refugees before they fled west, as the once-great Harappan cities began to fall apart due to changing climates and rivers drying up. Others believe they were made by the Indo-Aryan speakers referred to in the Rig Veda who came sweeping down the northern plains just as the Harappan Civilization was declining.

Some suggest these objects were the skilled work of indigenous tribes that had inhabited the area since a time even before either of these groups appeared.

Lately, studies of the objects have revealed something even more mysterious. Many of the objects, although skillfully cast, were not really meant to be used! The long, elegant swords were paper thin and would have bent easily. Solid axe heads were completely blunt and showed no evidence of having been used at all. Deadly-looking metal harpoons with sharp tangs were unnaturally large and of little practical use. Most scholars now believe the metal objects were made and buried for religious or ritual purposes. The wheeled Daimabad bronze chariot may have been used as part of a procession carried out for such a ritualistic practice.

Meanwhile, there is exciting news. Recent excavations at Sanauli, Uttar Pradesh, have revealed a huge burial site or necropolis, with over 116 burials dated to the late Harappan phase around 2000–1800 BCE. The bodies were buried in legged wooden coffins that were sheathed in copper and accompanied with elaborate copper grave goods that echo the style of the copper hoards—swords, torches, helmets, shields, and jewellery. Plenty of clay pots were found and, most spectacularly, the remains of two full-sized chariots that would have once been decorated with thin sheets of shining copper!

With these discoveries, we may be closer than ever to identifying the skillful makers of those beautiful but mystifying bronze and copper hoards.

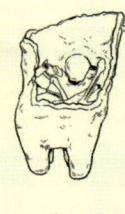

9

Man in a Clay Jar

Human burial, Inamgaon, Maharashtra, c. 1000 BCE

When archaeologists first found this strange clay jar that you see in the illustration, they were puzzled. The jar looks like a rather stout person with a big belly standing on four short legs. Inside, they were startled to find the seated skeleton of a man! He was about forty years old, in a rather cramped position with his knees drawn up against his body and his chin pressed against his chest. He was buried, seated like this, in the clay jar almost 3000 years ago!

The jar had been buried in the courtyard of a large five-roomed house in the site of Inamgaon, Maharashtra. Inamgaon was part of a complex of almost 100 sites found in the river valleys of present-day Maharashtra and northern Karnataka that were occupied by the earliest farming communities of the Deccan region. The excavations at Inamgaon have revealed fascinating details of the lives of these early farmers.

From about 1600 BCE onwards, they settled in the area, making their neat little rectangular mud houses with courtyards for their cattle and kitchens with fire pits. They grew barley, wheat, and rice in fields that

were watered by irrigation canals. Although they kept goats, sheep, and pigs, they also hunted wild animals and fished in the river nearby.

Based on the objects found in the houses, scholars believe one section of the settlement would have housed only artisans. These were craftspeople who made pottery, beads, lime, and ornaments of various kinds. They worked mainly with stone tools, but they knew how to make copper implements too—axes, knives, and fish hooks. To obtain copper, traders had to travel long distances to the nearest known sources of the metal, in areas now in Rajasthan. There, they would offer their pottery and beads in exchange for copper ingots. Their trade network included groups of hunter-gatherers from whom they sourced forest produce and even the later Harappans, who supplied them with exotic stones and shells.

In the centre of town, in bigger and better built houses, lived the well-to-do and the more prosperous farmers. It was here, in one of the largest houses with an attached granary, that they discovered the man in the clay jar.

Who was he and why had he been buried in this manner?

More than 200 burials were uncovered at Inamgaon, and they turned up some interesting information about these lively, farming people. All the burial pits were dug into the floors of the houses and courtyards. Most of them were of tiny children, encased in pots placed mouth-to-mouth. Adults were placed in an extended position, many of them didn't have feet. It is believed this was because they did not want their spirits wandering around! Some of the burials had clay vessels and beads placed in them for the use of the dead.

A study of the skeletons revealed, although they all seemed to eat well with plenty of grains, animal, fish, and dairy, those in the central part of town seemed to have better nutrition than those living in the outlying areas. The little children suffered from many deficiencies and adults lost their teeth fairly early in life. Over time, their living conditions changed, but their burial practices did not, indicating they had developed certain deep-rooted beliefs and traditions that they did not wish to change.

As for the man in the jar, since he seemed to have been singled out for a special burial, it appears he was important, perhaps a chief, a religious figure, or a clan head. It is hard to say since this was the only burial of its kind. But it certainly gives us an exciting insight into the lives of these prehistoric farmers and their unique practices that were so different from what we know of previous groups.

10

Fiery Forge

Clay brick metal-smelting furnace, Naikund, Maharashtra, c. 700 BCE

If you think the object in the illustration looks like a *chulha* or cooking furnace, you are not wrong. Only this particular hearth was used to cook—not food, but iron! It was found by excited archaeologists among the remains of a metal-working workshop at Naikund, a site in present-day Maharashtra.

What was so exciting about a metal-smelting furnace?

Smelting is the process of applying heat to a solid metal ore until it melts and a pure base metal can be extracted. The process required a furnace capable of reaching high temperatures.

It is believed ancient Indians discovered the use of iron more than 5000 years ago, when nuggets of meteoric iron were melted in their copper-smelting furnaces to make the occasional, precious object. But it was another 2000 years before they began to use iron as a more common metal of choice for making objects of everyday use. This change marked the beginning of the Iron Age.

Excavations at Naikund, on the banks of the River Pench, threw up some very interesting information. Archaeologists have found evidence of a thriving agricultural community dated to around 800 BCE. The people there grew rice, barley, and lentils and, like the early farmers of Inamgaon, they kept herds of cattle, sheep, and goat while continuing to hunt wild animals. But there were a few surprises.

Horses made a sudden appearance. As did a whole range of iron implements like knives, axes, hoes, chisels, nails, clamps, fish hooks, cauldrons, bangles, and even nail parers! And weapons like swords, daggers, spears, and arrowheads. Unlike the peaceful Harappans and the folks at Inamgaon, the inhabitants of Naikund seemed equipped for battle.

Life seemed to have changed, and death seemed to have changed too. Because, instead of in-house burials like those of Inamgaon, the people of Naikund took their dead away across the river to a barren area. There, they were buried with iron weapons, beautifully made black-and-red pottery vessels, and bead necklaces for their use in the afterlife. Some of the dead were even accompanied by their horses, which were buried in full regalia of elaborate copper and iron ornaments. Nearby, burial sites even had rather dramatic evidence of violent deaths—skeletons of men with arrowheads and spearpoints still embedded in their chests! The burials were marked by a circle of huge stones known to scholars as megaliths, from the Greek megas (great) and lithos (stone).

The increased use of iron seemed to have coincided with a time of major change as larger population groups looked for places to settle down and grow their own food. Iron implements were sturdier than copper, helping to clear and cultivate land. They also made for better weapons that were useful when hostile neighbours or cattle raiders attacked. And tough iron implements were able to carve out those megaliths used as burial markers. All of these were important clues to changing lifestyles, beliefs, and cultural lives.

Interestingly, at around the same time, settlements of people with similar ideas began to pop up all over, from Kashmir and north-eastern India to Madhya Pradesh and Maharashtra, with a particularly large concentration of them in the south, areas that are now located within the states of Tamil Nadu, Karnataka, and Kerala. They all seemed to have been familiar with the use of iron.

Which is why the iron-smelting furnace at Naikund was such a thrilling find. It was discovered in pieces. Within the remains of a workshop were the small, curved bricks of its chimney and parts of a cylindrical terracotta pipe used to blow air into the furnace. Scattered around were scraps of iron ore and coal, required to feed the furnace to temperatures as high as 1534°C and chunks of slag, the waste product that remains when pure iron is extracted from ore. Based on these pieces, archaeologists were able to reconstruct the original look of the furnace and gather information on how these people quarried ore, the smelting and smithy techniques they used, and the composition and purity of the iron.

Centuries later, Indian ironsmiths gained fame the world over for their great metallurgical skills, from the bafflingly rust-resistant Iron Pillar of Delhi to the wootz steel of southern India, which travelled to the world as Damascus steel, fashioning some of the most famous fighting swords in history. The techniques for these marvels were refined over the centuries and probably began with this fiery little furnace at Naikund.

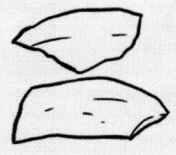

11

Glistening Black Pottery

Broken pottery, Ganga Valley, c. 500 BCE

These gleaming black potsherds, or broken pieces of pottery, once formed part of an exquisite pot made somewhere in the Ganga river valley around 500 BCE. The pot would have been wheel-thrown, made with finely worked clay and very thin, giving off a pleasing metallic twang when struck. But the most striking feature of the pot is revealed in these pieces you see in the illustration—the deep, glossy black finish. Potsherds like these were first unearthed by archaeologists at excavations in Sarnath, near present-day Varanasi, and at Takshashila or Taxila, in what is now Pakistan.

Believing it was found only in the north, archaeologists named this type of pottery Northern Black Polished Ware or NBPW for short. But later, they discovered NBPW in many other parts of India and even in Bangladesh and Sri Lanka! Archaeologists also noticed it came in a variety of colours, including brown, red, and deep blue. Bowls, dishes, cooking *handis* or pots, vases, and lidded jars were all made with so much care and attention to detail that scholars believe they would have been expensive even then and, hence, rather exclusive.

You may wonder, why the fuss over a few broken bits of pottery?

Pottery is one of the oldest arts. Humans first learned how to shape coils of wet clay into vessels for storage. Sun baking and then firing made the vessels waterproof and, hence, useful for storage of grains and water. Storage was important for survival, especially in times of shortage. And luckily, fired clay does not perish, so it can be used to date various periods of history using methods such as carbon dating. This is why pottery is an important source to examine and understand the past.

As far back as Harappan times, wheel-made pottery was common. The Chalcolithic farmers in central India even buried their dead in gigantic ceramic pots.

So, what is so special about NBPW?

NBPW is associated with a most interesting period, one that shaped almost all of the history that followed.

In the first millennium BCE, the Ganga–Yamuna doab was a time of hectic activity. For centuries, people had been moving to these densely forested, marshy lands between the two major rivers in northern India.

Some were refugees. Floods, earthquakes, and changing river courses sent entire populations from the once-thriving Harappan cities fleeing to the east in search of safer places in which to settle down.

Others were smaller groups of people speaking an Indo-Aryan language. They came through the north-west mountain passes of the Himalayas searching for fresh pasture for their large herds of cattle. They brought with them horses and sacred hymns in old Sanskrit, which they carefully committed to memory and recited as they moved towards the Ganga valley.

At first, they set up small agricultural settlements called Janapadas, which literally means the land where the *jana* (people) set their *pada* (foot), and settled down. These were tribal republics with elected chiefs. But, by the sixth century BCE, things began to change dramatically.

The changes may have begun with the new iron tools these groups made. The implements were hardy, helping them clear forests much quicker. They were also useful to plough fields more effectively. Agriculture became so successful that there was plenty of extra produce to sell in the market towns that began to spring up around this time. Many people no longer had to grow their own food and were free to specialize in crafts of their choice—like weaving, pottery, and metal work—or to become traders and merchants, exchanging these goods.

Others cleverly grabbed the chance to become leaders, taking the surplus food and redistributing it, becoming rich and powerful through the taxes they collected for doing this job. They hired officials and armies and issued silver coins. They guarded the trade routes to the north-west and southern India. With increasing prosperity, they became more ambitious, using force to grab other Janapadas, merging them into larger states called Mahajanapadas.

Religious texts such as the Buddhist Sutta Pitaka and the Jain Bhagavati Sutras name sixteen great Mahajanapadas, including some that become familiar to us later on, such as Gandhara, Kasi, Kosala, and Magadha.

New wealth was poured into Mahajanapadas, which in turn led to the rise of big cities. Excavations at ancient capital cities like Kaushambi and Rajgir show they were fortified with enormous brick walls and deep moats filled with dangerous creatures to fend off jealous enemies. The cities were well-planned, with big brick houses, sophisticated drainage systems, terracotta ring wells, and soakage pits. All these would have needed enormous resources and labour to build.

Somewhere amidst the buzz of these great new cities, potters spun out the glossy black pottery on their wheels. NBPW is commonly found in most of the Mahajanapadas, almost like a trademark of the cities of the day. It was refined luxury ware, made for the wealthy who could afford it. Merchants carried them along the new trade routes, making sure they were available far and wide in India's first kingdoms.

12

From Prince Siddhartha to the Buddha

Multi-panelled stone sculpture, Sarnath, Uttar Pradesh, c. 400–500 CE, depicting events from 566 BCE onwards

More than 2500 years ago, when the first city-states and small kingdoms were forming in the Ganga valley, a male child named Siddhartha was born at Lumbini near Kapilavastu, now in southern Nepal. Siddhartha was a prince, born to the chief of the Shakya clan. The multi-panelled sculpture shown in the illustration, although made almost a thousand years after Siddhartha's death, recounts in detail some of the main events of his life.

Who was this prince, and why was his life important enough to be remembered in sculpture so many years later?

The formation of the Mahajanapadas or the first city-states on the subcontinent brought about great social and economic change. Society was now more complex, with people trying out all sorts of new professions and ways of living. There were priests and rulers, warriors and traders, craftspeople and farmers, herders and fisherfolk. For possibly the first time, there were marked social differences with some becoming very rich and others who remained quite poor.

During this period, priests composed the later Vedas, providing people with guidance on how to live their lives and outlining the rituals necessary for a meaningful existence. The Upanishads were also being compiled, with deep questions relating to the meaning of life, death, rebirth, and what, if any, was the true meaning of life.

The priests decided to organize people into *varnas* or groups based on their occupation—priests were Brahmanas, warriors were kshatriyas, traders and farmers were called vaishyas, and the lowly—those who were excluded from almost everything except serving the other three groups—were called shudras. As time passed, these divisions gradually turned oppressive, imposing an unreasonable belief that a person's varna was solely determined by birth, thereby restricting individuals to the professions practiced by their forefathers.

These new rules and ideas were not accepted by everyone. At this time, many thinkers emerged who tried to understand the changes around them, each in their own way. They looked at things differently. Travelling far and wide on the new trade routes that were opening up, they gathered in groups, discussing and debating on a whole range of questions, trying to convince others of their way of understanding the world.

It was in this atmosphere of changing ideas that Siddhartha was born. Based on texts written almost a hundred years after his death, we know that despite growing up within the sheltered walls of a luxurious palace, the young prince managed to catch glimpses of the suffering in the world outside. These instances had a deep impact on him, which is why he decided to leave his family, giving up his royal life, to search for the true meaning of life. He wore the simple clothes of a wandering ascetic and carried a bowl with which he could beg for scraps of food to survive. He wandered for years, depriving himself of all worldly comforts and meditating deeply in search of this truth. One day, when he was near starvation, he realized these extreme methods had not made him any wiser. He decided it was better to follow a middle path. Siddhartha finally attained enlightenment and came to be known as the Buddha. He began to teach the *dhamma*, or the path of righteous living.

The Buddha's teachings highlighted that human suffering and sorrow stem from the constant craving for more, driven by desires. This constant craving causes unhappiness that can only end by following a path of moderation. Every person is responsible for their own salvation through good and right actions rather than relying on rituals and sacrifices or status based on birth. This was a practical approach in which individual effort and compassion as human beings were emphasized.

These values appealed to people who were confused by all the changes they saw around them, and soon the Buddha gained scores of followers. For more than forty-five years, he travelled across

Multi-Panelled Stone Sculpture Showing Key Events from the Buddha's Life

northern India, accompanied by groups of disciples, teaching his insights. After his death, the message of Buddhism spread to other parts of India, inspiring kings and commoners, traders and artists to produce some of India's finest philosophies, literature, and art.

Now let us take a look at the image of the sculpture again. The Buddha is believed to have lived from around 563 BCE to 483 BCE. This sculpture dates to much later, around 400 CE, and was found near Sarnath. In the bottom panel, we see Siddhartha's birth and early life. At the bottom-left corner, we see him riding away from his palace on a horse, giving up his former life by cutting his long hair with a sword. The second panel from the bottom shows his struggle to find the meaning of existence through deep meditation and penance. Panel three shows the Buddha's first sermon after his enlightenment, said to have taken place in the deer park at Sarnath, near Varanasi. Finally, at the top is the *mahaparinirvana*, when the Buddha gives up his bodily existence. This sculpture is a moving piece that presents the pivotal events in the life of one who eventually became one of the most influential spiritual figures in the world.

13

Bahubali Standing Still

Copper alloy figure, Karnataka, c. sixth to seventh century CE

The metal figure shown in the illustration on the next page is only eleven centimetres tall. It depicts a prince named Bahubali, who, according to the Jain tradition, attained the status of a *siddha*, or perfection, due to his right conduct, faith, and knowledge. Bahubali, a legendary prince of the kingdom of Podanapura in southern India, got into a great fight with his brother Bharata for the throne of the northern kingdom of Ayodhya. Instead of the usual war, Bahubali and Bharata fought a public duel of wits and strength. Bahubali, with his strapping body, was clearly going to win. But just as he was about to crush his elder brother in a wrestling lock, he was overcome with remorse. It suddenly dawned on him that the worldly power he was fighting for was worthless.

Quite abruptly, he left the field, gave away all his worldly possessions—including his kingdom, his wealth, his precious ornaments, even his clothes—and retreated deep into the forests. There he stood in motionless meditation in a yogic pose known as *kayotsarga*, which literally means being unmindful of the body. Legend has it that he was so unaware of the world while doing his penance that vines and creepers wound up over

his body, insects crept all over him, anthills formed around his legs, and the elements lashed at him. But Bahubali stood stock still in the midst of it all for more than a year until he finally attained *moksha* or liberation and became a siddha or pure soul.

Jain tradition has it that Bahubali was the son of Rishabhanatha, the first Jain Tirthankara, a guide or teacher who saved souls by helping them across the river of existence. There were twenty-three such legendary teachers before the final one.

The twenty-fourth and final Jain Tirthankara was Vardhamana, later known as Mahavira. He was born in 599 BCE at Kundagrama near Vaishali, located in present-day Bihar, north of the River Ganga.

The first millennium BCE was a period of intense religious and philosophical activity, particularly in the Ganga valley. Vardhamana and Siddhartha or the Buddha were contemporaries; their birthplaces were not very far apart.

Although Jain philosophy had been in existence long before Mahavira's birth, he is considered the founder of the Jain religion. The legends of the Tirthankaras that preceded him were already well known. But Mahavira was a historical figure, born into an aristocratic family, and like the Buddha, he gave up his worldly life to pursue a spiritual path. For twelve years after he left home, Mahavira wandered alone, leading a life of extreme penance, meditating on spiritual questions until he finally attained enlightenment.

In these years, he gained many followers to whom he taught the importance of individual effort in seeking the truth and gaining freedom from the cycle of births and rebirths. To do this, he believed one had to give up completely on domestic life and abandon all rituals. Mahavira taught that the whole world, including plants, animals, and tiny insects, have souls and should not be hurt or killed, and even non-living things such as air and water should not be harmed. Ahimsa or the non-injury of all living beings was one of his most important instructions.

Mahavira's teachings, like those of the Buddha, struck a chord with people from all walks of life. They found they could understand him easily because he used Prakrit, the language of the common folk. Both men and women in large numbers gave up everything to join the Jain sangha or monastic groups. They led extremely simple lives, often giving up even their clothes and relying on begging for survival. They vowed not to kill or harm even the tiniest of creatures, to not lie or steal or to keep family ties.

Jainism is considered one of the most ancient of India's religions. Centuries after Mahavira's lifetime, it spread from the Ganga river valley to other parts of India. In Gujarat, Rajasthan, Tamil Nadu, and Karnataka, we can see its influence in beautiful art and sculpture, temple buildings, and a wealth of literature in various languages.

Jain traditions and ideas have impacted history since the sixth century BCE. The legend of Bahubali and his representation in art are important legacies of the Jain religion. In the tenth century, inspired by the faith, a massive fifty-seven-foot-high statue of Bahubali was carved out of a single block of stone at Shravanabelagola, a town near Bengaluru in Karnataka. One of the largest free-standing rock-cut images in the world, this statue shows Bahubali in the same kayotsarga pose as the tiny metal image. Vines and creepers climb their way up his mountainous stone legs and anthills as high as buildings group around his feet. To this day, every twelve years, massive crowds of devotees gather to watch and worship as the statue is ceremonially bathed in milk, curd, and ghee.

Inscriptions near Shravanabelagola suggest the founder of the great Mauryan kingdom, Chandragupta Maurya, gave up his throne in the later part of the third century BCE and accompanied a Jain saint named Bhadrabahu to southern India, where he spent his last years as an ascetic.

14

Kuviranatan's Pot

Potsherd, Keeladi, Tamil Nadu, sixth to fifth century BCE

Once again, we find ourselves looking at indestructible potsherds, broken fragments of pots and other ceramic containers from thousands of years ago. This particularly vibrant piece in the illustration is from a Black and Red Ware pot from the Keeladi site near Madurai in Tamil Nadu. It is believed to be more than 2500 years old and has intrigued archaeologists because of the inscriptions etched on its surface. Right there on the shoulder of the pot, written in Tamil using the Brahmi script, is the name of its owner—Kuviranatan!

This potsherd is an important key to understanding the development of civilization and human settlements in southern India.

We know that continuous human activity in southern India goes back a long way, with some artefacts dating back to over a million years ago. Material remains excavated in Palaeolithic settlements such as Attirampakkam and Pallavaram, numerous cave art sites such as those at Edakkal, and the mysterious giant stone megaliths associated with iron-using people in places like Hire Benekal support this theory. But puzzlingly, at the start of the Early Historic Period beginning in the sixth century BCE, when cities were coming up all along the River Ganga basin, no one really knew what was happening down south. There were no signs of big settlements, fortified towns, or cities in the areas of present-day Kerala, Tamil Nadu, southern Andhra, Telangana, and southern Karnataka.

Relying on the writings of the Tamil Sangam—a massive assembly of poets who gathered in Madurai between 300 BCE and 300 CE—scholars believe the Early Historic Period in this area began only around the fourth century BCE with dynasties such as the Pandyas and Cholas.

Then, in March 2015, came a huge discovery. On the banks of the River Vaigai, a few kilometres south of the great city of Madurai, archaeologists discovered Keeladi. Through several seasons of excavations, they found the remains of a sprawling city. Carbon samples found on the site were dated to as early as 580 BCE. This meant the Early Historic Period in southern India could, in fact, have begun 300 years earlier than previously believed!

What did the archaeologists find?

In Keeladi, they found signs of an advanced people who lived in a well-planned city with large brick houses, sophisticated drainage systems with ring wells and terracotta drainage pipes running along the broad streets. They engaged in a wide range of activities, from agriculture and cattle rearing to pottery, ironwork, brick making, and even spinning and dyeing fabric. Many of them could afford gold ornaments, beautiful bead and ivory jewellery, and were affluent enough to be able to spend time playing board games and even a form of hopscotch. It was also evident they had a wide trade network.

So, who was Kuviranatan of Keeladi, and why were archaeologists so pleased to have found a piece of his pot?

Apart from telling us of the skilled potters of Keeladi, the potsherd with its etched inscription gives us amazing information on the development of language and scripts in India.

Languages can be written in various kinds of scripts. The Brahmi script goes back to the third century BCE and was used in north India to write the languages of Prakrit (like Ashoka's edicts) and Sanskrit. In southern India, Brahmi was used to write the early form of the Tamil language. All these languages later developed scripts of their own.

Interestingly, many Keeladi potsherds were inscribed with names in the Tamil Brahmi script *after* the pot had been fired. This meant the owners inscribed them after purchase from the potter, indicating that there was a high level of literacy even among the common people.

In the layers below where these potsherds were found, archaeologists found others with scratch marks that no one could read. These un-deciphered marks, known as graffiti to scholars (from the Italian *graffiato* or scratched), shaped like ladders, fish, spirals, tridents, or the sun, bear an astonishing resemblance to the un-deciphered symbols of the Harappan Civilization. Two civilizations—separated by thousands of kilometres and over a thousand years apart. How did they come to have similar writing styles? Were they once connected in some way? And did the graffiti script eventually evolve into the Brahmi script seen on this potsherd? Scholars are still trying to figure this out.

Meanwhile, we know that Kuviranatan, who once owned this pot was probably an important person because scholars tell us the 'atan' at the end of his name was an honorific, a title that conveys courtesy or shows respect to the person. Rather like using Mr before a name or 'Ji' after it. Kuviran, a gentleman who lived at a time when urban life was shaping itself on the banks of the River Vaigai.

15

A Rock Speaks for King Ashoka

Inscribed rock edict, Girnar in Junagadh, Gujarat, third century BCE

At the base of Mount Girnar, one of the highest peaks in Gujarat, is a huge rock that seems to ooze out of the earth. More than twelve-feet high and a sprawling seventy-five feet wide at the base, its smooth surface is covered with lines of engraved writing. This boulder reveals an important story from Indian history.

However, Colonel James Todd, an officer in the army of the British East India Company, did not know that. When he first noticed it in 1822, all he could make out were the strange letters of some unknown script running up and down the surface of the stone. They looked like gibberish. But they interested the colonel enough for him to have them copied and sent to James Prinsep, an assistant at the East India Company's mint—a factory that manufactures coins for currency. And this was where the story took a rather dramatic turn.

Prinsep was an avid scholar of Indian studies, deeply interested in Indian coins and scripts. For many years, he had been working on a puzzle. A series of mysterious inscriptions had been reported by Company officials, surveyors, and explorers from far flung places in central and western India. Most of these were inscribed on large rocks and pillars. Although no one could understand the language and the script looked like a string of stick figures, everyone agreed the inscriptions looked ancient. What were the words written on those towering pillars and huge rocks, and who had written them? When copies of the Girnar rock inscriptions reached Prinsep, he was already working round the clock, obsessed with finding answers.

In 1837, overworked and ill, Prinsep finally had his eureka moment. By comparing inscriptions from different regions, he cracked the code of the stick figures. James Prinsep had deciphered the Mauryan Brahmi script! Scholars call this one of the most important moments in the study of Indian history. And you will soon see why.

The first few words Prinsep translated from a pillar read 'Thus spake King Devanamapiya Piyadasi', a name unknown in Indian history at the time. After some frantic searching, scholars found a clue in a Buddhist text—written in Pali—from Sri Lanka where a king called Devanamapiya Piyadasi was praised for being a devout Buddhist and friend of the Sri Lankan monarch. His other name was—Ashoka!

This was none other than the grandson of Chandragupta Maurya and ruler of one of the first empires of India—Magadha, the region that is now in and around present-day Bihar.

Once the script could be read, it turned out the pillars and rocks were etched more than 2000 years ago, during Ashoka's lifetime! Amazing details of the empire of Magadha began to emerge from these readings— about how large the kingdom was, how rich and how powerful its rulers were. On the pillars and rock surfaces were messages from the emperor himself to his subjects, inscribed and placed at public places for them to read or to have read to them, since many ordinary people were possibly

illiterate, by special travelling officials known as dhamma mahamattas. In the inscriptions, Ashoka asked that the people follow the path of dhamma, a way of life full of compassion and respect for all fellow beings on earth.

But the most astonishing message of all was inscribed on the Girnar rock!

Eight years into his reign, around 257 BCE, Ashoka conquered the eastern state of Kalinga, in present-day Odisha, in a great and bloody war. Instead of crowing about his success, as rulers often did in those times, Ashoka did the opposite. Horrified at what he saw on the battlefield, he told his subjects how sorry he was for all the suffering, death, and devastation he had caused! We learn this from the inscriptions on the Girnar rock. He vowed to change, to look after the welfare of all his subjects, and take up the way of dhamma and non-violence. And he begged other kings, his family members, and all his subjects to do the same. Eventually, it is said, Ashoka became a Buddhist. It is a deeply touching, personal statement of a monarch giving up war after victory—an action quite unmatched in history.

The Girnar rock inscriptions enabled scholars to not only rediscover one of India's greatest historical figures but also gain insight into his thoughts.

However, there's more!

Apart from Ashoka's edicts, there are two other inscriptions on the same rock. Around 150 CE, the Kshatrapa ruler Rudradaman I wrote of the great Sudarshan Lake, a reservoir constructed originally by Ashoka's grandfather, which he had repaired at great cost. Two hundred years later, the Gupta king Skandagupta inscribed his own contribution towards restoring the lake. The inscriptions record the fate of the reservoir over a span of an incredible 1000 years!

It is not surprising then, that many call the Girnar rock inscription one of the most extraordinary written records in history. Today, the all-important rock is sheltered within a building to protect it from the elements.

16

Four Roaring Lions

Stone pillar capital, Sarnath, Uttar Pradesh, late third century BCE

The roaring lions shown in the illustration on the next page probably look familiar to you. Graphic illustrations of this stone carving feature on official seals, documents, currency notes, and coins in the country—a universally recognized symbol of the Republic of India.

The Lion Capital, as it is called, is more than 2000 years old and was made during the reign of Mauryan Emperor Ashoka in the third century BCE to sit on top of a pillar or column. The four stone lions sit back-to-back, which is why one of them is not visible when viewed from the front. They are polished to perfection and carved in exquisite detail. As you gaze at them, you can almost feel the rough fur of their manes and see the twitch of their whiskers. They represent royalty but their roars were intended to spread the dhamma, the 'Four Noble Truths' of the Buddha, across the land.

The lions are seated on a round drum. Walking clockwise around the drum are a horse, an ox, an elephant, and a lion. In the middle is another familiar symbol, a twenty-four-spoked chakra. This is the 'Wheel of Law' that we see in the centre of the Indian flag. The drum sits on a carved inverted lotus flower. The lions once held a huge carved spoked chakra on their shoulders, a piece that is now missing. The capital would have once crowned the top of a twelve-metre-high stone pillar at Sarnath, installed in the midst of the deer park where Buddha gave his first sermon. Today, it is in the Sarnath museum, and only a broken fragment of the original pillar is found embedded in the ground nearby. The Sarnath pillar is one of many hundreds, many of them with similar lion capitals, made on the orders of King Ashoka.

Why did Ashoka want giant pillars at all?

This may have something to do with the scale of his kingdom. Towards the end of the third century BCE, Ashoka found himself ruling vast territories. These were so vast that there were governors for different provinces. To guard the frontiers, there was a huge army, and to collect resources to run the empire, there were tax collectors and revenue officials. Merchants travelled on roads and rivers that were maintained and taxed by the state, and craftspeople sold their wares in huge marketplaces. Large areas of dense forests were cleared for cultivation and for animal herding. The once-modest city-state of Magadha in this period became India's first empire.

Ashoka's Lion Capital

In keeping with the size of Ashoka's empire and the immense amount of wealth flowing into the state treasuries, even the art changed. Rather than the small, personal art objects of the past, Ashoka could now afford to commission massive monuments, such as palaces and pillars.

The particularly savage battle at Kalinga, which took place at the height of his power, had caused an abrupt change in Ashoka. He decided to give up all forms of violence and turned to the teachings of the Buddha for solace. Influenced by the Buddhist path of dhamma—a way of life that treated all living creatures with compassion, he decided to work for the welfare of his people, for justice, peace, and goodwill throughout the world.

It was a whole new outlook for the powerful king! Wanting to share these unique thoughts with his subjects, Ashoka chose a rather spectacular method.

Gigantic stone pillars were cut, carved, and polished to a mirror sheen in workshops around the Mathura region using the distinctive Chunar sandstone. Crowned with carved capitals featuring bulls, elephants, or lions, they were inscribed with personal messages from Ashoka to his subjects. The edicts talked of the monarch's concern for the welfare of his people, his new policies, the justice system his empire practiced, and his intention to follow a path of non-violence. The immense pieces, some of them weighing up to fifty tonnes each, were then carefully packed and carted to the far corners of the vast Mauryan Empire, ranging from central to southern India, Nepal, and as far as Afghanistan. They were set up along important trade routes or places of pilgrimage where large crowds were likely to gather. Ashoka's messages were inscribed in at least three different scripts and many different languages so that people from various parts of the empire could read them. And for those who could not read, the pillars were accompanied by officials known as dhamma mahamattas, who would read the messages out loud for their benefit.

All this took a lot of planning, resources, and a large workforce. And that is what Ashoka had in plenty.

In 1950, when India became a republic, the founding fathers of the Indian Constitution realized the new nations' values of tolerance, non-violence, and belief in social justice, peace, and goodwill towards all were perfectly symbolized by the ancient Lion Capital of Ashoka—which is how it was adopted as the national symbol.

17

A Sculpted Jataka Tale

Sculpted medallion on the
Bharhut Stupa, Madhya Pradesh,
second to first century BCE

After the Buddha died around 483 BCE, his followers began to write down his teachings. They were compiled into the Tripitakas—which literally mean 'three baskets'—each holding different instructions and ideas of the Buddha. In one of these baskets, known as the *Sutta Pitaka*, there is a surprise—more than 500 entertaining stories brimming with animals and humans, heroes and villains, action and adventure! They are called the Jataka tales. Each story describes the previous lives of the Buddha as a Bodhisattva. A Bodhisattva is one born in a human or non-human form who can attain enlightenment at any time in their lifetime but prefers instead to live on in their worldly body. They do this in order to teach lessons on good behaviour to the people of the time.

Why did the Buddhist scriptures include these stories?

Humans learnt how to tell stories a long, long time ago. In prehistoric times, as they sat by the flickering firelight in their caves and rock shelters, they told visual stories by drawing animals, human figures, and symbols on the walls of their dwellings to describe their daily experiences, transmit instructions, or give warning of potential danger. Perhaps because this information helped them to survive their dangerous lives, enabling people to remember information and make sense of their world, this form of communication struck a chord in human hearts.

As time went on, there was a shift to oral traditions. Across cultures, oral chants, prayers, songs, and poems were passed down the generations by word of mouth. The popular form of tales and stories came later, with storytelling often playing a central role in community life.

When religious teachers wanted to reach out to larger audiences, they often used folk tales to engage the attention of their listeners. The Jataka tales deliberately included many such stories that the common people could identify with, by working the Buddha's messages into them.

Many of these tales were narrated by professional storytellers. Wandering showmen drew scenes from the more popular ones on cloth scrolls and walked from village to village, entertaining audiences with illustrated storytelling sessions that often lasted all night.

And then, around the first century BCE, at Bharhut in central India, an amazing new concept of a stupa began to take shape that was made completely from bricks and stone.

At the heart of the stupa was a dome said to contain the relics of the Buddha, possibly his ashes or bones. Around it, stone workers had carved beautiful railings and four richly decorated *toranas* or gateways. Pilgrims from faraway villages and towns would make the long journey to visit the stupa. Perhaps they were accompanied by a guide-monk explaining things as they walked slowly round, gazing in awe at stone recreations of episodes from the Buddha's life, taking in the spiritual atmosphere in the process. And maybe they would call out to each other in excitement when they recognized familiar characters from their favourite stories carved into the stone gateways. Was that not what the wandering showman had performed for them back in the village? We can only speculate.

Sculpted scenes from the Jataka tales are one of the highlights of the Bharhut stupa.

The illustrated medallion below tells the Mahakapi Jataka, or the story of the Great Monkey King. The Bodhisattva was once a Great Monkey, leader of a large troop that lived on a mango tree on the banks of the River Ganga. The fruit of the tree was divinely delicious, and the monkeys took great care that none of them fell into the river and were wasted. But one day, the king of Benares (now Varanasi) heard from a fisherman that the monkeys were eating the best fruit in his kingdom.

Angry that he was being denied these delicious fruit by a band of monkeys, the king rushed to the spot with his soldiers, ordering his archers to shoot down the monkeys. The monkey troop was panic-stricken as arrows rained down on them. The Great Monkey, or Bodhisattva, remained calm. He fashioned an escape bridge made of bamboo to reach another tree across the river. But he miscalculated the distance, and the bridge fell short! The Great Monkey stretched himself across the gap, urging

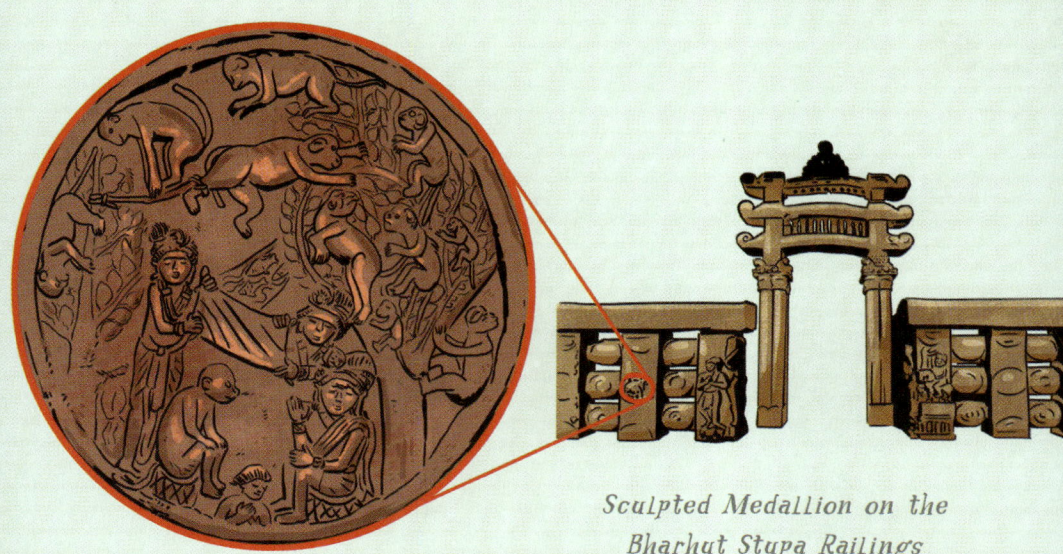

Sculpted Medallion on the Bharhut Stupa Railings

his companions to use his back to dash across to safety. The king was amazed at this noble deed and had the Great Monkey brought down to safety. But alas, by now his back had been broken by a particularly wicked monkey! He survived for just enough time to tell the king about how the duty of a righteous ruler must be to put the happiness of his subjects and his kingdom above all. The king gave the Great Monkey a royal funeral.

What is most interesting is the way the artist has depicted different episodes from the story, all in one medallion. And we can imagine hundreds of wide-eyed pilgrims absorbing the sacred lessons of the Buddha as they examined this piece.

18

The Village of Uruvela

Sculpted pillar panel, Stupa at Sanchi, Madhya Pradesh, first century BCE

The famous Sanchi stupa in Madhya Pradesh is a treasure trove of sculpted stories from the life of the Buddha. One such story, known as the Conversion of Kashyapa of Uruvela, is depicted on a pillar of the eastern gateway.

After renouncing his royal life as a prince of Kapilavastu, the Buddha gave up all worldly pleasures and wandered, seeking enlightenment. It is said that some years later, in the kingdom of Magadha, which is now in present-day Bihar, he and his companions came upon a tiny village named Uruvela on the banks of the beautiful River Nairajana. Charmed by the beautiful countryside, a shaded grove of trees, and the serene river flowing by, the Buddha decided to settle down to meditate under a peepul tree. He asked a grass cutter to give him a sheaf of kusha grass to sit on. Just then, a farmer's daughter named Sujata was passing by. Shocked at the gaunt appearance of the starving monk, Sujata rushed home and brought back a bowl of milk, rice, and honey. The Buddha ate the bowl of rice gratefully because, by now, he had realized that extreme penance was not the way to enlightenment. His five companions, however, did not understand this. They thought his behaviour was unbecoming of a monk seeking salvation and leaving him alone, they walked away.

Nourished by this simple meal, the Buddha went into deep meditation where he finally saw the 'truth'. A few weeks later, he went to Sarnath to give his first sermon. When he returned to Uruvela, he met the Kashyapa brothers, well-known ascetics themselves, impressed them with his wisdom, and converted them to his way of thinking. The place of the Buddha's enlightenment, the little village of Uruvela, came to be known as Bodh Gaya.

Based on the style of construction and inscriptions found on the gateways at Sanchi, scholars believe that the original brick dome-like stupa that housed the relics or physical remains of the Buddha was constructed by Ashoka, the great Mauryan emperor. The elaborately carved *toranas* or gateways came almost 200 years later, during the time of the Satavahana rulers of the first century BCE.

The Conversion of Kashyapa is one of many incidents from the Buddha's life that are sculpted on the Sanchi gateways. Three panels on a pillar tell the whole story. But we are concerned only with the topmost panel that is depicted in the illustration on the facing page. And what we see here is life in the little village of Uruvela exactly as it was more than 2000 years ago!

By the banks of a large lotus pond, we see a few huts with thatched roofs, an open-air shrine under a tree and a somewhat palatial house with balconies where people sit and watch the world go by. Down at the pond, women wash and fill water pots while buffaloes float lazily by, their heads bobbing between brightly coloured lotus. Cattle, goats, and woolly sheep graze on the banks.

A woman squats, winnowing grain in a shallow basket while her companion stands, pounding the husk out of the grain with a pestle and

mortar. Another is grinding with an oblong stone called a quern on a large stone base or saddle. And somewhat strangely, there is a woman standing at a table and rolling out something. She seems to be making cakes or rolling out dough for bread. But scholars find her standing posture highly unusual for an Indian setting.

Apart from village life, if we look carefully at the sculptures on the Sanchi gateways, we see more scenes of everyday life. Grand royal processions and huge multi-storey, pillared palaces set amidst lush vegetation. There are cities surrounded by crocodile-infested moats with balconied houses where people in various costumes, jewellery, and elaborate hairdos go about their everyday business. We see tiny details like furniture, cooking vessels, and musical instruments like drums, flutes, and trumpets. There are various types of transportation like horse chariots, bullock carts, and boats, as well as weapons of war like spears, tridents, and swords.

While the intention of the Sanchi stupa was to preserve the relics of the Buddha and depict episodes from his life, the masterful sculptors have provided us with an illustrated book of life in those times.

19

Demetrius Wears an Elephant Scalp

Silver coin of Demetrius I, north-western India, 200–185 BCE

Around 326 BCE when Alexander the Great's exhausted and homesick army forced him to turn back from the gates of India, somewhere in the region of the River Jhelum, he literally marched away from his dream of conquering the fabled land of riches. Over a hundred years later, another Greek ruler decided to try his luck. The only difference was that Demetrius I was not a Hellenic Greek from Greece but a Bactrian Greek. Bactria is an area between the River Amu Darya and the Hindu Kush mountains in northern Afghanistan. The image featured on the coin on the next page depicts Demetrius I. It is an amazing portrait of a king who lived more than 2000 years ago. In the image, he wears a strange hat, but we'll come to that in a bit.

Bactrian Greeks or Graeco-Bactrians, as they are called, were originally exiles from the Persian Empire who settled in Bactria centuries ago, way before Alexander came along. They held on to their Greek roots, retaining the language, religion, clothing, lifestyle, and even their city plans. They prospered in this fertile region and profited from their location that was situated along major trade routes. Much of what we know of the Graeco-Bactrians comes from the beautiful coins they minted with detailed portraits of the rulers on them that were later found among the ruins of their cities.

Indians had regularly interacted with them as far back as Mauryan times, calling them *Yavanas*. Chandragupta Maurya was said to have married a Yavana princess. Ashoka had some of his rock edicts inscribed in Greek for the benefit of the Greek populations living in the north-western frontiers of his empire. The Mauryas were a powerful dynasty, and as long as they ruled, the Graeco-Bactrians did not venture into the boundaries of India beyond the areas that are now Pakistan and Punjab. But in 185 BCE, when the last Mauryan ruler was assassinated, the kingdom looked unstable, and the Greeks saw their chance.

Demetrius moved his base to Sirkap, near Takshashila or Taxila in present-day Pakistan, acquiring large areas along the Indus valley and Punjab. From this base, his armies swept down into the Gangetic plains,

Silver Coin of Demetrius I

capturing the cities of Mathura, Saketa (present-day Ayodhya), and even the capital of the Mauryan Empire—Pataliputra. Another branch of his army worked their way to central India, taking the prosperous trading city of Ujjain. The Greeks now controlled some of the most important cities in India. It was probably around this time that Demetrius minted these coins with his portrait, wearing this rather unique headdress shaped like an elephant's head. The elephant was an ancient symbol of India, and the 'scalp cap' represented Demetrius's conquest of Indian territories.

No one really knows how long they held these territories. But by the first century BCE, the Graeco–Bactrians were cut off from their original home in Bactria by invaders known as the Scythians. They decided to stay put in the Punjab region, making north-west India their new home. Scholars refer to these people as the Indo-Greeks.

The Indo-Greeks immersed themselves in various aspects of Indian culture. They issued bilingual coins in both Greek and Brahmi scripts. Some replaced images of Greek gods, like Apollo and Zeus, on their coins with those of Krishna, Balarama, and Lakshmi, making these the earliest representations of the Indian deities. The Indo-Greeks were generous donors to Buddhist cave monasteries as well. At least one ruler, Menander I, a former general in Demetrius's army, converted to Buddhism. We find a carved Greek figure lounging casually on a pillar on the Bharhut stupa. He has on boots and a tunic with a Greek-style headband across his curly hairstyle. A group of enthusiastic Greek devotees accompanied by their own band appear on the northern gateway of the Sanchi stupa, while sculpture and art in the northern region of Gandhara take on a distinct Greek flavour.

In the town of Besnagar, near Bhopal, Madhya Pradesh, there is a carved pillar dated to around the second century BCE and inscribed with a unique calling card. A six-line Prakrit inscription in Brahmi script mentions this was set up by a man named Heliodorus, the Greek ambassador of the king of Taxila who was sent to the court of the Shunga king—the successors of the Mauryas. Heliodorus describes himself as a Bhagavata, a devotee of the god Vasudeva, another name for Krishna or Vishnu. This was, in fact, a Garuda pillar. Garuda is an eagle and the vehicle of Vishnu, but its carved image is now missing from the top of the column. Nearby, archaeologists found the remains of a structure they believe was once a temple dedicated to Vishnu, the earliest one of its kind.

Heliodorus, the Greek ambassador, had adopted the god Vasudeva as his own, just as many of his countrymen had adopted the ways of India as their own. Like the coin of Demetrius I, this is another important indication that the Greeks and Indians were in regular and, most often, friendly contact at this time.

20

The Enchanting
Chauri-Bearer

Polished Chunar sandstone figure, Didarganj, Bihar, first to second century CE

On the banks of the River Ganga near Patna in present-day Bihar, there was a small village called Didarganj. One day, in October 1917, Ghulam Rasul, the maulvi of the local mosque, noticed a large, flat stone slab sticking out of the mud on the riverbank. Curious, he dug it out. The jutting stone turned out to be the base of a spectacular life-sized statue of a beautiful woman carrying a chauri or fly-whisk.

The Chauri-Bearer or the Didarganj Yakshi, as she came to be known, is undoubtedly one of the finest pieces of ancient Indian art ever found. Elegantly dressed and perfectly coiffed, she stands gracefully, holding a chauri over her right shoulder with a hint of a smile. Her left hand is missing and her nose is damaged, which is not surprising considering she had been buried in the mud for hundreds of years.

Scholars immediately began to debate the age of the statue. Since it was found in isolation, they had to rely on the material and style of the statue itself. The free-standing statue is made of a single slab of tan-coloured Chunar sandstone, polished to a mirror-finish gloss. The skills and decorative touches used are associated with the Mauryan period, just like Ashoka's shining lions. This similarity in style led some scholars to date the piece to the end of the Mauryan period, around the third century BCE. While others have dated it to a period a couple of centuries later. However, most agree that she was a yakshi.

Yakshis and their male counterparts, yakshas, go back a very long way.

Imagine life in very ancient times. As people walked through dense forests where wild animals roamed, weathered crop-destroying storms, crossed raging rivers, and perhaps fell ill with mysterious ailments that seemed to have no cure, they must have felt a real sense of danger all around them. Perhaps to help them cope with the mysterious or the unpredictable, they worshipped deities known as yakshas and yakshis. These were formless guardians of trees, lakes, and ponds, or those residing in forests, on mountains, or along the highways. Some were friendly and helpful, others were mischievous or downright troublesome. All of them had to be pleased or pacified in some way, and the common folk would appeal to them for boons or for protection against evil. There were yakshis associated with fertility, childbirth, and plentiful harvests. Yakshas were often tree or water deities or connected to wealth and treasure.

Soon, people started making small stone and terracotta images of these deities either to worship or as votive offerings in gratitude for boons granted. Both yakshis and yakshas were well-dressed and prosperous-looking figures, reassuring their devotees of their strength and powers.

From the third century BCE, worship of these semi-divine beings was widespread and popular among the common folk. Along with the portable terracotta and stone pieces, there were now larger statues which were meant for community worship. In the Bihar and Mathura regions, powerful-looking life-size stone yakshas have been found, some of them clutching bags of money or medicine in their hands, ready to grant favours to their devotees.

The beauty and skill of their workmanship indicate that they were probably sponsored by wealthy clients and made at workshops where the artists were trained for uniformity in style.

But when the more formal religions like the Brahmanical traditions, Buddhism, and Jainism came up, each of them claimed these popular semi-divine beings as part of their own pantheon of gods.

You can spot yakshas and yakshis posing gracefully in all their finery on the *toranas* or gateways of the Buddhist stupas at Sanchi, Bharhut, and Amaravati. Or carved along with Jain Tirthankaras on the rock faces or hill shrines of Tamil Nadu. In fact, each of the twenty-four Jain Tirthankaras were assigned one guardian yaksha and one yakshi of their own. And later, with the building of temples, these beings appear as protectors of the Brahmanical deities all over India, sculpted or painted on temple walls or as bronze images. Scholars believe that the images of the yakshas and yakshis were inspiration for later depictions of the Buddha and deities like Lakshmi.

When the Didarganj Yakshi was unearthed, local villagers immediately propped her up under a bamboo canopy and began to worship her as a deity. However, local administrators and archaeologists of the British colonial government soon arrived on the scene to carry the statue off to the newly established Patna Museum. Clearly, ancient memories of yakshi worship still lingered in the minds of the common folk.

The Didarganj Yakshi

21

The Formidable Lady of Chandraketugarh

Terracotta moulded plaque, Chandraketugarh, West Bengal, c. first century BCE

The illustration depicts a tall lady standing in a pillared hall, towering above her attendants as they scurry respectfully behind her with fans and fly-whisks. She is magnificently dressed in plenty of jewellery, with strings of flowers around her wrists and a heavy waistband. The large umbrella held over her head and the gesture—of her lowered hand with an open palm—remind us of a goddess granting boons. What is most unusual, though, is her hairdo. It is an elaborate and probably very heavy affair, and if one looks closely, one can see that it is held together with some rather unexpected hairpins. In fact, the hairpins are weapons—an entire arsenal, including swords, axes, arrows, and tridents.

Who was this woman, and why was she so heavily armed?

This is a terracotta plaque from the early historic site of Chandraketugarh in West Bengal. The site is actually a cluster of villages located around the Ganga delta, not far from present-day Kolkata. The name Chandraketugarh

The Terracotta Plaque from Chandraketugarh

comes from a local legend of a king named Chandraketu who is said to have once ruled in these parts. The place first came to the notice of archaeologists when locals began unearthing antiquities in large numbers in the early twentieth century. However, the barren mounds that exist there today have been excavated in fits and starts.

Although detailed reports are still to come, it appears that the site has been continuously occupied since before the time of the Mauryans, around the sixth century BCE to almost the twelfth century CE. Rivers have changed course since its earliest occupation, but Chandraketugarh would have once been connected to the River Ganga, making it ideally located as a centre of trade. Excavated mud ramparts and walled structures indicate that the area once held a large population. Other artefacts, like punch-marked gold and silver coins, seals, pots inscribed in Brahmi and Kharosthi scripts, and figurines of ivory and bronze, are clues to the trade and commercial activity of the place. Some scholars believe that Chandraketugarh is the same place as the Gangaridae mentioned in *Geographia*, an atlas of the world, written by the Graeco-Roman geographer Ptolemy in the second century CE, and that it was probably a major trade centre of Indo-Roman trade.

But the most intriguing finds of Chandraketugarh were the exquisite terracotta objects and plaques, like the one in the illustration here. Large numbers of them literally popped up everywhere, many of them dating back to 200 BCE. A lot of the artefacts were quickly collected by local antique collectors to save them from robbers carting them away to be sold in the international art market.

The terracotta objects range in colour from brick red to browns and greys. But what was unusual was that these were not individual pieces made by a rural craftsman for a local market. Many of the themes are repeated, sometimes with small modifications, leading to the conclusion that they were manufactured from moulds. This was finely made, mass-produced ware to cater to a larger number of customers in an urban centre.

The scenes depicted on the plaques provide valuable clues into the social and cultural life of the time. There are women and men who look like nature spirits, known as yakshis and yakshas. They are elaborately dressed in sheer fabric and jewelled waistbands, the men with ornate turbans. There are squat figures of turbaned grimacing dwarves, winged humans, and realistic-looking animals and birds, all carved with a high degree of skill. There are also a range of images from everyday life. Heavily bejewelled women dance or stand about in lush gardens with lotus ponds. One plaque shows a wealthy family in what could be a modern-day studio portrait with a well-dressed father and mother posing formally with a curly-haired child holding a pet dog on a leash, while other household pets like ducks and a monkey wander casually around them.

As for the tall lady on this plaque, does she remind you of a certain goddess with weapons? Scholars believe that in a time before gods and goddesses were depicted as images to be worshipped, this was an early form the goddess Durga, she of the multiple weapons acquired from the other gods in order to slay the demon buffalo, Mahisha. The pillared hall she stands in may be a shrine and the plaque may have been used as part of household decor or as a religious icon to be worshipped in a household shrine.

At Chandraketugarh, we have many exciting clues to the rich, vibrant, and cosmopolitan society that once lived here. Today, however, the desolate mounds await more excavation and research to further understand this long-vanished civilization.

22

Naganika Sends a Message

Copper alloy Satavahana coin, Junnar region, Maharashtra, c. first century BCE

The copper alloy coin depicted in the illustration on the facing page tells an unexpected tale. It was issued around the first century BCE in the western Deccan by the Satavahana king, Sri Satakarni. His name in the Brahmi script appears around the rim of the coin. But occupying pride of place, right in the centre of the the obverse, or heads, side of the coin and enclosed by a rectangle, is the name of his queen, Naganikaya or Naganika, as she is commonly known. Over 2000 years ago, a queen was powerful enough to have her name on a coin!

Who was she, and who were these Satavahanas?

After the collapse of the Mauryan Empire, a number of regional rulers saw it as an opportunity to claim their independence. The Satavahanas were among the first of these ambitious chieftains. Around the first century BCE, they emerged around the northern Deccan, in an area that is now in present-day Maharashtra, Madhya Pradesh, and northern Karnataka. At this time, across the Deccan plateau, there was growing prosperity. Large tracts of the fertile black soil were being brought under cultivation,

Both Sides of Naganika's Coin

towns were growing into cities, and specialized craft guilds were producing goods that traders were carrying along river routes and on the Dakshinapatha, the Great Southern Highway—a road that connected the northern areas to the ports of the western coast.

Here, foreign merchants waited, impatient to load up their ships with textiles, muslin, finely carved ivory, and precious gemstones from the Deccan heartland, sailing back to meet the huge demand across the Roman Empire and Southeast Asia. There were profits to be made from these commercial networks through tolls and taxes and the Satavahanas intended to do just that. Their capital, Pratishthana, present-day Paithan, was a major point on the Dakshinapatha and they also controlled the important western ports of Sopara and Kalyan.

With so much at stake, naturally, the Satavahanas did not go unchallenged. Other equally determined chieftains were constantly at war with them. Chief among their enemies were the Shakas, a group originally from Central Asia but now ruling parts of India in areas that are in present-day Gujarat and northern Rajasthan. The astute Satavahanas decided that it was best to quickly make some powerful friends. Sri Satakarni married Naganika, a princess from a tribe of fearsome warriors known as the

Maharathis, who controlled large parts of present-day Maharashtra. With their backing, the Satavahanas were firmly on their way to defending their rapidly expanding empire.

Meanwhile, there is evidence that Naganika played an important role at the Satakarni court. The coins with her name on them were a vital clue.

There were more clues to come. At Naneghat, a narrow pass that cuts through a rocky gorge in the Western Ghats connecting the Deccan plateau to the ports on the coast, archaeologists discovered a rather special rock shelter. It was probably meant for traders to rest as they navigated the steep slopes of the pass. Deep inside, along the back wall was a niche in which eight life-size figures had been carved in relief. The features of the figures had crumbled with time but luckily their inscribed names remained—Naganika, her husband, sons, father, and father-in-law. This was a complete royal portrait gallery!

Running along the walls of the shelter are inscriptions that are now considered one of the oldest and most important historical records of the time, dating back to the first century BCE. Apart from describing the king's victories at war, the inscriptions talk of the works of Naganika—how she assisted her husband in managing the kingdom when he was alive and how, after his death, she took over the throne as their sons were too young to rule. She continued Sri Satakarni's work, performed ritual sacrifices with the aid of Brahmanas, and made lavish donations of cows, silver, horses, and elephants.

Naganika was not the only formidable Satakarni woman. Later Satavahana kings commonly took on their mothers' names, like Gautamiputra, the son of Queen Gautami, one of the most powerful of the Satavahanas. Queen Gautami, like her ancestor Naganika, also details proudly the sacrifices performed by her son and how they gave respect to the Brahmanas. The inscription, strangely, is on the walls of a cave being donated to a Buddhist monastery! Those were socially complex times and this intermingling of religious declarations was not uncommon.

The Deccan was milling with rival chieftains, power-seeking tribes from Central Asia and Bactria, fortune-seeking merchants from far-off lands, all jostling for position. The Satavahanas could not rely on just military might to keep their subjects happy. They had to convince them that they were legitimate rulers, ordained by the gods. One way to command obedience to their royal selves was to patronize the Brahmanas and have themselves included in one of the higher castes. Another strategy was to gain popular support, especially from the wealthy people of the day, most of whom were Buddhist merchants.

So, it appears that while the men went out doing battle to retain their rich territories, the remarkable Satavahana women decided how to keep ahead of the competition. Through coins like this one, Naganika made sure people knew she was in charge!

23

A King with Two Capitals

Life-size stone statue of King Kanishka, Mathura, Uttar Pradesh, c. first century CE

This life-size stone statue, illustrated on the facing page, was unearthed in 1911 in the ploughed fields of Mat village, near Mathura in present-day Uttar Pradesh. Currently preserved in the Government Museum of Mathura, something about the way the figure stands is awe-inspiring. Although the head is missing and so are the arms, he still looks impressive in his belted coat and strapped boots, clasping a lethal-looking broadsword in one hand and an intricately carved mace in the other. His attire and posture tell us he was not just a warrior and a man of action but also a very powerful person. Although discovered in north India, the figure seems to have wandered far from home, dressed as he was in a style common to horse-riding Central Asian nomads! Luckily, there is a Brahmi inscription running along the folds of his coat. And just as we suspected, the inscription reveals that this is indeed the statue of a powerful person—a king named Kanishka, the great Kushana.

The Kushanas' original homeland was in the Central Asian pasture lands beyond the Hindu Kush mountains. They were known as the Yuezhi, and sometime in the early second century BCE, they were harassed out of their homelands by a confederation of rival tribes known as the Hsiung-Nu. But, as it turned out, this was not a bad thing because the hardy Yuezhi tribespeople managed to move southwards where they set up a kingdom for themselves in areas that are now northern Afghanistan. By the time Kanishka became king in around 78 CE, the Kushanas, as they came to be known, had established a kingdom that stretched all the way from Afghanistan, Pakistan, and Kashmir, even reaching deep into the Ganga basin of northern India. It was so large that Kanishka found he needed two capitals to run his vast empire. He set up one at Mathura and the other at Purushapura, in modern-day Peshawar, Pakistan.

The Kushana kingdom sprawled across the heart of the famous Silk Route—an over 6000-kilometre network of land- and sea-trade routes linking China with the Mediterranean. The Kushanas controlled the caravans filled with textiles, gemstones, and spices that joined the route from India. They held the seaports along the western coast as well as a shorter, but somewhat dangerous route through the Karakoram mountains into China. All this was profitable business and the Kushanas flourished.

From Buddhist records, it appears Kanishka was an ardent devotee of the Buddha. He sponsored Buddhist

The Stone Statue of King Kanishka

monks and artists heading to China and Central Asia, set up monasteries and rest houses for them, making travellers more confident of using the difficult Karakoram route. He built a stupa at Purushapura that was so magnificent that it was said to be one of the wonders of the ancient world. The Fourth Buddhist Council, a huge gathering of Buddhist scholars and monks organized to compile and record the teachings of the Buddha, was held under his patronage in Kashmir.

Because the Kushana kingdom was so vast, the population consisted of a variety of people. There were Indians, Persians, Greeks, Bactrians, and Central Asians, each with their own culture and religious practice. Kanishka, despite being a Buddhist himself, was wise enough to be open-minded to all this diversity. As a result, the coins from his era depict not just Buddhist icons but also Brahmanical deities, such as Shiva and Nandi, the Persian gods Mithra and Atash and the Greek sun god, Helios. In one recently found inscription in Afghanistan, Kanishka instructs one of his officials to build a temple to Nana, a West Asian goddess. Graeco-Bactrian and Indian artists mingled, creating unique new styles of sculpture at the time and Kanishka presided over a great fusion of thoughts and ideas.

Where the Kushanas did differ from previous kingdoms was in their fondness for making larger-than-life statues of themselves. Until the Kushanas came along, most early Indian art focused on generic themes. The Buddha was depicted as a series of symbols indicating his presence rather than as a physical form and there were almost no royal portraits, even of the kings who had funded the production of the artworks. Kanishka commissioned free-standing statues of himself and his father, Vima Kadphises, and the remains of both have been found near Mathura. Other massive statues of Kushana rulers have been found in Afghanistan. Scholars debate whether these were installed in temples as attendants to the main deities. There is also an alternate theory that the Kushanas could have wished to depict themselves as godlike to be worshipped by the people, which is why the colossal statues were created.

On his coins, Kanishka is shown as a powerful warrior, armed with a sword and lance, with flames coming out of his shoulders. The inscription on this headless statue declares this is 'Mahārāja Rājadhirāja Devaputra Kāṇiṣka' or 'the Great King, King of Kings, Son of God, Kanishka'.

Monarchs at the time wanted to be seen as nothing less than the offspring of gods.

24

The Buddha in Graeco-Roman Style

Schist stone statue, Gandhara, north-western Pakistan, first to second century CE

We know, of course, that the statue in the illustration on the facing page is of the Buddha. The statue was sculpted around the first or second centuries CE in an art style that came to be known as Gandhara, named after the region by the same name in north-western Pakistan where it originated. But the statue itself would have come as quite a surprise, even to the Buddha's most ardent devotees at the time.

This is because, for more than 400 years after his death, artists had been somewhat reluctant to represent the Buddha as a human figure. Instead, they preferred to use different symbols to represent and depict significant events from his life. When devotees walked along stupa railings or gazed at the carved gateways and came across the image of a pair of footprints, a peepul tree, or an empty throne, they understood the artist's intention and believed that they were looking at the Buddha. It was only around the first century CE that actual figures of the Buddha began to be produced. The statue in the illustration is among the first ever humanlike representations of the Buddha.

However, what could be the reason behind the Buddha's resemblance to a Greek god?

Gandhara had been at cultural crossroads for centuries. Once described as one of the important Mahajanapadas or city states, it was ruled by the Persians till around the fifth century BCE, later conquered by Alexander the Great, brought under Mauryan control, and then taken over by the Indo-Greeks. But it was under the Kushanas, from the first to fifth centuries CE, that Gandhara saw its real glory. The Kushanas used Gandhara's geographical position to their advantage, turning it into a hub of important trade routes that connected China, India, and Central Asia with the Mediterranean. Merchants and craftspeople from Persia, China, India, and Bactria mingled in the prosperous urban centres of Gandhara, exchanging ideas and opinions along with goods. Buddhist monks, particularly in the reign of Kanishka, set up monasteries and translated important Buddhist manuscripts to supply the increasing demand from China and Central Asia as Buddhism spread across these regions. In this great melting pot, a unique school of art was born, later named the Gandhara school of art.

For centuries, artists of the region trained in the classical Greek and Roman traditions catering to the tastes of their Graeco-Bactrian and Indo-Greek masters. Beginning in about the first century CE, they began to incorporate Indian, and particularly Buddhist, themes into their art. They sculpted in stone, ivory,

Stone Statue of the Buddha in the Gandhara Style

metal, and plaster-like stucco, portraying not just the traditional narrative scenes from Buddha's life but also, for the first time, images of the Buddha himself, who began to be depicted as a strong, almost muscular figure as is evident in the Gandhara statue, with its wavy hair and sharp features. In his flowing robes with carefully sculpted folds, he could almost be mistaken for the Greek god Apollo! He has a serene expression, one leg slightly bent, his now-broken but once an open palm gesturing the *abhaya mudra*, reassuring his followers and asking them not to be fearful. His elongated earlobes reveal his origins as a prince who once wore heavy ear ornaments, and his hair—piled in a topknot—indicates a style that was associated with wise men known as the *ushnisha*. A flat stone halo behind his head emphasizes his divine status.

Hundreds of such Buddha images have been found all over the Gandhara region. The Buddha is shown in various poses—standing, sitting, in deep meditation, and even in a state of starvation due to fasting while searching for enlightenment. Gandhara artists also sculpted elaborate Bodhisattva images, portraying them as sleek, moustached figures with rich robes and ornaments, said to be modelled on royal princes of the time. They took pride in showing emotion on their faces and in the details of their dress and accessories. Amongst these Buddhist themes, they would often slip in images associated with Roman art, such as winding grape vines, chubby flying cherubs with flower wreaths, centaurs, and Greek gods, such as Zeus, Apollo, and Athena!

Meanwhile, in faraway Mathura, the southern capital of the Kushanas and an important trade and pilgrimage centre, artisans already familiar with carving life-size statues of their monarchs now turned their attention to sculpting the Buddha. Using the speckled red sandstone from the area around Sikri, near present-day Agra, they created powerful-looking, broad-shouldered Buddha statues with strong limbs and smiling faces. These images seemed to owe their style to the nature deities or yakshas that had first appeared on stupa railings around the same area, and the style they used came to be known as the Mathura school of art.

The Gandhara and Mathura schools used very different styles to represent the Buddha. However, the message conveyed through them was the same. These were not just beautiful images made for ornamental reasons. They were figures that were expected to be respected and worshipped as gods.

25

Dinnerware from Rome

Potsherds of red Arretine ware, Arikamedu, Puducherry, c. first century BCE to second century CE

The potsherds you see in the illustration have travelled a long way. They once formed part of fine red tableware, platters, cups, and bowls with moulded decorations, originally made in the workshops of Arezzo in Italy sometime between the first century BCE and the middle of the first century CE. Large numbers of the pieces, carefully packed and loaded into the holds of sailing ships, made their way to the Coromandel Coast of southern India. Not far from present-day Puducherry, sailors used a sea inlet to sail up to a safe harbour on the right bank of the Ariyankuppam river. There, on the wooden jetty of a trading station named Arikamedu, traders would unload their wares.

Commercial ties between India and the West, particularly the Roman Empire go all the way back to the first millennium BCE. It is said the Roman Emperor Caesar Augustus received trade missions from India around 25 BCE. While both overland and maritime trade routes reached northern and western India, Arikamedu provides the earliest evidence of Indo-Roman

trade on the eastern coast. Arikamedu was known to ancient sailors as Poduke Emporion or Poduke trading station.

It was around the mid-eighteenth century when archaeologists began to notice intriguing artefacts at the abandoned site of Arikamedu. A gemstone engraved with the face of a man identified as Caesar Augustus and typically Roman-style amphorae, clay storage jars with two handles commonly used to transport liquids, were found at the site. Scholars wondered what these distinctly Roman pieces were doing in faraway southern India and how had they reached there.

When excavations finally began in the 1940s, archaeologists were stunned by what they found. It was clear that Arikamedu had been occupied from third century BCE onwards. It was a large settlement with brick houses, walled courtyards, ring wells, tanks, warehouses for storage, and the remains of a wooden jetty with rope fragments, probably used to secure docking ships.

In the lowest levels of the settlement, excavators found shards of the typically pinkish-yellow-coloured amphorae. They came from the Mediterranean area and were used to transport wine, fish sauce, and oils. Sangam literature written around these times refer to how sweet-scented wine was brought on the ships of the yavana, foreigners, and served to noblemen on special trays of gold.

Archaeologists also found Roman lamps, glassware, and semi-precious stones with intaglio—a typically Roman engraving style. Arikamedu itself seemed to be a major production centre of fine cotton cloth and muslin, and a prominent bead-manufacturing hub, producing fine beads of gold, shell, and terracotta for export. All products that the Romans would have wanted to carry back with them.

What interested scholars the most was the pottery that was found at the site. Apart from the amphorae, there were shards of what is called rouletted ware. The pottery was decorated with distinctive spiral patterns in a technique known as rouletting. Although the technique originated in the West, it is believed much of this style of pottery was locally produced since large quantities of it were found along the east coast in areas with a strong ancient tradition of pottery making. Did this mean that Roman craftspeople may have lived and worked at Arikamedu, influencing local craftsmen with their style?

As for the fine red tableware from Italy, also called Arretine ware, the potsherds had something important to reveal. A number of the pieces were stamped with the potters' family seals. The base of the flat dishes bore names like Vibie, Camvri, and Itta. These were traced back to the families that manufactured the pieces in Italy, giving scholars not just the origin of the pieces but a date with which to work out how old this trade was. Most Arretine pieces were made in Italy between the first century BCE and the second century CE. Thus, the trade with Arikamedu now had a date!

Scholars initially believed Arikamedu was a Roman trading post with substantial settlements of Roman traders and merchants who imported goods, such as wine and tableware, for their own use. But recent studies have revealed the trade from Rome to India was generally conducted by Egyptian and Arab merchant-sailors and agents. What is clear is that the ties between the Roman world and Arikamedu went beyond the commercial interests of trade. There was also interaction and an exchange of skills and crafts that influenced these communities that lived so far apart.

After the fall of the Roman Empire, Arikamedu turned its attention to trade with the East, to China and the Southeast Asian empires. Trade flourished for another 500 years, and the town was only finally abandoned around the sixteenth century.

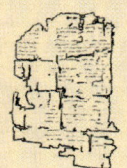

26

A Trade Deal from Muziris to the Mediterranean

The Muziris Papyrus fragment, Egypt, mid-second century CE

This brittle fragment of papyrus from the second century CE is one of the most important bits of information on ancient south Indian trade relations with the Mediterranean world. It originated in Egypt, and the text on both sides of the page is written neatly in Greek. The fragment is the remnant of a bigger document, now lost. But what this single page reveals is quite extraordinary.

On one side is a contract between a banker and a merchant. The banker, in the Egyptian town of Alexandria, lends money to the merchant to finance his trading expedition to the port of Muziris on the Malabar Coast of India. The money is to be paid back in a year. The borrower assures the banker that once back from India, he will be responsible for the onward transportation of the goods from the port (possibly Berenice on the Red Sea coast) westwards across the desert by camel train to Koptos on the banks of the River Nile. The whole cargo would then sail down the river to the major Egyptian port of Alexandria. There, Greek

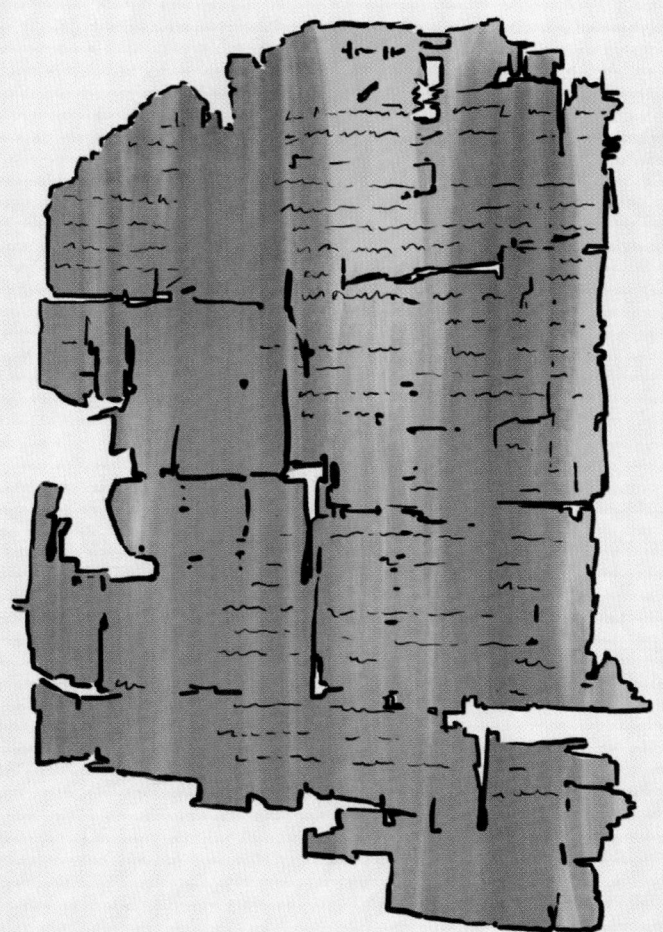

The Muziris Papyrus Fragment

and Roman merchants would be waiting to take the goods ahead to the Mediterranean kingdoms.

The papyrus is torn and damaged, and some details are tantalizingly missing, such as the names of the signatories. A rough translation of the merchant's undertaking to the banker, with missing words in brackets, reads like this:

'I will give to your camel driver 170 talents, fifty drachmas for use of the road to Koptos, and I will convey (your goods) inland through the desert under guard . . . to the public warehouses . . . at Koptos and I will place them under your ownership and seal . . .

'I will load (them) aboard at a required time on a seaworthy boat on the river, and I will convey (them) downstream to the warehouse . . . at Alexandria.

'. . . if, on the occurrence of the date of repayment specified in the loan agreements at Muziris, I do not then rightfully pay off the aforementioned loan in my name . . . you will possess and own . . . and transfer to where you wish and sell . . . (the goods).'

On the flip side of the page is part of a detailed list of calculations made by the merchant on the customs duty and taxes due on each item of cargo imported from India, possibly the same shipment mentioned in the contract. Once again, scholars have had to work hard to fill in the missing gaps in the writing on the fragmented document. They do not always agree, but the following is some of what the papyrus reveals.

In the middle of the second century CE, the merchant on his ship, the *Hermapollon*, made an early winter start from Muziris, sailing out towards the Red Sea. The ship's hold, by some estimates, was capable of carrying a staggering 635 tonnes of cargo. It was packed with eighty containers of Gangetic nard, an essential ingredient in perfumes and certain medicines; over three tonnes of elephant tusks; several tonnes of malabathron, a fragrant leaf used to flavour wines and sauces; small ivory pieces; tortoise shell; and bolts of fabric. But the bulk of her cargo consisted of over 500 tonnes of pepper!

It looks like the *Hermapollon* was a very large ship. In fact, in the early centuries of the Common Era, ocean-going vessels between Egypt and the southern Indian coast were the biggest the world had ever seen. There was a reason for it. In the words of an anonymous Greek-Egyptian merchant who wrote a handbook for merchants engaged in Indian

Ocean trade, 'very big ships sail to these emporia (markets) on account of the weight and the volume of the pepper and malabathron.'

Malabar pepper, sometimes called 'black gold', was considered a great luxury in those days. It was used as currency and traded for gold, so valuable that it made the long, risky journey to India worthwhile.

Apart from pepper, there were other products from India that the world wanted—fine textiles, cotton, sandalwood, precious and semi-precious stones, pearls, ivory, and tortoiseshell. In return, foreign merchants brought in gold, glass, coral, rare metals, silks and linens, wine, and olive oil. India was well located midway between the western and eastern markets. Internal trade routes and waterways were also developed so that traders from the interiors could make their way to port towns that dotted the peninsular coastline.

Literary sources and excavations speak of vibrant, cosmopolitan times between the third century BCE and third century CE when Arab, Persian, Greek, East African, and Phoenician merchants flocked to ports like Arikamedu and Puhar on the east coast and Muziris on the west coast. Some even set up permanent townships of their own.

The Muziris Papyrus gives us a most unexpected glimpse into the nitty gritty of big business in those times.

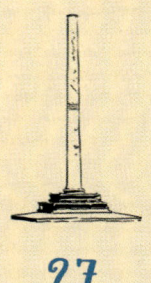

27

The Pillar of Many Voices

Polished sandstone pillar, Prayagraj, Uttar Pradesh, third century BCE, fourth century CE, and sixteenth century CE

In earlier chapters, we read about the Mauryan Emperor Ashoka's stone pillars—magnificent, gleaming sandstone columns that conveyed to us the words of one of ancient India's greatest rulers. The Allahabad pillar is yet another of these edict-bearing stone pillars erected by Ashoka in the third century BCE, but with an interesting twist.

It was originally made at the sandstone quarries of Chunar, near present-day Varanasi. Once engraved with the edicts of Ashoka, it was first set up at Kaushambi, an ancient town near present-day Prayagraj, formerly called Allahabad. A few centuries later, it made the fifty-kilometre journey from Kaushambi to Allahabad where it stands today within the ramparts of the fort. The pillar is over ten metres tall, with neatly inscribed rows of Ashoka's words in Prakrit language using the Brahmi script winding around the column. However, the capital has gone missing.

But there is more!

Directly below Ashoka's edict on the pillar there is another finely carved inscription. This one was written in ancient Sanskrit, using a later form of the Brahmi script called the Gupta-Brahmi script. It is a poem or a *prashasti*, literally meaning 'in praise of', composed by a man named Harishena. The poem sings the virtues of King Samudragupta.

Samudragupta was part of the illustrious Gupta dynasty that ruled large parts of northern and central India from the fourth to the sixth centuries CE. The heart of their empire covered areas once ruled by the Mauryas, with Pataliputra as their capital. But soon, they came to dominate an area that covered almost the entire subcontinent.

The Gupta period was a time of an outpouring of artistic and literary achievements. The Puranas—religious tales of gods, goddesses, and stories about the creation of the world that had been known for many centuries—were compiled and written down. The Ramayana and Mahabharata, and stories from the Jatakas and Panchatantra that, until now, had been a purely oral tradition, were also being transcribed at this time. Among the elite, Sanskrit became the chosen language over Prakrit.

The Guptas were patrons of Brahmanism, an early form of Hinduism. Artists vied with each other to produce beautiful terracotta, stone, and metal art depicting various Brahmanical deities, particularly Vishnu. The earliest free-standing Hindu temples and life-size deities appeared at this time. This was also the time of a host of achievements in the fields of medicine, mathematics, and literature. The great Sanskrit poet and playwright Kalidasa and the astronomer and mathematician Aryabhata are believed to have lived during Gupta times.

Not all of this cultural achievement was entirely due to the Guptas. Many regional kingdoms at the time were equally sophisticated, funding highly refined creations themselves. The Vakatakas of the Deccan, for instance, were contemporaries, and were engaged in sponsoring the beautiful paintings in the caves of Ajanta from the fifth century CE.

Samudragupta was possibly the most successful Gupta king, ruling in the mid-fourth century CE. And almost everything we know about him comes from the prashasti of Harishena on this pillar. Harishena was an important minister at the Gupta court and obviously a part-time poet. He describes Samudragupta's family, his military campaigns and conquests, his personal achievements as a warrior and ideal ruler, his talents as a poet and musician, and even his looks. One long verse describes every battle scar on his body!

Apart from his deep admiration for Samudragupta, Harishena presents a most interesting picture of the Indian subcontinent. We are told that after conquering the rulers closest to the Gupta heartland, Samudragupta took on the eastern kingdoms in Assam, Bengal, and the lower Himalayas. Their rulers were crushed and made to travel to the Gupta court to pay their tributes. Then he marched south, snaking along the eastern coast of present-day Odisha as far down as present-day Kanchipuram in Tamil Nadu. Twelve defeated southern rulers were pardoned after they had surrendered and were allowed to go back to ruling their kingdoms. However, the forest people of central India were not so lucky. They were defeated and enslaved. So, although the Guptas did not physically create an all-India empire, they managed to dominate most of it through a network of different kinds of relations with all the states of the time.

We get all this information from just one inscription on a pillar.

Many centuries later, on this very pillar, the sixteenth-century Mughal Emperor Jahangir decided he needed to write something too. Overwriting part of Ashoka's edicts there is a Persian verse, finely inscribed by Jahangir's favourite calligrapher as you can see in the illustration, telling us all about Jahangir's own great ancestors! Why would an immensely

wealthy Mughal choose to *reuse* a pillar for an important inscription of his own? Perhaps by now, the pillar itself had taken on an air of importance.

Three monarchs over three millennia from perhaps three of north India's greatest dynasties—Maurya, Gupta, and Mughal—make their appearance on the Allahabad pillar certainly making it one of the most unique sources of Indian history.

28

Bearer of the Lotus

Mural painting of Bodhisattva Padmapani, Ajanta Caves, Maharashtra, late fifth century CE

The Bodhisattva Padmapani is probably one of the most beautiful paintings you will ever see. The name roughly translates as the bearer of the lotus, and this painting, as depicted in the illustration, is considered one of the masterpieces of world art. Surrounded by attendants, musicians, and monkeys frolicking in the abundant foliage, the Bodhisattva seems unbothered by the ruckus around him. His expression is sublime and his eyes reflect an inner calm. The vivid, glowing colours make it hard for us to believe that the painting is almost 1500 years old. Why, then, is this tucked away inside a dark cave in a remote location where hardly anyone can view it?

To find an answer, we have to travel back to the second century BCE when Buddhist monks first started hollowing out caves in the rocky hills along the Western Ghats. They needed monasteries for the growing congregation of monks and nuns and remote places like these seemed ideal. The rock faces were skilfully carved into spacious chaityas, halls meant for prayers and worship, and viharas, which were the living quarters for the monks.

Many of the caves were located along the famous Dakshinapatha trade route, offering rest stops to the caravans of traders who walked these paths. There is evidence of the close links between the Buddhist monks and the prospering merchant class of the time. Inscriptions reveal many of the caves were sponsored by wealthy merchants, shipping agents, crafts guilds, royalty, and even *Yavanas* or foreigners. Some of the cave sites were well-known trading stations along the caravan route, with rest houses and other facilities for the merchants.

More than a thousand such caves have been found at places like Junnar, Karle, Bhaja, and Bedsa in present-day Maharashtra. Most of them were made between the second century BCE and seventh century CE. However, as time went on, they were slowly abandoned and then completely forgotten.

Then, in the early nineteenth century, a hunting party, scrambling down the forested slopes of the Waghora river valley, unexpectedly stumbled into a huge stone-pillared hall. Although in semi-darkness, they were astonished to find themselves surrounded by the most exquisite, colourful paintings. These were the long-deserted Ajanta caves! And on the walls were scenes from the everyday lives of people who lived thousands of years ago. Princes and princesses in splendid costumes accompanied by playful children and their attendants; grand processions watched by crowds of awestruck commoners; lush gardens teeming with animals and mythical creatures; wandering hermits; depictions of stories from the Jataka tales; and beautiful Bodhisattvas with their serene expressions of deep compassion.

Eventually, twenty-eight caves were discovered. They had been made in two phases. The earliest caves date back to the second century BCE sponsored by the Satavahana rulers and a later group between the fourth and sixth centuries CE, funded by the Vakatakas, who were rulers in the Deccan. Interestingly, both dynasties followed Brahmanical traditions and did not think it unusual to fund Buddhist monasteries.

The caves are majestic, with soaring vaulted ceilings carved with rafters made to look like wood and long, pillared halls with stone stupas at their far ends. But it was the paintings that caught the world's attention. These, the earliest surviving mural paintings in India, were unmatched anywhere in the ancient world—their elegant style, the realistic expressions of the subjects, the technical finesse of creating three-dimensional effects and perspective with shading, and the warm mineral colours that still glowed almost 2000 years later.

Scholars found the techniques of the Ajanta paintings had travelled with the ideas of early Hinduism and Buddhism along with merchant caravans, influencing art in Afghanistan, Central Asia, China, and Japan. They headed south to Sri Lanka and Southeast Asia as well, where the classical art of the region traces its roots to the painting styles of Ajanta. Many artists of the modern art movement in India, including Nandalal Bose, Asit Kumar Haldar, and Amrita Sher-Gil, are said to have been influenced by this art.

While ancient paintings have been discovered all over India—from the Hindu and Jain caves of Karnataka, temple walls of Tamil Nadu, palaces of Kerala to monasteries in the high Himalayas of Ladakh and Kashmir— it is at Ajanta that we witness the birth of the classic Indian painting. The artists had learned their techniques through a verbal tradition handed down through generations and over centuries. They chose to remain anonymous, never signing their masterpieces. They were content to let their skills and their deeply spiritual vision of the world speak through their work. Within the cool, dark interiors of the rock-cut caves, pilgrims and seekers were left to discover these treasures for themselves.

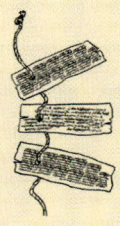

29

The First Book on Ayurveda

Birch bark manuscript, China, fourth to early fifth century CE

Early in 1890, Lieutenant Hamilton Bower of the British Indian Army was on a top-secret mission. He was hunting down a murderer on the run. The fugitive, a rather dodgy Pathan trader, was accused of killing a Scottish business associate in cold blood two years earlier. Following treacherous trails through the frozen Himalayan passes, Bower made his way to the northern edge of the Gobi Desert. There, in that desolate terrain, Bower and his small party set up camp at Kucha, an old oasis town in present-day Uyghur region of China, which was once an important hub on the Silk Road.

A few days later, they had a visitor. The man carried a small package of ancient-looking manuscripts. He claimed they had been found in a nearby stupa and offered them for sale. The manuscripts looked rather ragged, but Lieutenant Bower decided to buy them anyway. As it happened, that was a smart move because these manuscripts turned out to be one of the earliest written works ever found from India.

The text was written on fifty-five oblong birch-bark leaves. As you can see in the illustration on the facing page, each had a hole punched in the middle of the left side of the leaf for the string that would have once bound them together like a book. Based on the ancient Sanskrit verses written in the Gupta-Brahmi script, experts dated the manuscript to the Gupta era, between the fourth and early fifth centuries BCE.

There were seven parts in all but scholars were most astounded by the first three, as these were on Ayurveda, the ancient Indian system of medicine. Although Ayurveda is said to date back to Vedic times, the medical treatises of Sushruta and Charaka, commonly known as the founders of the system, were known only in oral form. The Bower Manuscript, as it came to be known, is the earliest surviving text on Ayurveda, even quoting the great sages Sushruta and Charaka and their works. The manuscript was written by four Buddhist monks who once lived in a monastery near Kucha.

What was this valuable manuscript doing in Central Asia?

The Bower Manuscript gave scholars a whole lot of information about what was going on in India at the time. It was evident that by the time of the Guptas, the literary tradition in India had really picked up steam. A number of works which had been passed down orally for centuries, including the Ramayana, the Mahabharata, the Puranas, and the Jataka tales, were finally being written down. Usually these were written in Pali and later Sanskrit, engraved on thin, flexible palm leaves with a stylus, and then smeared with an ink made of charcoal soot and vegetable juice for the words to stand out. The pages of the manuscript were punched with holes, threaded with string, and bound with wooden covers.

The Buddha's message had been travelling to Central Asia for many years with merchants and pilgrims and there was already a large population of devotees in those parts. With the stability of the Gupta period, India was a hub of busy international trade routes. On the busiest of these routes, caravans loaded with spices, cotton textiles, pearls, and precious stones

made their way to Central Asia and China. They returned laden with ivory, jade, and silk and accompanied by pilgrims travelling to India, eager for knowledge of the Buddha from his birthplace.

Once in India, the Chinese pilgrims found other equally interesting works on various subjects, such as mathematics, astronomy, medicine, botany, philosophy, and the arts, to take back to their home country. Indian monks often accompanied them on their return to China, living in monasteries and caravanserais along the way, spreading the word of the Buddha and working on manuscript translations. Many of these important works would have been lost to us but for the work of these monks and pilgrims.

And that is how the Bower Manuscript came to be buried in a stupa in that remote Central Asian town. After it was discovered, there was a great flurry of exploration, bringing masses of ancient Buddhist manuscripts tumbling out of monasteries and caves along the Silk route. One of these, the library of manuscripts at Dunhuang, another key trading post on the edge of the Gobi Desert, is considered one of the most important archaeological discoveries ever!

Within those fragile manuscript leaves, scholars discovered the ideas of ancient India and its beliefs, values, and knowledge that was shared so freely, spreading to all parts of the known world at the time. Lieutenant Bower never did find the ruffian he was looking for, but through this discovery he opened up a great treasure trove of priceless information for future generations.

30

The Monumental Varahas

Stone relief at Udayagiri and stone sculpture at
Eran, Madhya Pradesh, fourth to fifth century CE

The illustrations in this chapter are of two stone boars. Both were
sculpted in the Gupta period, but they tell very different stories.

By around the third and fourth centuries CE, things were changing in the
religious lives of the people. Ideas about gods and worship began to
grow around earlier traditions, slowly developing into what we now
know as Hinduism. People chose individual deities, worshipping them
with *bhakti* or devotion. Cults of worship grew around the gods Shiva and
Vishnu. Shiva was now represented in either the symbolic form of a *linga*,
indicating his energy and strength, or in human form. Vishnu appeared
in his avatars—human or animal forms—that he is said to have taken on
whenever the world was threatened by dangerous forces. Depending on
the danger, he appeared as one of ten avatars, including in forms such
as a tortoise, a fish, a dwarf, a warrior, or a boar.

It was around the same time that the Puranas began to be compiled.
These were well-known stories about kings and queens, gods and
goddesses, and the creation of the world. They had been circulating

for centuries in their oral form, told and retold by bards, pilgrims, and merchants, changing in details as the storytellers travelled and came across new ideas and local beliefs across the land. Now, for the first time, the Brahmanas took it upon themselves to write these stories down in Sanskrit, in a form that would be simple enough to read out to the common people who may not have been literate.

Sculptors and artists were inspired to experiment, representing these gods and goddesses in new, elaborate forms. Each deity was depicted with a specific set of costumes, ornaments, and weapons to make them easily recognizable by the worshipper. The familiar Hindu icons of today were originally visualized at this time.

And that is how the first of these images came to be created. You can see in the illustration below—a spectacular thirteen-foot-high relief of Nar Varaha, Vishnu as a half-man, half-boar, emerging from a cave wall at

Stone Relief of Nar Varaha at Udayagiri

Udayagiri, near Vidisha in central India. It forms part of a complex of rock-cut caves from the Gupta period, portraying mainly Hindu deities.

The scene depicted is based on a story in the Puranas about how the gods and demons fought for control of the universe. In the confusion, a demon named Hiranyaksha tried to drag the earth goddess Bhudevi deep into the cosmic ocean. She was saved when Vishnu, in his boar avatar, came to her rescue.

Here on the cave wall, a powerful-looking, sculpted Vishnu with a human body and a boar's head is seen rescuing Bhudevi, plucking her from the churning ocean waters. The scene shows neat rows of gods, sages, and royalty standing on wavy lines (depicting the ocean), shouting out praises, and applauding Varaha's brave deed. Kneeling amidst the waters is another figure. Sadly, it is missing a head, but going by his well-groomed appearance, some scholars believe that this is the royal

The Monumental Stone Varaha at Eran

donor himself, Chandragupta II, son of Samudragupta and also known as Vikramaditya!

The Guptas were well-known patrons of Vaishnavism, worshipping Vishnu as their chief god. It is believed that this dramatic, sculpted tableau is a not just an object of worship but a symbolic depiction of the Guptas' vast conquests. The muscular Varaha figure is a reminder to the viewer of their power and their role as protectors of their subjects.

Meanwhile, at Eran, not far from Udayagiri, there is another Varaha from a later date. This Varaha is different. Standing solidly in front of a long-destroyed shrine, it is a mountainously huge, eleven-foot-high boar. Fine carvings decorate the massive body, including figures of over one thousand sages arranged in rows with Bhudevi hanging delicately from the Varaha's right tusk. Although it now stands in the open, it is believed to have once been housed in a shrine of its own. This temple complex was made by a local governor, Dhyanavisnu, in memory of his family and dedicated to the 'ruler of the earth'—Buddhagupta of the Gupta dynasty in the year 485 CE.

However, on the boar's broad chest, there is another, more interesting inscription. The first line is a dedication to a *maharajadhiraja*, the king who is foremost among the great kings. This king of kings was not a Gupta, but a Huna named Toramana! Hunas were the fierce nomadic warrior groups from Central Asia who had taken over large swathes of northern India at this time. By the time the temple complex was completed and the Varaha sculpted, the Hunas had replaced the Guptas as the rulers of the land. The devout governor had a new boss. Thus, changing times were reflected in a sculpture that combined a religious and political statement, all in one.

31

A House for the Divine

Stone shrine, Sanchi, Madhya Pradesh, late fourth to early fifth century CE

Sanchi 17 is an unremarkable stone building that stands quietly in a corner of the Sanchi stupa complex in central India. Surrounded by other, far more dazzling buildings, you would hardly notice it if you were to visit the place.

So, why is this modest stone structure considered one of the most important buildings of ancient India?

Sanchi 17, depicted in the illustration here, is possibly the oldest surviving free-standing stone temple in India. It was built in the early fifth century CE, during the Gupta period. But here there are no dramatic towering shikaras and elaborately carved interiors that are usually associated with temples. Instead, you will find a simple, small, flat-roofed shrine or sanctum with a four-pillared porch. It is undecorated except for the inverted lotuses carved on the pillars and the prancing lions that appear to be supporting the roof. Although originally used for Buddhist worship, Sanchi 17 bears traces of the basic style seen in most Hindu temples that were built in later periods.

We already know that by the time of the Guptas, modes of worship were slowly changing. Vedic rituals and outdoor fire sacrifices had earlier formed an important part of the prevailing Brahmanical religion and the Guptas, although supportive of Buddhist and Jain practices, were mainly patrons of Brahmanism. Many Gupta inscriptions and coins refer to these rituals. Vibrant stories of gods, goddesses, and heroes from the Puranas and epics were being written down at this time, which captured the imagination of the common people. Skilled artisans were inspired to create beautiful images of these characters. The yakshas and nagas of the Buddhist stupas were slowly being edged out by sculptures of Vishnu in his various avatars and Shiva and Durga in the forms in which we see them today.

Where were these deities to be housed for devotees to worship them?

No one really knows when the earliest temples devoted to Brahmanical gods were constructed. In the earliest days, way before Gupta times,

Sanchi 17

these temples probably consisted of caves hollowed out of rock faces, something that was present in the Buddhist and Jain traditions.

The famous Heliodorus stone pillar inscription of the second century BCE was once the centre of a temple complex dedicated to Vishnu. At Udayagiri, Madhya Pradesh, there is a small, early Gupta rock-cut cave shrine fronted by an open, pillared outer hall, which is part cave and part free-standing temple. It is against this backdrop that, finally, we find a stand-alone temple made with dressed stone bricks at Sanchi, named temple number 17 or Sanchi 17 by archaeologists.

There would certainly have been temples of this kind dating back to an earlier time, but they may have been built with perishable materials like wood, thatched roof, brick, and terracotta, which is why they would not have lasted too long. These would have been simple structures too, with a small room known as a garbhagriha or sanctum, in which to place an idol of the deity. From here, a single doorway would lead to a porch or mandapa where gathered devotees could catch a glimpse of their gods as they came in to worship.

By the fifth century CE, the Guptas ruled vast territories, their treasuries filled with taxes from their expanding kingdom. As a way of showing off their new wealth and status and perhaps also to indicate they were closely related to the gods and heroes of the stories from the Puranas, they began to fund the construction of more elaborate temple complexes. The beautiful Dashavatara temple at Deogarh in present-day Uttar Pradesh was built in the Gupta period. Similarly, the unusual brick temple at Bhitargaon, near the city of Kanpur in Uttar Pradesh, with its high tower above the shrine, reminds us of the later shikaras of north Indian temples.

The evolving temple building styles of the time reflect the great changes taking place during Gupta times in the artistic, religious, and social aspects of life. It was a time when new features and innovations developed that gave us the visuals we now associate with Hindu religious practices, more than 1600 years later.

Temples gradually expanded into elaborate, richly funded affairs. And yet, no matter how complex they became, they always retained, at their heart, the small sanctum for the deity and the pillared porch that was first observed in Sanchi 17.

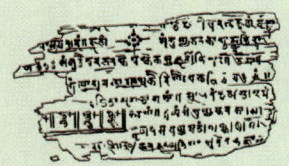

32

The First Written Zero

Birch-bark manuscript, Bakhshali, Pakistan, fourth century CE

In the summer of 1881, near the village of Bakhshali, not far from the ruins of the ancient university town of Taxila in present-day Pakistan, a farmer was digging along a ruined stone enclosure when he unearthed an ancient-looking manuscript. There were about seventy leaves of birch bark, most of them falling apart with age and densely packed with inked writing. The fragile package was handed over to the authorities for examination and translation. Then came a stunning announcement.

The manuscript was essentially a handbook of mathematical rules, problems, and instructions, possibly for the use of merchants and traders, written in a language which included elements of what is called Buddhist Sanskrit, Prakrit, and Old Kashmiri. The problems were written in verse and the solutions laid out in carefully worded prose with elaborate explanations. The topics covered were fractions, profit and loss problems, mensuration, linear equations, square roots, and geometric progressions. The manuscript was believed to have belonged to the third or fourth century CE, making it the earliest Indian mathematical text ever found!

But there was more. Throughout the manuscript, scattered within large numbers—poised above and below fraction lines and included within long multiplication sums—were large dots. They were symbols for zero, and it appeared that the Brahmana who originally wrote the manuscript, described as 'the son of Chajaka ... king of calculators for the use of Vasistha's son Hasika', was using zero quite confidently as a number for mathematical operations. These were the earliest written representations ever found of that all-important number—zero!

Ganita-shastra, or mathematical science, has been a highly advanced subject in India since ancient times. Using a combination of philosophical concepts, advanced astrological knowledge, and smart number skills, ancient Indian mathematicians managed to formulate many of the fundamental concepts of mathematics that are still accepted today.

Going back all the way to Vedic times, numbers were not just numerals but were spoken of in tracts of verse. Brick altars for sacrifices were built with guidelines from the earliest manuals on geometry of the time. By the fifth century CE, the number notations we are familiar with had appeared, and the decimal system had been discovered that allowed the use of extremely large numbers based on the use of a decimal point. Indian mathematicians also invented the earliest forms of algebra. Among the many recorded accomplishments of the famous astronomer Aryabhata was a value of pi correct to four decimal places. In the Jain traditions, deep interest in the cosmos led to discussions on geometry and the arithmetic of large numbers.

And then there was zero.

No one really knows who invented zero or when. A pre-second century BCE Sanskrit text by Pingala uses a symbol he calls *shunya*, empty or void, which is possibly the earliest reference to the concept of nothing or zero. Texts written in the sixth and seventh centuries by astrologers and mathematicians like Varahamihira and Brahmagupta show they were already using the zero. Many of these texts were based on knowledge from much earlier times when scholars had memorized this knowledge and passed it on in spoken form until, finally, in some later period, someone decided to write it all down.

Other ancient civilizations, such as the Mesopotamians and the Mayans, understood the idea of using a symbol to denote 'nothing' as a concept.

However, it was in India that the dot hollowed out into the circle, the widely accepted symbol for zero, and more importantly, where it was first used for independent mathematical operations. A number in its own right, in one stroke, the zero made large numbers easy to count and handle. From India, important mathematical ideas made their way to West Asia with Persian and Arab scholars and traders, carrying the concept of zero along with them. Today, it's hard to imagine our world without zero.

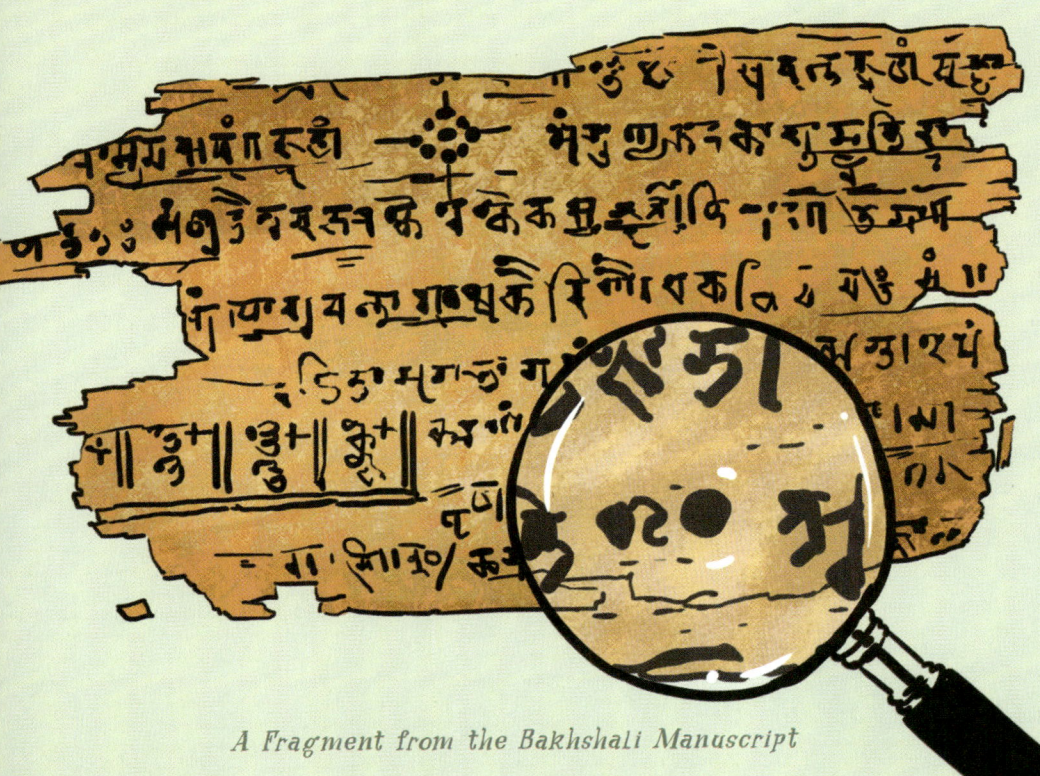

A Fragment from the Bakhshali Manuscript

The Bakhshali manuscript now rests in the Bodleian Library at the University of Oxford, England. Its fragile pages are preserved in a special folio with transparent windows to view the manuscript without the need to physically handle it. There is some unresolved controversy over the age of the manuscript. Based on the language and script and the mathematical concepts discussed, some historians believe that the Bakshali manuscript could be a later copy of a more ancient text written around the fourth century CE. Scholars continue to research the language and script, scouring it for more information.

But for now, the Bakhshshali manuscript is considered the earliest mathematical manuscript from India, one that provides written evidence of what is considered the greatest invention in the history of mathematics.

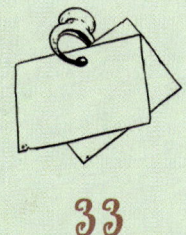

33

Prabhavatigupta Donates Land

Copper-plate inscriptions, Pune, Maharashtra, late fourth century CE

In the late fourth century CE, Prabhavatigupta did something rather unusual. She decided to donate land and a village named Danguna to a learned Brahmana named Chanalaswamin. It was unusual because it was generally thought that women in those days did not have the freedom to own property. But Prabhavatigupta was no ordinary woman. She was royalty, the widow of a Vakataka king and the queen regent, actively ruling the Vakataka kingdom—an area that is now in northern Madhya Pradesh and north-eastern Maharashtra—on behalf of her minor sons. What was even more surprising was that she made sure everyone knew she was also the daughter of the powerful Gupta king, Chandragupta II! Prabhavatigupta was both a Gupta princess and a Vakataka queen.

All this information comes to us from a pair of copper-plate inscriptions. The two flat rectangular pieces of copper inscribed in ancient Sanskrit were found in the early twentieth century. They belonged to Balwant Bhau Nagarkar, a coppersmith from Pune who claimed they had been a family heirloom for as long as he could remember. Unfortunately, scholars had barely made the translations from Sanskrit before the original Poona plates, as they came to be known, suddenly disappeared, leaving us with just the ink rubbings that you see in the illustration! However, we can make a reasonable guess as to what they would have looked like from a number of other such copper plates that have been found in various parts of the country.

Copper-plate inscriptions were quite the fashion, particularly from the fourth to seventh century CE. This was a time when chieftains and warrior kings jostled for power, looking to create independent kingdoms and styling dynasties of their own. In order to show their new-found power, they began to grant large tracts of land to various influential groups of people, mainly Brahmanas, trade guilds, religious and charitable institutions, and to temples.

The people who benefited from these donations were expected to develop the land, often in remote, previously uncultivated areas, and hand in some of the benefits in the form of taxes or agricultural goods to the royal donor. Through these transactions, the economy gradually evolved. The overlords increased their hold over larger areas of land and also increased their revenues without having to worry too much about collecting taxes directly from their expanding kingdoms. The donations to the Brahmanas also guaranteed the prestige of these chieftains as the Brahmanas would then perform all the necessary rituals to make sure the chieftains were declared as kshatriyas of high status with 'royal' lineage, no less!

Most copper-plate inscriptions consist of a few flat, rectangular copper plates held together with a heavy copper ring bearing a royal seal or emblem. The plates are engraved with closely packed lines of writing generally in Sanskrit but also, depending on where they were found, in Prakrit, Tamil, Kannada, and Odia. They usually begin with rather grand

Ink Rubbings of Queen Prabhavatigupta's Copper-Plate Inscriptions

verses praising the donor and talking about their family history before going on to describe the details of the actual donation.

The land grants were often very specific, with references to village boundaries and geographical features like ponds, lakes, and rivers, agricultural produce, transportation, temple buildings, rural life, and various crafts and professions.

While these were centuries of great, sweeping changes, there are relatively few archaeological and historical records of these years. These copper-plate inscriptions contain a wealth of information which reveal rare insights into everyday lives of the common people in those days.

As for Queen Prabhavatigupta, this was not the only donation that she made. Her name appears in at least two other copper-plate inscriptions and one temple wall, providing details of her background as a Gupta princess, her marriage into the up-and-coming Vakataka family and her extraordinary, perhaps two decade-long, reign as regent for two minor sons after the early death of her husband, the Vakataka ruler Rudrasena II. Her detailed inscriptions are links to understanding how the Vakatakas rose through turbulent social and political changes, to become one of the most prominent dynasties of the time.

34

Xuanzang's Epic Journey

Painting on silk, Tokyo, Japan, fourteenth century CE

Early in the seventh century CE, a young Buddhist monk named Xuanzang lived in Chang'an, the capital of the Tang kingdom in eastern China. He was a devout Buddhist who was dedicated to his studies. However, the more Xuanzang studied the Buddhist texts available in China at the time, the more dissatisfied he became. These texts were filled with errors in translation and contradictory ideas. Monks were often confused as to what the real teachings of the Buddha were. After much thought, Xuanzang came up with a plan. Why not travel to India, the birthplace of Buddhism? There, he could meet Indian teachers and source original texts. He could bring back these authentic manuscripts and translate them himself, putting an end to the prevailing confusion.

The idea was a bold one. In addition to the long, dangerous journey through unknown lands, Xuanzang also had to plan how to sneak out of the Tang kingdom. At that time, due to widespread civil unrest, crossing the frontier had been forbidden by King Taizong. In 629 CE, Xuanzang secretly started on an epic sixteen-year journey in which he would walk more than 16,000 kilometres and visit more than 100 kingdoms.

The journey to India was long and challenging. Xuanzang traversed desolate landscapes, sandy deserts, and frigid snow-clad mountains. He was attacked by bandits, lost all his belongings, survived an attempt on his life, and wandered about lost in the vast Gobi Desert. Four years later, after unimaginable hardships, Xuanzang managed to make his way to the eastern banks of the River Ganga, the land of the Buddha.

He spent more than ten years in India gathering an enormous collection of 657 Buddhist manuscripts, holy relics, and statues of Buddha. By the time Xuanzang returned to China, he was a legend. But before he could re-enter his homeland, the monk sent a message to King Taizong. He explained the important reason for which he had left the kingdom without his permission, what he had done in the years he had been away, and begged his forgiveness. Eight months later, eager to hear stories of the faraway land of the Buddha and to see Xuanzang's rare and precious collection, King Taizong granted him an audience. Xuanzang

was received with great honour, entering the capital city in a ceremonial parade, cheered on by crowds of people who had lined the streets to welcome him.

Xuanzang became one of the most important translators of Buddhist scriptures, with his works spreading to the neighbouring kingdoms of Korea and Japan as well. After his death, he stayed alive in the people's imagination through folktales, theatre, puppet shows, and art. In the illustration on the previous page, a fourteenth-century Japanese painting depicts Xuanzang walking with a bamboo backpack filled with scrolls of scriptures.

Apart from his translations, Xuanzang also wrote an account of his travels called *Records of the Western Regions Visited during the Great Tang Dynasty*. It is considered one of the most important accounts of life in seventh-century India.

He entered the Indian subcontinent from what is now eastern Afghanistan and wound his way through Pakistan and Kashmir to the sacred spots associated with the Buddha's life in the Ganga valley. Xuanzang wrote down these experiences in great detail. The landscape, the climate, the people, Indian laws and social customs, governments, religions, the caste system, food habits, attire, architecture, languages, taxes, measurements, writing systems, burial practices, and even the prevailing personal hygiene practices!

He spent several years at Nalanda University, in what is now Bihar. His account describes the grandeur of this centre of Buddhist learning, which was set in a sprawling campus of beautifully decorated monasteries and massive libraries filled with precious palm-leaf manuscripts. More than 10,000 students, many of them from other countries, were taught by 2000 master scholars. Apart from Buddhist studies, over a hundred lectures were held every day to teach Sanskrit, the Vedas, mathematics, logic, grammar, medicine, and several other disciplines. The students were provided housing and food rations of rice, milk, and butter, most of which were donated by nearby villages who were responsible for the upkeep of the university.

Xuanzang travelled extensively in India. With his great learning and charisma, he soon caught the eye of the reigning kings of the time— Harsha of Kannauj and King Kumara of Kamarupa, in present-day Assam. Xuanzang's first-hand account of meetings with these kings and their conversations on Chinese culture are some of the most unique accounts in Indian history.

Centuries later, in the nineteenth century, *Records of the Western Regions* became an invaluable guide to historians and archaeologists. Following Xuanzang's route and excavating at places mentioned in his account, they found, to their great surprise, that everything the intrepid traveller had recorded was just as he had described.

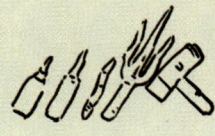

35

A Mason's Tools

Stone carving, Papanatha Temple, Pattadakal, Karnataka, mid-seventh century CE

The entire landscape of the Indian subcontinent is dotted with thousands of ancient temples. Most of these feature beautifully appointed complexes with pillared shrines, carved towers, and *mandapas* or open halls. The walls are covered with exquisitely sculpted deities and relief panels with stories from mythology. Built on a massive scale, they were expensive projects sponsored most often by kings, queens, or wealthy merchant guilds.

Have you ever wondered who imagined these creations? Who planned them and how did they build them?

The names of the clever architects, skilful sculptors, and anonymous masons whose hard labour built these creations have been, most often, lost in time. Which is why this particular panel on the wall of the Papanatha temple at Pattadakal, in present-day north Karnataka, is a surprise.

The Papanatha temple is part of an unusual group of temples along the River Malaprabha. It was built during the time of the powerful early Chalukya rulers who ruled the area from the sixth to the eighth centuries CE. As you can see in the illustration, instead of celestial or mythological figures, this panel on the temple wall features carved chisels—an implement that carpenters or stonemasons use. The stonemasons might have used chisels exactly like these to shape the massive stone blocks needed to build the temple. Or they may have been the implements of choice of the sculptors responsible for the exquisite carvings of the temple. We learn about the name of the architect who built the temple from an inscription in Kannada located nearby—Revadi Ovajja. Revadi lived in the mid-seventh century CE and belonged to the guild of the Sarvasiddhi acharyas, master craftspeople who designed temples. He was assisted in his work by the master sculptors Baladeva and Devarya.

The Early Chalukyas—called so to distinguish them from later dynasties who ruled further east and were also known as Chalukyas—dominated this part of the Deccan for over two centuries. Although they spent much of their time battling neighbouring kingdoms, they managed to sponsor interesting experiments in temple building on several sites along the River Malaprabha. Perhaps they wanted to show the people how rich and powerful they were or to impress upon them their closeness to the gods. These are among the first temples funded by royals.

The earliest temples look more like caves, emerging out of huge sandstone cliffs like the Buddhist chaityas or rock-cut monasteries of old. In the ancient towns of Aihole and Vatapi (later known as Badami), there are free-standing temples built in a variety of styles. While some are in the southern Dravida style with a pyramidal tower of carved tiers called a vimana, others are in the northern Nagara style with a curvilinear tower or shikara. The mixture of styles seems to indicate that there was much experimentation in different distinct styles of architecture. Did the craftspeople and architects come here from different parts of India?

Masonry Tools Carved onto a Wall of the Papanatha Temple

In the middle of the seventh century, the Chalukyas moved their capital to the town of Pattadakal, continuing their experiments in temple architecture styles. Among the oldest of the temples built here was the Papanatha temple. Nearby, scholars were excited to discover the remains of a stone quarry.

In the quarry, there are clear signs that this was where hardworking masons cut and dressed the stones required for the temples at the Chalukyan capital. On the steep sandstone cliffs, some rock faces have straight lines of deep, wedge-shaped holes. It appears the quarrymen were marking out where they intended to cut out slabs of rock from the cliff. Wooden pieces would have been inserted into these holes and doused with water, expanding them and splitting the rock. The masons would have then hammered out the split pieces in huge chunks to be dressed as blocks for the temple walls.

Along the smooth-rock surfaces, there are scribbled inscriptions, including names like Bhribhrigu and Vira Vidhyadhara. We can only conjecture if these were the names of masons. There are inscribed doodles of birds and animals as well as sketches of arches and doorways, almost as if sculptors were sketching rough ideas for the final carving to be done on the temple walls. There are remains of what could have been the living quarters of the workers. One interesting rock surface has a series of even stroke marks in groups of seven. Scholars believe that these could be part of an 'attendance register' of sorts which the overseers used to calculate payments that were due to the masons! And most incredibly, buried underneath the rubble, an ancient steel wedge was found along with a heavy hammer head that would have once been used to split rock slabs.

The chisels carved on this slab at Papanatha was perhaps a reminder, a way of honouring the hard work of the masons and craftspeople involved, not only in the making of a magnificent temple, but also in making the Chalukyan kingdom a bridge of ideas connecting the north and the south.

36

Ravikirti's Song of Praise

Temple wall inscription, Aihole, Karnataka, 634–635 CE

On a windswept hill in the ancient town of Aihole, north Karnataka, is the Meguti Jain temple. It was built between 634 and 635 CE, by the poet of the Chalukya court, Ravikirti. Ravikirti also put his poetic talent to use in a famous inscription on one of the temple walls, that you see in the illustration. In nineteen lines, written in Sanskrit using an old Kannada script, he wrote a *prashasti* or song of praise. It was in honour of the entire Chalukya family but specifically listed the great qualities of the reigning king, Pulakeshin II.

The Aihole inscription, as it came to be known, gives an unbelievably detailed account of the conquests of Pulakeshin II, possibly the greatest of Chalukya kings and lord of almost the entire Deccan at one time. Ravikirti tells us how Pulakeshin II wisely first secured his own throne in an area that is now northern Karnataka after an evil uncle tried to grab it for himself. Then he worked his way up the western coast, using his navy to take islands and important ports on the coastline. Eventually, after subduing the kingdoms of southern Gujarat and Rajasthan, he stopped on the banks of the River Narmada. Here, he was to confront one of the greatest challenges of his life.

Meanwhile, King Harsha of Kannauj was by now the ruler of almost all of north India, with a kingdom that stretched as far as Bengal and parts of Assam. Pulakeshin II, the young upstart from the Deccan, had grabbed all the western ports that Harsha wanted. So, he had to be stopped! With his massive armies, limitless wealth, and great experience in battle, Harsha had assumed the task would be simple. But he had underestimated the ambition of his young opponent, Pulakeshin II.

In the winter of 618 CE, Harsha's army marched to the banks of the River Narmada. Records of the time describe a great clash in the forested Vindhyan foothills, with terrible bloodshed and hundreds of fallen war elephants. Harsha realized he could not win and retreated north, leaving the Deccan to the Chalukyas. In the words of Ravikirti, 'Harsha had his joy (a play on the word *harsha*, which also means joy) melted away by fear' on account of the fierce Pulakeshin II!

Xuanzang, the Chinese Buddhist scholar who had travelled widely in India at that time, wrote about Pu-lo-ki-she, as he called him. He hailed him as such a powerful ruler that even Harsha, with all his resources, was unable to defeat him. He praises Pu-lo-ki-she as a just and generous ruler. This is quite unusual, since Xuanzang was not given to praising anyone who was not a Buddhist. He was also Harsha's friend and confidante. So this praise was even more surprising.

Pulakeshin II did not stop there. He continued east, conquering parts of modern-day Odisha and Andhra, before marching south. Crossing the River Kaveri, he forced the kingdoms of the south—the Cholas, Pandyas, and Cheras—to accept his offer of friendship. But it was here, in Tamilakam—the region that is now Tamil Nadu—that he made a formidable enemy. Pulakeshin II chased the Pallava king and forced him to take refuge in the fort of Kanchipuram. Humiliated in defeat, the Pallavas never forgot this insult. It set off a whole series of tit-for-tat wars and plenty of bloodshed that continued over the course of an entire century!

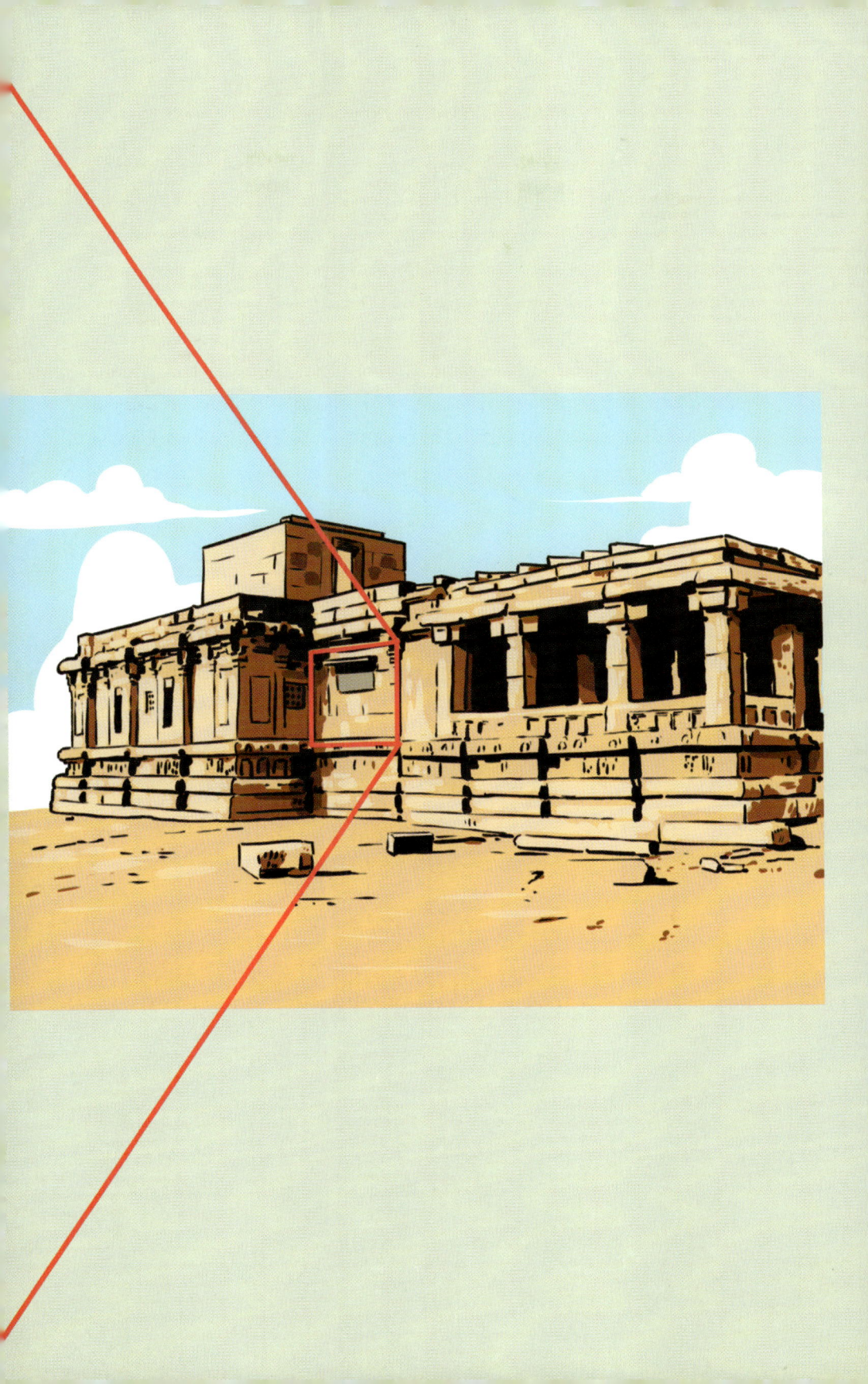

Pulakeshin II returned to his capital, Vatapi (later known as Badami), reigning in great splendour after his many conquests. Soon enough though, the Pallavas started seeking revenge. In 642 CE, Narasimhavarman I marched to Vatapi, defeated the Chalukyas, and ransacked their great capital. Pulakeshin II is said to have died in this battle. There is a triumphant inscription on a rock, now rather defaced, behind an old temple in Vatapi that boasts of Narasimhavarman's great victory, calling him Maha-Malla or Great Wrestler. He later took on the title Vatapikonda or the 'conqueror of Vatapi'. The Pallavas occupied the place for over thirteen years until one of the sons of Pulakeshin II was able to grab Vatapi back for the Chalukyas.

The Aihole inscription speaks of Pulakeshin's triumphs. Not long after, another inscription at Vatapi speaks of his defeat.

37

Real-Life Events in Pallava Times

Sculpted wall panels, Vaikuntha Perumal Temple, Kanchipuram, eighth century CE

Running along the walls of a raised verandah in the Vaikuntha Perumal temple at Kanchipuram, dating back to the eighth century CE, are rows of unique sculptures. Among all the gods, goddesses, mythical figures, and beasts sculpted on the walls and ceilings of the ancient temple, these rows depict scenes from real-life events. There are more than 500 panels placed in two rows, separated by a band. Each scene is framed in its own panel, giving the walls the effect of a sequential comic strip. The sculpted scenes depict the life and times of the Pallavas, the rather dazzling dynasty that ruled in the areas of what is now southern Andhra Pradesh and northern Tamil Nadu from the late third to the ninth centuries CE.

The Pallavas seemed to excel in every field. They were ruthless warriors, carving out a large kingdom for themselves in the fertile river valleys along the coastal belt of this region. Constantly holding off their arch enemies, the Chalukyas and the Pandyas, on the battlefield, the Pallava rulers still managed to find time for culture and the arts. Many of them were outstanding playwrights and poets themselves. Others were musicians and builders. The Pallavas were also responsible for the great spurt of construction in the seventh century CE. At the port town of Mamallapuram, also known as Mahabalipuram, the five carved stone rathas, the Shore temple, and the magnificently sculpted rock relief known as 'The Descent of the Ganges' are considered some of the most important sculptures of ancient India.

Mamallapuram, under the Pallavas, was one of the most important ports in the world at the time. Ships laden with spices, sandalwood, precious stones, cotton cloth, ivory, and other luxury goods sailed to China. Expeditions were sent out to Sri Lanka and Southeast Asia including present-day Indonesia, Cambodia, Vietnam, and Laos. Traders, merchants, craftspeople, and temple priests set up colonies in those places, influencing their cultural and artistic lives. Pallava-style temples, inscriptions in Tamil, and kings who declared themselves devotees of Vishnu were common in Malaya and Java. Tamil literature is full of stories of merchants and adventurers sailing in ships so laden with treasures that the vessels were in danger of breaking into pieces! In the eighth century, even the otherwise reclusive Tang Chinese emperor set up military and trade ties with the Pallava court.

The Pallavas were enterprising and resourceful. So, it came as no surprise that they did something rather unusual when their young king Parameshwaravarman II died in battle without leaving an heir in 731 CE. A delegation of nobles and soldiers sailed from Mamallapuram to the kingdom of Champa, present-day southern Vietnam. There, a long-lost branch of the Pallava family had been ruling the kingdom of Champa for many years with the Pallava surname Varman. The high-powered delegation made them an offer—the Pallava throne at Kanchipuram! After much discussion, the king of Champa's youngest son, twelve-year-old Pallava-malla, agreed to make the journey back to Kanchipuram with the nobles. Young Pallava-malla was crowned Nandivarman II and ruled over the Pallava kingdom for the next sixty-four years!

It was his idea to build the Vaikuntha Perumal temple. It is probable that it was his idea as well to recount all the main events from the history of this extraordinary dynasty in sculpted panels along the walls of the corridors. The busy scenes begin with the gods Shiva, Vishnu, and Brahma blessing the Pallavas copiously for their long and prosperous reigns. There are grand coronations scenes of no less than eighteen of the Pallava kings. Some even bear labelled descriptions of the event—kings sit grandly at court with their queens, fanned by *chamara* or fly-whisk bearers and protected by *chattras* or decorated umbrellas. Courtiers bow deeply, messengers dash back and forth, and foreign ambassadors are received with honour. They are entertained by groups of dancers and musicians and are amused by wrestling matches and animal fights.

However, it is not all pomp and glory. There are also many battle scenes, some quite gory, with trampled soldiers, rampaging elephants, and lines of prisoners being hauled off into captivity. The victory over the great Chalukyan capital is shown in detail, with large amounts of loot being carried back to Kanchipuram. Back home, the king and queen, bearing baskets of fresh flowers, give thanks at the temple for their victory.

Nandivarman II even made sure that his long journey from Champa was depicted on the panels. There are sailing ships, rides through dense jungles, and finally a grand reception at Kanchipuram befitting a newly coronated king.

These sculpted panels, as represented in the illustration on the next page, are not only the first depictions of historical events in Indian art but also show that, whereas royalty had previously been granting funds for the construction of temples and other religious structures, they were now commissioning these grand buildings in which they wished to record their own stories!

Nandivarman II Holds Court

38

A Hero's Death

Hero stone, Begur, Karnataka, early tenth century CE

The Begur Hero stone is considered one of the most important objects that has survived from the early tenth-century Deccan. The flattish chunk of granite, over six-feet high and almost as wide, was found at Begur, a town not far from present-day Bengaluru. The inscriptions in Old Kannada and detailed carvings on the stone reveal some fascinating information from this time.

The early tenth century CE was a time of great conflict in the southern regions. The big dynasties like the Chalukyas, Rashtrakutas, and Gangas from what is now southern Karnataka, fought each other almost constantly, vying for land, water, treasure, taxes, and anything that would make them more powerful. In these battles, when their armies were exhausted or simply too busy, they often had to draw on the resources and manpower of local chieftains or ordinary folk, offering them great rewards for loyalty to their king.

In the carved scene on the Begur Hero stone, we see one such warrior. He wears an elaborate headdress and rides a horse, leading his troops into battle against an elephant-mounted and heavily armed enemy. According to the inscription, this is the Battle of Tumbepadi, in which the chieftain known only by the title of Nagattara is fighting on behalf of the Ganga king.

As you can see in the illustration of the stone below, the battle scene is rather gory. A trumpeter walks ahead of sword- and spear-wielding soldiers as they slash their way through enemy ranks. The badly injured

The Begur Hero Stone

war elephant is running amok, crushing bodies underfoot. Vultures and wild animals feast on wounded soldiers while the goddess of victory known as Rana Bhairavi stands far above watching over the grim scene. Despite his brave efforts, the Nagattara is killed in battle and replaced by a comrade.

The story does not end here, though.

Carved above the battle scene, we see that the heroic, but now-dead, Nagattara has ascended to heaven. There, as a reward for his bravery on the battlefield and service to his king, he is shown being waited upon by many attendants and entertained lavishly by *apsaras* or female celestial beings.

The history of commemorating dead people with large stones goes way back to almost 1000 BCE when giant stones known as megaliths (from the Greek *megas* or giant and *lithos* or stone) were first used to mark burial sites. By the fifth century CE, stone memorials were erected in many parts of India, but most commonly in the south—especially areas that are now in Karnataka and Tamil Nadu. But by the tenth century CE, they were not merely used to mark burials. They were known as veeragallus or nattukals and were carved with the name or image of a person who died performing a brave deed—in other words, a hero. With kingdoms constantly at war, the ordinary folk often had to defend their villages against various dangers on their own. Or, as in the case of the Begur Hero, they came to the defense of their overlords or kings.

While the Begur hero stone is considered unique for its large size and detailed pictorial representation, hero stones are typically flattish, about three to five feet high and carved in horizontal panels meant to be seen from the bottom up. The lowest panel is usually where the action is. A hero defends his village against attackers or thieves or fights off cattle raiders or wild animals like tigers and boars. In the central panel, he dies in action and ascends to heaven. Finally, the topmost panel shows him being honoured by the gods for his bravery.

Interestingly, the heroes in question are sometimes women, leading bands of men in raids or avenging the deaths of their family members. Some stones depict battles at sea, and others honour brave hunting dogs that fight alongside their masters and perish in the process. Some large stones depict events of an important person's life; others pay tribute to women who became satis or those wives who voluntarily chose to follow their heroic husbands. Others commemorate monks who perform the Jain tradition of *sallekhana*, meditating and slowly starving to death. Many of them have inscriptions in ancient languages describing the scenes that have been depicted.

You can still see hero stones, half-buried under trees in remote places along a highway, near village tanks, or collected and stored in the courtyards of temples. They carry an immense treasure-trove of information on those turbulent times. Unlike most other records which tend to focus on important people, in these stones we finally catch a glimpse of how the common people lived, their social and religious customs, languages, household goods, clothes, and jewellery, and even their pets! And, as in the case of the extraordinary Begur Hero stone, we see their battle techniques and how heroic they were required to be in the service of their rulers.

39

Didda Takes Charge

Bronze coin of Queen Didda, Kashmir, tenth century CE

A well-worn coin with slightly jumbled-looking figures on both sides, rather surprisingly, reveals the story of one of the most remarkable characters in Indian history—Didda, the queen of Kashmir. Didda sat on the throne of Kashmir for almost fifty years, first as regent for her minor son when her husband Kshemagupta died in 958 CE. Nearly twenty years later, she was still a power to reckon with, taking sole charge of Kashmir from 979 to 1003 CE.

On the obverse or the heads side of the coin, we can just about tell that a man, probably a king, is standing at an altar performing some kind of ritual. On the reverse or tails side of the coin is a seated female identified as Ardochsho, the Kushana goddess of good fortune, said to be like the goddess Lakshmi—the goddess of wealth and prosperity. She holds a small crown in her right hand and a long-stemmed lotus in the other. The legend or writing on the side of the figure says 'Sri Didda'.

The legend on the coin would have been just another name if it were not for a twelfth-century chronicler called Kalhana.

Kalhana belonged to a prominent family of Kashmir. His forefathers had once served at the royal court. Kalhana himself was quite scholarly and was considered a gifted poet, so it did not surprise anyone when, in 1150 CE, he came out with a book. Unexpectedly, Kalhana did not write a book of poems. Instead, the *Rajatarangini* (*River of Kings*) was possibly the first-ever purely historical chronicle to be written in India, and Kalhana is sometimes considered India's first historian. Using all the resources available to him at the time, including manuscripts, coins,

Bronze Coin Bearing the Name of Queen Didda

inscriptions, monuments, and the fading memories of the older scholars in his family, Kalhana reconstructed the history of Kashmir, complete with rulers, battles, legends, and real events from the earliest times till the twelfth century. All this information was set against a backdrop of beautiful descriptions of Kashmir told in the most poetic language, with plenty of action, intrigue, and drama thrown in. It is here, within the pages of this most unusual book, that the name of Queen Didda shows up!

According to Kalhana's account, Didda came from a long line of royalty. Her father ruled a mountainous state, a region in present-day Poonch in Kashmir, strategically located on an important trade route. Didda was said to be very beautiful, but she had a hobbling limp. Determined not to let this hamper her, Didda would have herself carried everywhere on the back of a very strong woman. No one expected very much of her. When she married Kshemagupta, the crown prince of Kashmir, everyone was surprised as it was considered a very good match, uniting two adjacent kingdoms into a powerful one in the region.

However, Didda's troubles had only just begun. Kshemagupta was a weak ruler, gambling and hunting his days away. As things began to go downhill, Didda decided to step in. It was she who issued orders and instructed the council of ministers on behalf of Kshemagupta. Unusual coins with the joint names of the king and queen were minted. When Kshemagupta died an early death, Didda refused to become a sati like his other wives and, instead, ruled as regent for their young son. Revolts broke out among the ministers and powerful landlords who believed it was unsuitable for a woman to be giving them orders. Didda remained undeterred. Following the early death of her son, she firmly crushed any resistance and eventually took over the throne herself.

Much as the men resented her, they could not deny that Didda was an able ruler and that Kashmir was peaceful and prosperous under her reign. As trade flourished, Didda founded new towns and monasteries and sponsored the building of more than sixty temples. This was when she minted new coins in her own name—Sri Didda, like this one.

Despite her success, Didda continued to face strong opposition within her own court, with powerful enemies plotting against her. They say she became increasingly ruthless. Kalhana even accused her of murdering her own grandsons in order to keep the throne for herself! Before she died in 1003 CE, after almost fifty years in power with twenty-two of them as an independent ruler, she nominated her brother's son as her successor.

Kalhana's account came more than a hundred years after Didda's death. He writes with a deep disapproval of her character and behaviour, which were so unconventional for those days. However, even he could not help but grudgingly admit, 'The lame queen, whom no one had thought capable of stepping over a cow's footprint, got over the host of her enemies just as Hanuman got over the ocean.' Today, Didda is a term still used in Kashmir when referring to a respected lady.

40

The Rani Who Was a Raja

Carved pillar bracket, Svayambhu temple in Warangal, Telangana, mid-thirteenth century CE

This is how Rudramadevi, queen of the Kakatiya dynasty, saw herself—a fierce warrior brandishing a dagger and shield, seated on a lion. Her title on this carved pillar bracket at the Svayambhu temple in Warangal fort is 'raya-gaja-kesari'—lion who rules over the elephant-like enemy kings. And that is what she was for the long years of her rule from 1262 to 1289 CE over the kingdom of Warangal, in present-day Telangana and Andhra Pradesh.

When Rudramadevi's father chose her as his successor, there was, as expected, quite a furore. In those times, a woman being put in charge of a kingdom was simply unthinkable. Realizing they would face opposition, the wise king Ganapatideva decided to present his elder daughter as a male. He performed the ancient putrika ceremony where a man could declare his daughter as a 'male heir'. Then he took to calling her Rudradeva, the male version of her name. Rudramadevi received training in the martial arts and, dressed in masculine clothes, accompanied her father everywhere to learn the skills required to rule a kingdom.

Queen Rudramadevi as Raya-Gaja-Kesari on a Carved Pillar Bracket

When Ganapatideva died in 1261, Rudramadevi took over as monarch. According to inscriptions of the time, she was addressed as maharaja. Her enemies, both within the kingdom and in neighbouring states, rubbed their hands in glee, imagining that she would be a weak ruler and easily defeated due to the 'disadvantage' of her gender. However, they were in for a surprise. The Yadavas of Devagiri, in what is now western Maharashtra, were the first to attack. They were astonished to find a horse-mounted Rudramadevi in full battle gear, leading her army from the front! Driven back and defeated in no time, the humiliated Yadava king later sheepishly claimed that he had 'allowed' Rudramadevi to win since he respected her as a woman! Rudramadevi marked her victory with this carving, illustrated on the previous page. Other powerful kings tried their luck as well but were forced to retreat by the determined warrior queen.

Throughout her long reign, when Rudramadevi was not fending off attacks on Kakatiya territory, she was busy facing rebellions and betrayals from her own noblemen. That did not deter her from ruling her kingdom well. She worked hard, initiating the building of great temples and public buildings, turning Warangal Fort into one of the most impregnable forts yet. She travelled the countryside, seeing to it that her subjects benefited from irrigation projects and tanks in their villages. Inscriptions reveal that there was widespread respect for this unusual 'king'. The famous Venetian traveller Marco Polo visited the Kakatiya kingdom during her rule. Filled with admiration, he described Rudramadevi as 'a lady of much discretion . . . a lover of justice, of equity and of peace . . . she was more beloved by those of her kingdom than ever was Lady or Lord of theirs before.'

At a remote village in the Warangal district, archaeologists have found a rare sculpted granite slab. It depicts Rudramadevi on a horse, clad in battle armour and brandishing a sword. Fighting her is her arch-enemy, the chieftain Ambadeva who had plotted against her for years. This was Rudramadevi's last battle where she died the honourable death of a warrior.

Just like Queen Didda of Kashmir, Rudramadevi of Warangal had managed to stand out in a world dominated by men.

There were others like them too, such as Tribhuvana Mahadevi of the Bhauma-Karas, a dynasty that ruled the eastern coastal areas of what is now Odisha for about two hundred years from around 736 CE. Ascending the throne in 846 CE, Tribhuvana commanded an army of over 30,000, and her 'lotus-like feet' are depicted as being 'kissed by the heads of feudatory chiefs, bowed down with devoted loyalty'. Of the eighteen known Bhauma-Kara monarchs, six were women who ruled in their own right, often despite having eligible male heirs. They were educated and powerful enough to follow their own religious beliefs. Some were Buddhist; others worshipped Vishnu or Sakti, the fierce goddess. They built wells, tanks, and roads, constructed temples and charitable homes, encouraged trade, promoted the arts, and made generous land donations recorded on a series of copper-plate inscriptions, which is how historians were able to learn more about the Bhauma-Karas.

Historical records of the time tend to either gloss over or even hide the achievements of these courageous women, leaving us to hunt for more information on them in coins, stray inscriptions, land grants, or on the pillar brackets of the temples they had built.

41

The Arrival of the Araghatta

Water wheel for irrigation, c. eighth century onwards

For a period from around 600 to 1200 CE, in what historians sometimes refer to as early medieval times, the Indian subcontinent was divided into many small kingdoms. These kingdoms popped up in every region, with their kings and queens constantly battling each other for more power, territory, or resources. It was a time of constant change.

What were the common people doing in these times? Those who were not drafted into the armies of these warring regional kingdoms were involved in many different professions. There were weavers, traders, potters, craftspeople, and most importantly—because everyone has to eat—there were farmers.

It appears that agriculture became one of the most widespread occupations at this time. Inscriptions on temple walls and on a large number of copper-plate inscriptions found all over the subcontinent give us detailed information on how rulers donated large pieces of land to groups of Brahmanas and other religious groups. These donations were usually of uncultivated wilderness or forested areas far away from towns. The grateful recipients were expected to move to those far-flung places. There are inscriptions that tell us how groups of Brahmanas moved from the Ganga basin in the north to southern India. Others moved east to what is now Bangladesh, West Bengal, Bihar, and Assam. There, they cleared and cultivated the land, making new village settlements and spreading agriculture over areas that were previously uncultivated or considered waste land. Most of these grants were tax free for the Brahmana settlers. In return, they worked with state officials to make sure that taxation on other rural groups, irrigations systems, and even judicial matters became more organized. All this added extra revenue to the state coffers.

Based on the available inscriptions, we know that sometimes the new settlers had to overcome hostility from forest dwellers and indigenous tribes that had been living in those areas long before their arrival. Sometimes, state officials had to intervene to settle matters.

Copper-plate inscriptions often describe villages of the time as well-organized places, with small houses constructed in the shade of fruit trees—such as jackfruit and mango—or clumps of bamboo in the eastern areas. These homesteads were surrounded by fields and pasture lands for herds of cattle and sheep. The boundaries of the villages were marked by mud embankments or rows of thorny bushes.

Interesting farming handbooks written at the time, including one famous tenth-century work called the *Krishi-Parashara*, detail everything from seeds, rainfall, soil types, and the parts of a plough to the best kind of manure for various crops.

However, with all this expansion of agricultural lands, the most important requirement was water. Although they were aware of the monsoon rains, the farmers knew they could be unreliable. Artificial irrigation was an

important part of the spread of agriculture. Rulers and chieftains often talked of how they had funded the construction of tanks and wells for villages. And there is evidence of cutting-edge technology in irrigation that was devised at the time.

One of these innovations was the water wheel, a clever device known as an *araghatta*, from a combination of Sanskrit words: *ara* meaning spoke and *ghatta* meaning pot. The araghatta was a large wheel, as you can see in the illustration, with earthen or iron buckets fitted along its rim at regular intervals, positioned above a deep well or tank. As the wheel was turned slowly, the buckets scooped up water, emptying it into a smaller tank on the way up. The water then travelled to the fields through specially designed channels. Inscriptions tell us that the wheel dated as far back as the early centuries of the Common Era and would have been a common sight all over the countryside during the time of expanding agriculture.

With the coming of the Turks in the thirteenth century CE, the araghatta design became more sophisticated. A horizontal wheel was attached to a gear mechanism, enabling the vertical wheel to turn with cattle or camel power and hence reach water at even lower levels. Later, this new contraption came to be commonly known as the Persian wheel.

Water wheels were particularly important in arid regions like Rajasthan where the water table was lower and access to water more difficult. It even features on a particularly beautiful carved stone panel from the eleventh century, now displayed in the Sardar Museum at Jodhpur. The panel depicts a group of soldiers, some on horses, casually gathered around a water wheel, waiting to quench their thirst. There is a wheel operator keeping an eye on the pots slowly rising from the well.

This water wheel became the basis of a complex irrigation system, enabling farmers on the subcontinent to grow summer and winter crops, ensuring supplies to the now-increasing population. They also began to grow a wide variety of crops, including rice, wheat, millets, sugarcane, and oil seeds. Texts refer to special 'oil men' called telikas whose job it was to crush the seeds to extract the oil. Sugarcane, then unknown to the rest of the world, was an important crop in the subcontinent, with most of the sugar being exported. And the increasing cultivation of cotton was the foundation of what was to become the famed Indian textile industry in the centuries to come. With the advent of the water wheel, the agricultural landscape of the subcontinent took on an appearance that we are familiar with even in modern times.

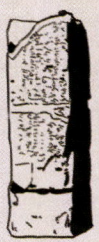

42

Five Hundred Lords of Ayyavole

Stone inscription, Sumatra, Indonesia, c. eleventh century CE

This stone in the illustration is about three feet high and cut in a roughly hexagonal shape. The inscriptions carved into it are in ancient Tamil. What is surprising, however, is that it was not found anywhere in India but far away, in the ancient port town of Barus on the island of Sumatra, Indonesia! Known as the Lobu Tua inscription of Barus, it dates back to 1088 CE and reveals the story of an interesting group of merchants from southern India. They called themselves Ainnurruvar or the 'Five Hundred Lords of Ayyavole', sometimes referred to as 'Five Hundred of a 1000 Directions'.

Indians have always been enthusiastic traders. From the earliest days, when the Harappans set out for Mesopotamia in boats laden with beads and pottery, to early historic times, when merchants sailed out of busy port towns with ship holds filled with spices, precious gems, exotic animals, wood, perfumes, and textiles, Indian goods have travelled a vast network of routes from Rome to China. Religious texts and folktales are

full of stories of merchants, sailors, trader caravans, port towns and the activities of *shrenis* or merchants' guilds.

The Ainnurruvar were one such guild, an association of merchants of whom we first find mention in an inscription dating back 800 CE. On the walls of a temple at Aihole in Karnataka, once a major cultural centre of the Chalukya kingdom, they are referred to as the 'merchant guild of the 500 Svamis of Ayyavole'. The appearance of a merchant guild at this point was not surprising. What fascinated scholars, however, was the power, organizational skills, and adventurous spirit of the Ainnurruvar.

The original 500 traders, thought to have been founded by a group of Brahmana traders, soon expanded to draw in other groups into their guild, including landlords, artisans, weavers, bankers, writers, messengers, and soldiers. They dealt with goods ranging from food grains to silk, textiles, animals, perfumes, and precious articles like metals, ivory, and gems. Membership of the guild was based strictly on occupation, which meant they accepted people from all castes and religions as long as they were skilled in that trade. As opportunities for trade increased during this time, the guild expanded their activities to other parts of southern India and even overseas to Sri Lanka, Myanmar, Thailand, and Indonesia.

The Ainnurruvar were expected to follow a strict code of conduct which included not just supporting fellow guild members but even in the practical training they acquired in defending themselves and their valuable goods from bandits along the trade routes. Regular meetings were called to ensure everyone knew and followed the rules of business. As they prospered, monarchs relied on them for loans and taxes. They were generous donors to temples and irrigation works. An inscription dated to 1055 CE describes the Ainnurruvar in detail.

'Famed throughout the world, adorned with many good qualities, truth, purity, good conduct, policy . . . and prudence; . . . born to be wanderers over many countries, the earth as their sack . . . by

land routes and water routes penetrating into the regions of the six
continents, with superior elephants, well-bred horses, large sapphires,
moonstones, pearls, rubies, diamonds . . . cardamoms, cloves, sandal,
camphor, musk, saffron, and other perfumes and drugs, by selling
which wholesale or hawking about on their shoulders, preventing the
loss by customs duties, they fill up the emperor's treasury of gold, his
treasury of jewels, and his armoury of weapons; and from the rest they
daily bestow gifts on pundits and munis . . .'—A History of India by
Burton Stein and David Arnold.

By the ninth century CE, the Ainnurruvar were influential enough for royal
families like the Pallavas and Cholas to collaborate with them. It is said
that the Chola invasions of both Sri Lanka and the Srivijaya kingdom
in Indonesia had more to do with keeping trade routes open for the
Ainnurruvar and other guilds than with a desire to conquer new lands.

Barus was famous for camphor and benzoin (a resin with medical uses),
which came from the forested highlands of the island. The town would
have been a busy mix of other foreign merchants, including Javanese,
Arabs, and Chinese. From the Lobu Tua inscription, we can conjecture
that the Tamil merchants of the Ainnurruvar met that day in 1088 at
a busy marketplace in the heart of a south Indian settlement to make
an agreement. They agreed to pay dues to various people, including
sailors, guards, and local merchants, whom they addressed as 'our sons'.
The inscription ends with a gentle reminder and an indication of the
guild's outlook:

'Thus we, the Five Hundred of the 1000 Directions, known in every
direction in all eighteen lands, had the stone inscribed and planted.
Do not forget the kind attitude, the kind attitude itself is a good friend.'

Perhaps it was this 'kind attitude' they encouraged that made the
Ainnurruvar one of the most successful merchant guilds of their day.

43

The Dancing Child-Saint

Bronze statue, Tamil Nadu, late fourteenth century CE

Between the sixth and ninth centuries CE in Tamilakam, the area that is now Tamil Nadu and parts of Kerala, some people began to question the way things were being done, particularly in religious practices. They wondered why only priests were allowed to communicate with the gods and why formal religious rituals were required. They felt ordinary people should be able to worship in their own way, with deep personal devotion to a deity. This questioning was led by ordinary men and women who, with their intense spirituality, came to be known as the Nayanars (saints devoted to Shiva) and Alvars (those immersed in devotion to Vishnu).

Across this period of three centuries, we know of sixty-three important Nayanars and twelve Alvars. They came from different places, backgrounds, and castes. Some were wealthy merchants, soldiers, and even royalty; others were 'low-born' peasants, hunters, and toddy-tappers. They all shared a common calling of single-minded dedication to their chosen deity. They spent their lives wandering through the countryside of southern India, visiting small local shrines, composing, and singing beautiful poems to Shiva or Vishnu. Some of them were contemporaries, walking and singing together. Others, particularly the women, travelled alone. Together, they created a new form of religious worship known as *Bhakti* or devotion.

The illustration below depicts a late fourteenth-century bronze statue from Tamil Nadu. It is the image of the happy, dancing child-saint, Sambandar.

Sambandar was a Nayanar, a child prodigy who lived sometime in the second half of the seventh century CE. Much of what we know of his life was written centuries later, when the writers may have wanted to present their favourite saint in a more favourable light. So, not all that we read may be accurate or true, but we can still get an idea of some of the main events of his life.

Bronze Statue of the Dancing Child-Saint Sambandar Nayanar

Legend has it that when Sambandar was a baby, his parents took him to a Shiva temple. Leaving him on the bank of the temple tank, they both went to bathe. Young Sambandar was hungry and started crying. By the time his parents came out of the water, they saw that Sambandar had already been fed. When asked where he got the milk, he pointed upwards. The goddess Parvati herself had heard the child cry and had descended from the heavens to feed him! And that is why he is often depicted with an empty cup in his left hand and the index finger of his right hand pointing upwards at the goddess who fed him. He is also depicted as shown in this figure, dancing happily in worship. For song, dance, and joy in worship became Sambandar's message as he took to walking from village to village, composing and singing songs in local shrines. Sambandar is said to have died aged only sixteen. But by that time, he had managed to compose over 10,000 hymns, of which only 384 have survived.

The Nayanar and Alvar saints made a real connection with ordinary people. Large crowds followed them as they walked across the countryside. The people understood the simple Tamil lyrics of the songs sung by these saints. They began to enjoy the new, more joyful ways of worship the saints presented and to welcome their message that everyone was equal before the divine. They were delighted when the saints visited their humble local shrines and identified them as the abodes of either Shiva or Vishnu. In these beautiful songs, we often get rare glimpses of the everyday lives of the time.

However, as time went by, the songs of the saints were slowly forgotten and those modest shrines fell into disrepair.

Luckily, when the Cholas came to power around the tenth century CE, they went about enthusiastically restoring the shrines associated with the saints. Many of the modest mud and thatch structures were turned into magnificent brick and stone temples dedicated to Shiva.

Quite by chance, an ancient manuscript surfaced with some poems by the three most famous Nayanar saints—Sambandar, Sundarar, and Appar. These were collected into the *Thevaram* which means 'garland of poems to the lord'. The great Chola king, Rajaraja Chola, ordered them to be sung at his new temple at Thanjavur every day. As temples became the hub of social and religious life in those times, the Nayanars and Alvars became part of the everyday worship of the people.

Today, in almost every part of Tamil Nadu, if you walk into a Shiva temple, you will see a group of sixty-three figures installed in the courtyard. In the case of a Vishnu temple, you will find a group of twelve. The endearing child-saint Sambandar still remains the most popular of them all.

In the centuries that followed, the idea of the poet-saint echoed across other places on the subcontinent. Figures like Basavanna in present-day Karnataka, Jnansehwar and Tukaram in what is now Maharashtra, Kabir and Guru Nanak, the founder of the Sikh faith, in northern India and Mirabai in present-day Rajasthan, challenged the strict rules of formal religion and society through their songs and poems. They sang in the local language, rejecting ritualism and social differences while encouraging worship of the divine through good deeds and personal devotion.

44

The Enduring Iron Pillar

Iron pillar, Mehrauli, Delhi, eleventh to thirteenth century CE

The iron pillar that stands in the Qutb Minar complex at Mehrauli in Delhi is certainly one of the great wonders of the ancient world. For over 1600 years, the tapering twenty-three-foot column, depicted in the illustration on the facing page, has stood there withstanding rain and sun, the blows of conquerors, and the touch of curious tourists. Inscribed on it are lines of Sanskrit in the Brahmi script that tell us that the pillar was erected to celebrate the battle victories of a certain king, Chandra, and that this was dedicated to the god Vishnu. Chandra is believed to be the Gupta king Chandragupta II who ruled northern India in the late fourth century CE.

It is thought that the pillar was originally located in central India and was brought to Mehrauli by the Delhi sultans in the early thirteenth century to decorate the new mosque complex they were building. Some scholars also believe, the move could have taken place much earlier, in the eleventh century, during the reign of the Tomara Rajput king Anangapala who founded Delhi and needed something with which to decorate his new capital, Lal Kot. It was once topped with a majestic capital, possibly a garuda—the bird-vehicle of Vishnu. However, apart from the missing capital, the pillar shows almost no other sign of ageing and deterioration. The inscriptions are still clear and readable and the iron—apart from a few small patches where there has been excessive contact with water—remains rust-free!

Scientists today are astounded at how over three tonnes of almost pure iron were forged into this column. Recent studies have revealed that the possible secret to its rust-resistant property is the high level of phosphorus in the iron. This forms a thin protective layer over the exposed iron surface, preventing corrosion. Who were the ironsmiths who understood this technology so many hundreds of years ago? And who were the craftspeople with the skills to fashion this great work?

To find answers, we have to go as far back as the Harappan times when metal objects were being produced with highly technical and artistic skills. Think of the widely admired 4000-year-old bronze dancing girl of Mohenjodaro and the beautifully made iron objects that came after—like spear heads, armour plates, daggers, fish hooks and bowls—found in the burial sites of southern India associated with megaliths or giant stones. Then, there is the famous life-size sixth-century CE Sultanganj Buddha from Bihar, now housed in the Birmingham Museum in England. Metallurgists still marvel at the special technique of hollow casting of pure copper used to make this image. In the town of Dhar, Madhya Pradesh, three broken fragments of an iron pillar were discovered, which when in one piece, would have once soared unbelievably high, to almost twice the height of the Mehrauli pillar!

The Iron Pillar

In southern India, as early as 200 BCE, ironsmiths were smelting iron ore with charcoal and glass at very high temperatures in clay pots. The result was a high-carbon steel, unmatched anywhere in the world. It came to be known as wootz steel, probably an anglicized version of the Tamil word for steel, *urukku*, which was a highly prized commodity. King Porus, it is said, chose to give Alexander thirty pounds—that is, over thirteen kilograms—of this valuable metal rather than conventional gold or silver. The famous twelfth century Moroccon geographer Ash Sharif Al-Idrisi wrote that Hinduwani or Indian steel was the best in the world. Arab traders carried steel ingots back with them from southern India. The ingots made their way to production centres in northern Iran and the Levant, where from around the tenth century CE, they were fashioned into the famous swords of Damascus. The European Crusaders of the thirteenth century were stunned by the deadly cutting edge of the Damascus swords which could pierce through the toughest metal armour. Curious about this excellent form of steel, Western scientists carefully studied its composition, leading to great inventions in the form of metal alloys in the eighteenth century.

The most amazing part about Indian metallurgy is the fact that these technical breakthroughs and high-quality metal works were not the output of huge factories or state-sponsored workshops. Most of these ideas came from traditional metal workers from tribal or indigenous communities, some of whom still work today, although they are increasingly becoming rare. Since very ancient times, these ordinary men and women would set up their clay and brick furnaces on the outskirts of towns or villages. They would scour the nearby forests for wood and metal ores. While men handled the smelting, the women pumped the bellows to feed air into the roaring fires needed to forge iron. All this required hard manual labour and great skill. Many of these tribes were nomadic, so once they made and sold their pieces, they would pack up and move on to the next village, looking for more work. The remnants of their work that exists today are tribute to the unsurpassed skills and dedication of these artisans.

45

Rajaraja Makes an Appearance

Mural painting, Brihadeshvara temple, Thanjavur, Tamil Nadu, tenth to eleventh century CE

In the dark, narrow passageway that surrounds the sanctum or main shrine of the Brihadeshvara temple in Thanjavur, a young historian came across a painting quite by chance. It was part of a whole expanse of brilliant murals dating back to Chola times, hidden under layers of crumbling plaster and later paintings. Uncovering them was a delicate task that took several years. Part of the mural depicts two figures standing in a larger court scene. In front is the venerable sage known as Karuvur Devar. Standing humbly behind him is a disciple. But this is not just any disciple. This figure is none other than the great tenth-century Chola king, Rajaraja Chola! At over 1000 years old, this is probably the earliest surviving royal portrait in India. And it tells us many interesting stories.

Rajaraja Chola was the man who ordered the building of this stupendously large temple.

Why did he need such a big temple? And more unusually, why did he choose to have his portrait painted on its walls?

Until the early medieval period, temples and other places of worship were not directly funded by royalty. Instead, their financing relied on donations collected from merchants, monasteries, and the working classes. Guilds of architects took on the task of building them. Kings and queens sometimes chipped in with grants of villages for the upkeep of these temples. By the eighth century CE, with the rise of powerful dynasties like the Pallavas and Pandyas who decided to pour some of their wealth into temple-building, the scale and style of temples changed. The landscape of southern India mushroomed with massive stone structures, elegantly planned and decorated with thousands of exquisite carvings.

In the middle of the ninth century CE, the Cholas came to power in the area that is now Tamil Nadu, with Thanjavur as their capital. With their advanced fighting skills, by the time of Rajaraja, the Chola empire extended across almost the entire southern Deccan up to the Malabar Coast and even overseas to Sri Lanka, the Maldive islands and parts of Malaya (present-day Malaysia). The royal coffers were filled to the brim with taxes from the

Karuvur Devar and King Rajaraja Chola

rich agricultural lands of the Kaveri delta, tributes from captured territories, plenty of war bounty, and taxes from wealthy merchant guilds.

So, Rajaraja had every reason to be pleased with himself, but instead, he found himself in a dilemma. Being the ruler of such a vast empire, he always had the lurking fear that an ambitious chieftain would rebel or the people of a faraway province would defy his royal instructions. What the king needed was a symbol, something that would convince his subjects that their king was not only powerful but also had the divine blessings of the gods themselves. It seemed like a good idea to build something awe-inspiring, such as a giant temple dedicated to Rajaraja's favourite deity, Shiva.

Construction began around 1004 CE. More than 130,000 tonnes of granite, one of the densest stones known, were hauled from a quarry seventy kilometres away. The temple was planned within a massive walled complex covering about forty-four acres of land and could be entered through two ornamented *gopurams* or gateways. The *vimana* or tower, over the sanctum was a marvel of engineering with thirteen hollow tiers of interlocking stones topped with an enormous capstone consisting of massive slabs of granite layered with brick and stucco to provide stability. On it was placed a gold-plated *kalasa*, a pot-shaped finial, taking the final height of the temple to a staggering 216 feet, making it the tallest structure constructed in its time.

In 1010 CE, the temple was finally completed. In a masterstroke, the king named it Sri Rajarajeshwara, or temple of the god of Rajaraja. As dazzled subjects looked on at this magnificent creation that bore their king's name, they could not help but think that he was indeed closely connected with the gods! Much later, the temple was renamed Brihadeshvara, which, even today, remains the popular name.

The temple became the centre of religious and cultural life, buzzing with hundreds of priests, cleaners, dancers, craftspeople, garland makers, and other tradespeople. Rajaraja's detailed instructions on how he wanted the temple to run were inscribed along the stone walls. Sprinkled through the vast temple, he added a few quiet messages about his connections with the deity. On the outer walls of the temple, Shiva is depicted in sculpted images as Tripurantaka, a fierce conqueror—just like the king himself. Also, on the walls of the narrow passageway around the sanctum, Rajaraja appears in the paintings standing among the gods. He and his three queens are depicted worshipping a dancing Shiva. And, as in the mural in the illustration, he pays close attention to his guru's words of wisdom. A subtle reminder to his vast empire and even his most faraway subjects: that their king was as wise as he was strong, and even the gods agreed!

46

The Lord of the Dance

Bronze Shiva Nataraja, Tamil Nadu, c. eleventh century CE

The figure in the illustration on the next page is perhaps a familiar one. You may have seen it in many places—museums, temples, homes, or even placed on stage during a dance performance. It is possibly the best-known representation of the god Shiva as Adavallan or Nataraja, the Lord of the Dance. This bronze free-standing statue belongs to the time of the Cholas, the dynasty that ruled in southern India from the ninth to the thirteenth centuries CE. The bronze Nataraja is considered one of the finest pieces of art ever made, carrying within it rich stories of philosophy, religious practices, devout royalty, and unmatched artistry.

Images of the Nataraja figure in stone and metal appear as early as the fifth century CE. However, it was only around the tenth century that this form became the favourite of the Chola family and the sculptures reached an unbelievably high level of creative expression.

In the bronze image, Shiva dances within a flaming circle that represents time, the Hindu belief being that time moves in a circle with no beginning and no end. He performs the *tandava* or cosmic dance that both creates

and destroys the world in an endless cycle. In his upper right hand, he holds a *damaru*, a small drum. With its rhythmic beat, he drums the world into existence. His upper left hand holds *agni* or fire with which he destroys the world. His lower right hand bestows blessings and his lower left hand points downwards at his gracefully raised left foot, indicating salvation. He stamps on a small figure called Apasmara, who represents ignorance. In this lifelike representation, one can almost hear the drumbeats as Shiva dances wildly, locks of hair flying, sashes billowing, bracelets and anklets jangling. It is a figure that conveys continuous movement and noise. At the centre of it all is his gently smiling face.

If we look closely at the figure, we will observe several holes on the stand. These give us a clue about how the image was originally intended to be used.

From around the ninth century CE, in present-day Tamil Nadu, there was a great spurt in temple building. Under the Cholas, small brick and thatch shrines that dotted the villages of the empire were rebuilt into grand stone structures. In the cities, kings commissioned splendid stone temples to house multiple deities. Running along the outer walls of these temples were niches to display portable bronze images of the gods in various forms—Vishnu as Krishna or Rama and Shiva as a wandering beggar or fierce conqueror. These figures were often shown accompanied by their wives and children. Depictions of the singing saints of the previous centuries, the Alvars and Nayanars, also found their place in these niches.

In the royal bronze-casting workshops, master craftspeople used a special method, now called the lost-wax technique, to cast these fine figures. An image was formed in wax and covered with a layer of fine, wet clay with a few carefully positioned holes. When the clay layer dried and became hard, the image was heated so the wax would melt and drain out of these holes (hence called lost wax). The centre would thus become hollow in the shape of the intended image. This hollow was then filled with molten metal—a specific combination of tin and copper, which formed bronze in the heating process. Once the metal cooled and solidified, the clay layer was carefully broken, revealing the solid bronze figure inside. It was a long process that required great technical skills. Some of the figures were almost five feet tall and weighed over a hundred kilograms. It is said the Dowager Queen Sembiyan Mahadevi, aunt of Rajaraja Chola, was a particularly generous donor who took a personal interest in the work of these skilled artists. To this day, their descendants continue to reside in the region and produce these images using the same tried-and-tested techniques.

Once installed in the temple niches, the images were treated as living personalities. Each had a personal retinue, including tailors, jewellers, garland makers, and parasol holders. They were bathed and dressed every day, and because they were in human form, the subjects could relate to them, worshipping them with deep adoration.

However, what was most unique about these images was that they were meant to be mobile. Every now and then, they would be dressed in their best silks and jewellery, and hoisted on to wooden poles by threading strong ropes through the holes at the bottom of the image. Then accompanied by chants and music, they would be taken out in a grand procession. Sometimes, it was to enact a picnic at a nearby garden; at other times, the trip would be a longer one to a seaside fair or simply a social visit to a nearby temple with a friendly deity. Even the birthdays and anniversaries of the deities were celebrated! On these special occasions, crowds would gather to catch a glimpse of their gods as they passed by, gaining their blessings by just gazing at their serene faces. Adavallan, or Nataraja, not only represented a high point in metal artistry but is also regarded as one of the finest representations of the divine in physical form, still venerated with as much fervour today as it was when it came out of Chola workshops in the eleventh century CE.

47

A Temple Town for the People

Inscriptions on stone, Brihadeshvara temple, Thanjavur, Tamil Nadu, eleventh century CE

A powerful, wealthy king in southern India builds the most monumental stone temple ever seen. It takes over six years to construct, but when it is finally ready to be inaugurated in 1010 CE, the Rajarajeshwara (later known as Brihadeshvara) temple at Thanjavur in present-day Tamil Nadu covers an area that is equivalent to the size of a township.

We can almost imagine what curious spectators at the time would have felt when they saw this temple complex for the first time. As they peeked through the towering gopuram gateways, they would have seen broad streets that seemed to go on forever, lined with brick double-storeyed houses. They would marvel at the airy, pillared mandapas and the sanctum at the far end with its distinctive gold-topped vimana. They would have heard of the bronze images being installed in the niches along the temple walls and of the massive stone Shiva linga within the sanctum. And they would have wondered amongst themselves, what would happen next?

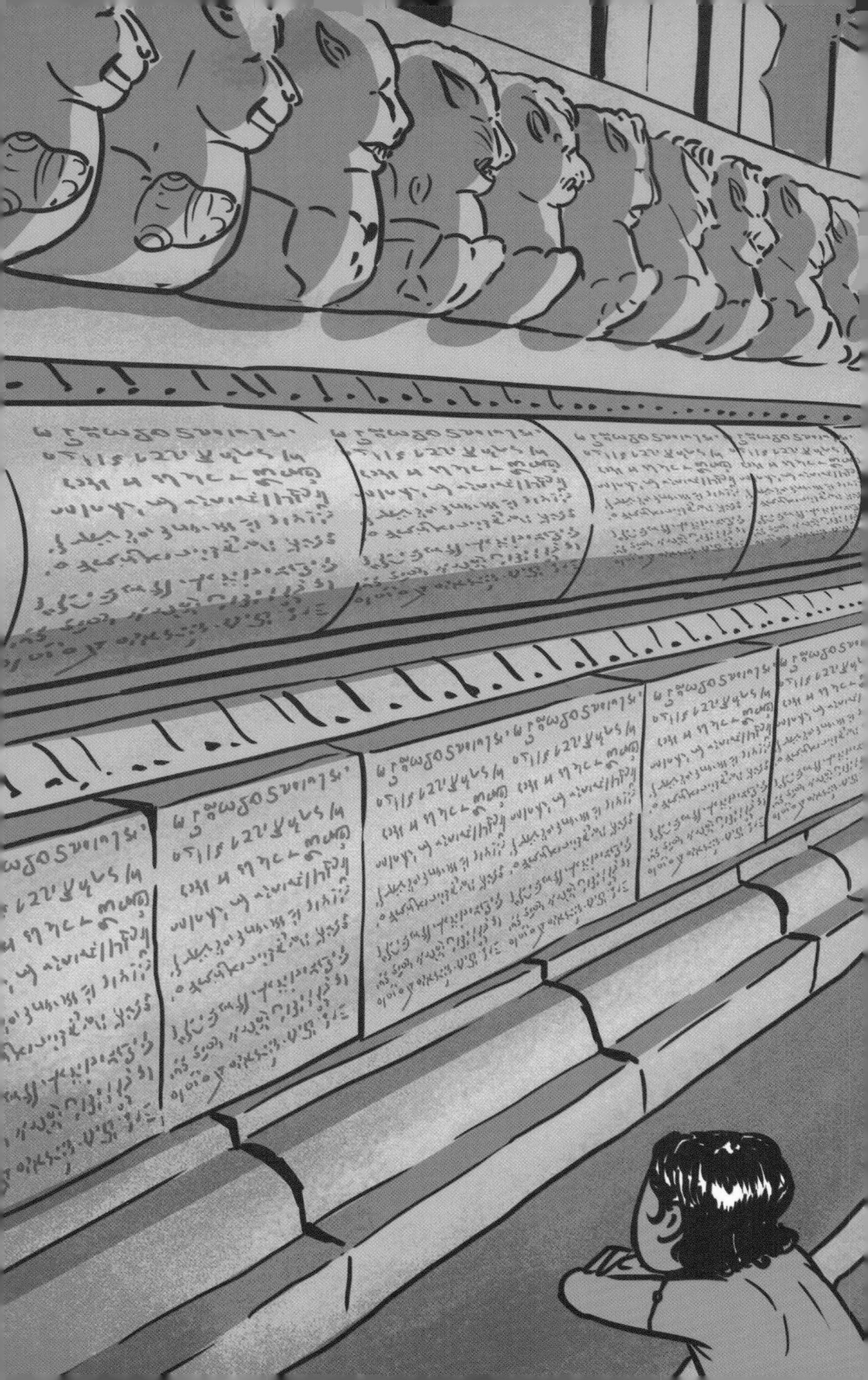

Who would be allowed to worship here? Would ordinary folk like them be allowed into this grand citadel?

The sheer grandeur of the temple and its phenomenal size would have been awe-inspiring and intimidating.

Luckily for his subjects, Rajaraja Chola was a man who was meticulous in his attention to detail, and he had not forgotten them. Not content with merely having this great complex made under his instructions, he knew exactly how he wanted to run the place. The illustration on the previous page depicts 107 paragraphs of beautifully inscribed Sanskrit and Tamil calligraphy running in lines along the base of the towering vimana. Incredibly, they are the words of Rajaraja himself, from more than a thousand years ago! And this is what they say.

To begin with, Rajaraja sounds satisfied with the way things have worked out. 'We, the emperor, have built this temple of stone in Thanjavur,' he declares. After some phrases on how powerful the Cholas are and how much territory they have conquered (almost all of peninsular south India and some overseas kingdoms in Sri Lanka, the Maldives, and Sumatra), the inscriptions go on to describe both the construction and the daily routine to be followed in running the temple.

They begin with the names of the architects and the master craftspeople responsible for the building of the temple. Then the names of those who financed the building through generous donations are listed—the king, his aunt, his elder sister, and his queens. Each of them commissioned spectacular bronze figures to decorate the niches along the temple walls and donated fine silks, gold jewellery, and precious stones like rubies, emeralds, diamonds, as well as strings of pearls, to adorn these idols. Every item, right down to the tiny gold ghee spoon donated by the king, was weighed, described, and accounted for by special accountants and jewellers. However, it was not just the rich who had their donations documented. Even the humble offering of the palace cook was recorded.

The inscription mentions a permanent staff of over 600 people, including priests, sweepers, barbers, tailors, musicians, painters, cooks, lamp lighters, garland makers, torch bearers, and parasol holders. In one extraordinary passage, there are details of the 400 dancing girls who were hired from various parts of the kingdom to dance for the deities. Their names and salaries, as well as the houses allotted to them along the new streets of the temple township, were also documented. The names and house numbers of the group of fifty musicians who were hired to sing the special Thevaram songs of the poet-saints were also registered.

Tradespeople and merchants from across the kingdom were specially instructed to source the produce required to run the temple. Shepherds travelled from afar with milk, butter, and ghee for the temple lamps and kitchens. Farmers brought in cartloads of rice, millets, and sugar cane. There were flower growers, salt makers, and betel-leaf vendors, along with guilds of craftspeople, to repair any damages to the temple complex. Villages from as far away as Sri Lanka were expected to send in tributes either in cash or in the form of produce to keep the activities of the great temple going.

The chief astrologer was in charge of ascertaining the right dates and auspicious times of day or *muhuratam* for the performance of rituals and festivals. They were all supervised by a head manager, a high-ranking Chola official, usually appointed by the king himself.

From all these detailed instructions, it certainly appears the temple was not just intended for religious rituals but served many other functions. With his flawless organizational skills, Rajaraja had managed to turn the complex into a hub of social and economic life where almost every citizen had a definite role to play and many depended on the temple for their livelihood. By pulling in dues from all over the vast kingdom, the temple was a symbol of Chola royal power and an arm of the administration. The neatly aligned inscriptions convey how the influence of the Rajarajeshwara temple spread across almost all of eleventh-century south India.

48

The Pious Gift of Queen Vihunadevi

Watercolour on palm-leaf manuscript, West Bengal/Bangladesh, early twelfth century CE

In the early twelfth century, a queen named Vihunadevi commissioned a monk to make an illustrated manuscript for her. She chose a well-known Buddhist text of the time known as the Ashtasahasrika Prajnaparamita or 'Perfection of Wisdom in 8000 Verses'. The manuscript would have run into many pages, each page carefully handwritten on the treated leaves of a special palm tree. The text would have been written in boxes on either side of the narrow, elongated page, leaving just a small box, not bigger than six centimetres wide, in the centre for a miniature painting. The leaves would have been punched on either end, bound with string, and held together between two wooden covers. Only a few pages of Vihunadevi's manuscript remain, the others lost over time. The illustration of the palm leaf on the facing page depicts just one page of that original work. The brilliant miniature painting depicts the Bodhisattva of compassion, Avalokitesvara, preaching to a female devotee.

The work shows that the artist not only had superb skills but also a great knowledge of the subject described in the text. From the quality of the work, scholars infer that this manuscript was made in the workshop of a great Buddhist monastery or mahavihara, as they were known, in eastern India. In these mahaviharas, artists and monks who were familiar with the texts could work together. The 'Perfection of Wisdom in 8000 Verses' was filled with chants, mantras, and invocations and was meant to be worshipped rather than read by a devotee wanting to attain blessings and protection against evil from the Bodhisattva Avalokitesvara. The making of the book itself was considered an act of worship.

Such fine work would have been an expensive project that only the very rich or royalty would have been able to afford. On another surviving page of the same manuscript, we read that this particular text is the 'pious gift of the queen Vihunadevi'.

A Page from the Ashtasahasrika Prajnaparamita

The queen was possibly a member of the Pala family, the dynasty that ruled for almost five centuries, beginning around the eighth century CE, in areas that are now in Bangladesh, West Bengal, Bihar, and Assam. The Palas were a powerful dynasty, and when they were not fighting their arch rivals—the Gurjara Pratiharas in the west and the Rashtrakutas from the Deccan—for control of the central Ganga river basin, they ran a prosperous kingdom.

The fertile, well-watered lands of eastern India gave them bountiful rice harvests. Along the eastern coast, their ports received Arab and Chinese ships as they made their way to Southeast Asia or Africa. They opened up land routes through the Northeast to Myanmar and north to Tibet.

The Palas were among the last of the great dynasties in India that supported Buddhism. They revived the famous Nalanda university, set up another great centre of learning at Vikramshila, in present-day Bihar, and at Somapuri, now in Bangladesh, reputed to be the largest Buddhist university even seen. Pilgrims and students flocked to these learning centres from all over Asia, including Sumatra, Cambodia, China, Sri Lanka, Nepal, Tibet, and Kashmir. They studied Mahayana Buddhism which was quite different from the Buddha's original teachings. Mahayana Buddhism emphasized the role of the Bodhisattvas, saintly beings who postpone their salvation to help ordinary people. It also included the use of mantras and magical spells for spiritual ends.

The Palas were enthusiastic patrons of the arts. During their rule, the art and iconography of Buddhism changed. Polished stone and bronze images of the Bodhisattvas were elaborately styled with multiple arms and legs, flowing costumes, and animated poses. Paintings influenced by the earlier Ajanta style were used in murals on temple and palace walls. Illustrated manuscripts with these tiny, detailed paintings were a popular form of devotion, often revealing the names of their donors, scribes, and the name and dates of the ruling king. Most of these belonged to the tenth and eleventh century CE.

But here is a strange fact: not long after the decline of the dynasty, in the early thirteenth century, invaders wiped out most traces of the Palas. It was as if their great Buddhist universities, their libraries filled with precious texts, their palaces decorated with murals, and their temples filled with great art work had never existed! So how do we know so much about them if these sources no longer exist? Apart from some inscriptions and writings of pilgrims, there was another unexpected source.

When foreign pilgrims and monks returned to their home countries, they carried copies of religious texts, portable images, and painted manuscripts. These objects later became a great source of information on Pala traditions and styles. This palm-leaf painting, the gift of Queen Vihunadevi, is a great example of that tradition that tells us of the last great phase of Buddhism and Buddhist art in India.

49

Black Gold

Black pepper or *Piper nigrum*, trade goes back to c. 2000 BCE

Is it possible that a humble spice could influence the history of India, and possibly, the world? In the case of black pepper—or black gold, as it was once known—it certainly is!

Piper nigrum is the botanical name of the dried berries of a climbing vine native to the Malabar Coast of present-day Kerala. Valued for its pungent taste and its benefit as a preservative, the use of this spice has been prevalent in Indian cooking and medicines since at least 2000 BCE.

When the Egyptian pharaoh Rameses II died in 1213 BCE, his nostrils and abdomen were stuffed with black peppercorns as part of the mummification process. Centuries later, archaeologists traced the origin of this pepper to the Malabar region. This means that even 3000 years ago, traders had carried Malabar pepper to Egypt.

The real boom in demand for pepper began after the Roman conquest of Egypt in the first century BCE. The Romans used pepper in everything. In meat and fish sauces, to spice up their wine, in medicines and tonics,

Black Pepper

even in their desserts! They just could not get enough of the spice. Using the Egyptians and Arabs as brokers, Roman ships began to sail across the Arabian Sea to the Malabar region, the only known source of pepper in the world at the time. In the early fifth century CE, the Roman geographer Strabo mentions a fleet of 120 Roman ships being sent on a round trip to India, sailing on the monsoon winds. They docked on the Malabar Coast, many of them at the legendary port of Muziris. To accommodate the huge demand for pepper, the Romans built larger ships with hold capacities of over 400 tonnes. Once in Rome, the spice was stored in special pepper warehouses and sold at unbelievably high prices to wealthy Roman households. Pepper was so precious that it was even traded and used as currency, which is how it came to be known as black gold.

Pepper was one of the first commodities to be traded across the world, opening up new trade routes connecting the Far East and Europe. Even after the fall of the Roman Empire in the fifth century CE, European cuisine just could not do without huge quantities of spices. By medieval times, pepper was a status symbol, and no self-respecting noble household would have a feast without dishes drowning in spices such as cumin, cinnamon, cloves, and especially pepper from Malabar.

This huge demand for pepper as well as other spices, textiles, and precious stones that came from the interior regions of the subcontinent meant the Malabar coastline was a busy, bustling centre with people from many different places mingling with each other to do business. Greeks, Egyptians, Arabs, Romans, and Chinese traders came here along with sailors, craftspeople, artists, and religious scholars. The rulers of the Malabar region welcomed them all.

Indian Christian legend has it that in 52 CE, Thomas, one of the twelve apostles of Jesus, is believed to have arrived at Muziris. He converted eleven prominent families to Christianity and built several churches in the area before moving on to the eastern coast of India, where he eventually died. The Syrian Christian community of Kerala trace their origins to these early Christian families. The Kottakavu Mar Thoma church in Paravur dates back to this time and is considered to be the oldest church in India.

In the first century CE, a community of Jews fleeing persecution in their homeland sailed to the Malabar Coast and was allowed by the king to settle in Kodungallur. This community built the Paradesi Synagogue in Kochi which still stands today. Here, in a sealed trunk, is an extraordinary document called the Jewish copper-plate inscriptions. The plates are inscribed in old Malayalam and dated to around 1000 CE, recording grants of land and other rights by the Chera king Bhaskara Ravi Varman to the Jewish merchant Joseph Rabban. Rabban belonged to a merchant guild of Jewish, Christian, and Muslim merchants from West Asia.

Not far from this church is the Cheraman Jama Masjid, said to have been built in 629 CE on the instructions of King Cheraman Perumal. It was believed that the king travelled to Medina and met the Prophet Muhammed, himself. He died on his return journey but sent instructions back home that his companions were to be given land and a place to practice this new faith. The Cheraman Jama Masjid is one of the oldest mosques in the world. People of all faiths often pray here, and children are brought here to perform the 'vidyarambham' ceremony, their initiation into reading and writing.

By the fifteenth century, fed up with the Roman traders' monopoly on the spice trade and the exorbitant pepper prices, the new maritime powers of Spain and Portugal decided to sail directly to the source of these spices themselves. Christopher Columbus sailed from Spain in the wrong direction and 'discovered' a new continent. The Portuguese sailor Vasco da Gama found his way to the Malabar Coast using a new sea route that skirted the coast of Africa. He landed in Calicut, modern Kozhikode on 20 May 1498, opening the floodgates of European colonialism in India. Small but potent, black pepper influenced not just the cultural life of India's western coastline, but also changed the trade history of the world.

50

An Ancient God of the Forest

Jagannatha, Balabhadra, and Subhadra carved from sacred neem logs, Jagannatha temple, Puri, Odisha, originally made c. twelfth century CE

By now, you will be familiar with how gods, goddesses, saints, and other figures of the Brahmanical and Hindu pantheons are generally depicted in art. From the earliest times, craftspeople and sculptors have been following the rules of the *Shilpa Shastras*, a collection of ancient texts that lay down the rules of how each craft is to be practised. These texts contain detailed guidelines on how to depict the gods, their facial features, their expressions, the position of their limbs, their attire and ornaments, and even how they should be posed. So, it is somewhat surprising to come across the unique-looking trio of deities from the famous Jagannatha temple at Puri, Odisha.

In the twelfth century CE, Anantavarman Chodaganga of the Ganga dynasty built a temple dedicated to Jagannatha—another name for Vishnu—which literally means 'lord of the universe' at Puri. At this time, a king building a temple was not an unusual move. What was curious was the choice of images in the sanctum or holy shrine. The images are life-size, with enormous heads, huge round eyes and squat, neckless bodies with stumpy hands but no legs. The idol with the dark eyes is Jagannatha. He is accompanied by his brother Balabhadra, with the white-rimmed eyes. The smaller figure in the centre is their sister, Subhadra.

Apart from their appearance, many other aspects of Jagannatha and his worship are different from what we know of Brahmanical practices from the twelfth century. The idols themselves are, most unusually, not made of stone or metal but from the wood of a neem tree. Since wood is perishable, every few years the idols are remade by a select group of wood workers in an elaborate ceremony which begins with finding suitable neem trees in the nearby tribal forests of Daspalla. They are said to be guided in their quest for these trees by prayers to the presiding deity of the Mangala temple in nearby Kakatpur village. Once the new idols are made, the old ones are buried in a special graveyard.

At certain times of the year, the temple priests called pujapanda nijog, or servers who perform the rituals, step back, and the deities are looked after

Balabhadra, Subhadra, and Jagannatha

by a special group of people known as the Daitas, or daitapati nijog. For a period, they take over the most sacred rituals including the tasks of clothing and decorating the idols and cooking them special foods. The daitapatis are not traditionally known to be priests but rather trace their origins back to ancient tribal groups known as the Savaras, indigenous inhabitants of the hills and forests of Odisha.

And, in another unusual custom, while, normally deities do not leave the sacred temple sanctum, once a year, Jagannatha and his siblings go out on a grand trip. Seated in specially constructed, towering wooden *rathas* or chariots, they are gently paraded along the main street of Puri by thousands of devotees. They are made to disembark at a nearby temple where they spend a short holiday. On their way back, they briefly halt to visit their aunt Mausi Maa's temple, who waits for them with their favourite sweetmeats.

What is the origin of these interesting deities and their unusual rituals?

From studies of inscriptions, old temples, and palm-leaf manuscripts, scholars offer the following explanation. As groups of Brahmanas were granted gifts of land by the kings of the newly emerging kingdoms in central India, they began to settle along the River Mahanadi that flowed down to the coast of what is now Odisha. While creating settlements of their own, they came into contact with groups of indigenous people who had already been living in the area for centuries before their arrival. Over time, and with increasing contact with the indigenous people, the Brahmanas slowly began to include the beliefs and rituals of the tribal people into the Brahmanical way of worship.

In the ancient forests of Odisha, groups of indigenous inhabitants known as Savaras worshipped a god of their own known in legends as Nilamadhava. His form was a pillar of neem wood, and he lived with his two siblings in a secret location deep in the forest that only selected people were allowed to visit.

Over time, the Savara tribal god was adapted into an incarnation of Vishnu in the form of Jagannatha. However, the image of the deity, his siblings, and the way he was worshipped retained many reminders of his tribal origins.

Beginning around 1000 CE, with the spread of settlers to remote, previously unexplored areas of the subcontinent, Brahmanical beliefs often encountered already-existing ancient religious traditions. In many such encounters, there was conflict and hostility towards accepting Brahmanical strictures on old practices. However, a number of deities across India were combined with these local beliefs, and turned into a fascinating blend of ancient practices, legends, and Brahmanical traditions. The shrines of these integrated deities have become important places of pilgrimage for people from all faiths and walks of life. The icons of Jagannatha and his siblings capture a period when two varied beliefs met and merged into one harmonious faith.

51

Victory Minaret

Sandstone-covered masonry tower, Mehrauli, Delhi, late twelfth century CE

The Qutb Minar is possibly one of the most recognizable structures in India. It was built in the last decade of the twelfth century CE in what was known as Dehli-i Kuhna or 'the old city', part of a complex of monuments in present-day Mehrauli, Delhi. With its unique fluted design, arched balconies—marking each of its five storeys and bands of exquisitely worked calligraphy—this sandstone-covered masonry tower is one of the tallest minarets of the medieval world. It has managed to survive the elements, earthquakes, and even the occasional lightning strike. And tells a remarkable story of changing times.

With the decline of the Guptas around the middle of the sixth century CE, warrior groups that later came to be known as Rajputs or 'sons of kings', began to carve out kingdoms for themselves in central and western India. One such group—the Tomara Rajputs—were the first to use the area that is now Delhi as a political centre. An eleventh-century Tomara king named Anangapala II built a fortified town known as Lal Kot and is even said to have relocated the famous Mehrauli Iron pillar to a temple courtyard here. Later, the Chauhans, another Rajput clan, took over.

Qutb Minar

Under the Tomaras and the Chauhans, Dhilli or Dihali, as it was referred to then, became an important commercial centre, with prosperous Jain merchants occupying the fortified town, constructing temples, and using specially minted coins called delhiwals.

Later in the twelfth century, the Ghurids from eastern Persia and Afghanistan, looking to expand their kingdoms, came pouring through the Himalayan passes. The legendary Rajput king Prithviraj Chauhan was defeated in 1192 CE, and the Ghurids took charge of Delhi. Their leader, Mohammed Ghori, went back soon after the conquest, leaving his former slave and trusted commander, Qutub-ud-din Aibak, in charge. Not long afterwards, Mohammed Ghori himself was assassinated, leaving Qutub-ud-din free to crown himself Sultan of Delhi in 1206 CE. He was the first of what came to be known as the Mamluk or Slave sultans because Qutub-ud-din and each of his successors had once started out as an enslaved soldier or Mamluk. It was the beginning of four centuries of rule by various dynasties of Turkic and Afghan origin, later jointly called the Delhi Sultanate.

On the ruins of the old citadel of Lal Kot, Qutub-ud-din Aibak built the Quwwat-ul-Islam Mosque, with a large courtyard for the faithful to gather in prayer. Standing next to the mosque was a minar that was to symbolize Ghurid victory over Indian territories. Qutub-ud-din died in 1210 when just one storey of his proposed grand minar had been completed. It was left to his successor, Iltutmish, to complete. Over the years, the complex grew as subsequent sultans added soaring decorative screens, gateways, and tombs to it, bringing architectural elements like domes and true arches into Indian architecture for the first time. Eventually, this became the Qutb complex, with what came to be called the Qutb Minar at the centre, showcasing some of the earliest Islamic- style architecture in India.

We can only imagine the baffled reaction of the local population at the time to this unfamiliar and yet spectacular architectural wonder. However, a closer look at the minar will reveal interesting details that could show that it was not all strange. On the Qutb Minar are carved bands of flowers, rows of temple bells, and wavy patterns associated with temple decoration! The columns of the mosque are made of salvaged pieces from demolished Jain and Hindu temples. There is an inscription on one of the gateways that reveals quite bluntly, 'The materials of twenty-seven temples . . . were used in (the construction of) this mosque'. Workers have cleverly reused doorways supported by brackets, typical of temples, and chiselled down sculpted figures since human representations were not allowed in Islamic art. Bits of the carved verses from the Quran in calligraphy look like they were made by someone unfamiliar with the script. Other parts of the complex feature *kirti mukhas*, fierce faces, meant to ward off evil and *kalashes* or pots that signify prosperity, usually seen on temple walls.

Scholars believe that while the Slave sultans came with new elements of architecture like the arch and an early form of the dome, it was Indian master builders who built the layout. Masons and craftspeople freely re-used the stones from the demolished temples, often merely reassembling pieces, which accounts for the typical temple motifs on the pillars and brackets. As time went on, some of these motifs, like the lotus and the *kalash* became an integral part of mosque and tomb building styles. With the blending of these elements, the building arts in India took on a whole new composite style.

The religion of Islam was not new to India. It had already made its way here quite soon after the death of the Prophet in the seventh century CE by way of traders, merchants, and occasional invaders. However, this time it had come to stay. Along with the Turkic and Persianate conquerors came social traditions, languages, art, architecture, food, and fashion from Central Asia, Persia, and Afghanistan. Northern India began to change and adapt these new ideas into its culture. So, while curious onlookers of those days may not have been quite as surprised as expected, the Qutb Minar remains an icon in the modern city of Delhi, a symbol of the syncretic culture that began back in the early thirteenth century.

52

The Doomed Tanka

Copper coin, Delhi, issued on the orders of Muhammad bin Tughlaq, c. 1329 CE

The copper coin shown in the illustration on the facing page is known as a tanka. It was minted around 1329 CE on the orders of Muhammad bin Tughlaq. The Tughlaqs were one of the five Turkic and Central Asian families that made up the Delhi Sultanate, which ruled large parts of India from the twelfth to early sixteenth centuries CE. They came on the scene in the early thirteenth century. This tanka tells the tale of a Tughlaq in a hurry.

Muhammad bin Tughlaq is one of the most controversial figures in Indian history. Even the manner in which he ascended the throne had a whiff of scandal about it. His father, Sultan Ghiyas ud din Tughlaq, had died when a temporary pavilion built to host a welcome party for him collapsed, burying him in the rubble. Some considered it an accident, others suspected foul play. There were whispers that the pavilion, designed under the personal supervision of Muhammad himself, had been tampered with.

By some accounts, the new sultan was said to be a well-educated man with highly cultivated tastes. He knew several languages, including Persian, Arabic, and Sanskrit, and was interested in subjects like

astronomy and mathematics. A famed calligrapher himself, he was also a generous patron of the arts. He had proven himself on the battlefield particularly in the conquering of Deccan kingdoms for the sultanate. He was impulsive and generous, often handing out bags of gold to beggars at his gate. Muhammad based appointments to his court on merit rather than high birth or religion. Much to the disapproval of the nobles and the *ulema* or religious heads, Muhammad included former barbers, cooks, and gardeners among his highest officials. He was quick-witted and impatient, often brushing aside good advice from his senior courtiers.

However, Muhammad hated opposition. To those who dared to oppose him, Muhammad showed a barbarous side of his character. Rebels were known to be flayed alive, their skins stuffed with straw, and put on public display. Since the sultanate now stretched from the Sind province (now in Pakistan) to undivided Bengal, southern India, Gujarat, and Malwa, these rebels surfaced regularly and were put down with ruthless punishments.

The unpredictable sultan was always full of innovative ideas. Many of them were based on good intentions but, due to either bad execution or bad luck, they ended in disaster. The Mongols, those fierce warriors from Central Asia, had already made several attacks on the Delhi Sultanate. They even besieged Delhi, leaving only after extracting a hefty ransom. Expecting another attack, Muhammad decided to increase the size of his army. The funds were to come from heavier taxes on the fertile lands between the Ganga and Yamuna rivers. Unfortunately, the increase in taxes coincided with a drought followed by a famine. Although the sultan organized a speedy import and distribution of grains, his suffering citizens blamed him for the drought.

It was then that Muhammad made another huge mistake. A shortage of silver was destabilizing the financial market in the Tughlaq kingdom. Having heard of the Chinese innovation of token-paper currency, which could be exchanged for a fixed amount of gold and silver, Mohammad ordered the minting of copper and brass coins called tankas. This was representative money, with the value of currency based not on the metal that it was made of but rather on a government guarantee of value. This was a very modern idea that is used to this day. However, unlike modern currency, the copper and brass tankas did not have any security features; they bore no special royal seals and were, therefore, easy to copy. In no time at all, according to the scribes of the time, every house became a mint, flooding the market with forged tankas! The situation got so out of hand that within two years, Muhammad had to buy back all the tankas in circulation, both real and fake, until mountains of useless coins piled up within the walls of the Tughlaqabad fort.

While the people were still reeling from that disaster, Muhammed decided that it would be a good idea to move his capital as far as possible to secure it from the invading Mongols. Delhi was to be his military capital, and Daulatabad, the administrative capital. This move was also to better administer his growing empire, by now stretching all the way up to Madurai in present-day Tamil Nadu. With hardly any notice, the court and all the important officers of Delhi were ordered to move to Devagiri or Daulatabad, 1400 kilometres away, in central India. But Muhammed had not reckoned on the unwillingness of the people. Despite generous compensation and arrangements for their comfort during the long journey, they complained, rebelled, and wrote spiteful letters against their sultan. After much suffering and financial loss, a few years later, the sultan ordered that the capital be moved back to Delhi.

When the sultan died in 1351 after a twenty-six-year reign, it was said that the citizens of his kingdom heaved a collective sigh of relief. Despite his reputation as a maverick, scholars now believe Muhammad bin Tughlaq was an original thinker, a man of foresight whose schemes fell apart due to poor implementation. The strategic move down south, although temporary, laid the seeds of the later powerful Islamic courts of the Deccan. And the system behind the notorious tanka came to be the norm in modern currency systems.

53

The Most Magnificent Raya

Bronze statue set, Tirupati Venkateshwara temple, Andhra Pradesh, 1517 CE

In the fourteenth century, an empire arose in the Deccan that was so brilliant and so dazzling that even 500 years after it was gone, people still told stories of its glory. The Vijayanagara Empire, in its heyday, stretched from the River Krishna to the southern end of the Indian peninsula. Its capital city was called Vijayanagara, literally meaning the 'City of Victory'.

Krishnadeva Raya was its most famous ruler. He ruled for almost twenty years, beginning in 1509 CE. Under him, the Vijayanagara Empire reached the height of its glory. He was a formidable warrior, conquering new lands in modern-day Odisha and Bijapur for his already huge empire and fending off constant attacks from both the Deccan Sultans and the Delhi Sultans. Despite the need to be constantly on alert against his unpredictable neighbours, Krishnadeva Raya's rule was known as a period of great prosperity. Trade, agriculture, and manufacturing flourished throughout the empire. In the sprawling capital on the banks of the River Tungabhadra, there was a flurry of construction. Magnificent buildings, market places, gardens, palaces, and temples came up, protected by no fewer than seven layers of fortified walls. Being an arid region, the king sponsored major irrigation works, including a network of canals and aqueducts to carry water from the river into the heart of the city. Vijayanagara was reputed to be one of the greatest cities of the medieval world, said to rival Rome in size and beauty.

The three bronze figures shown in the illustration below depict Krishnadeva Raya and his two wives, Chinnamadevi and Thirumaladevi. The statues were installed at a *mandapam* or hall in the famous Tirupati Venkateshwara temple in Andhra Pradesh. Krishnadeva was a devotee who made several pilgrimages to the shrine and, it is said, donated these images himself in 1517 CE. Here, the king looks elegant and serene,

Krishnadeva Raya and His Wives, Chinnamadevi and Thirumaladevi

perfectly turned out, with his distinctive conical cap and an almost divine air about him. However, a Portuguese traveller named Domingo Paes had visited Vijayanagara during the rule of Krishnadeva Raya and had this to say of his looks: 'The king is of medium height and of fair complexion and good figure, rather fat than thin; he has on his face, signs of smallpox.' So, it appears that the bronze figure is really a projection of how Krishnadeva wanted his subjects to see him and probably does not represent his true likeness.

This was not unusual in those days. Throughout history, rulers liked to project themselves in art as physically powerful and with close connections to the gods. It was one way of not only convincing their subjects that they had the right to rule over them but also to thwart any potential rebellions.

Krishnadeva Raya ruled over an empire during changing times. Apart from his reportedly million-strong army that was constantly vigilant, Vijayanagara was a cosmopolitan centre of commerce. Adventurers and fortune seekers came from all over the subcontinent. Foreign merchants and visitors, including Arabs, Jews, Persians, Portuguese, and Italians travelled here. They brought with them goods from all over the world to trade and to marvel at the prosperous city with its grand streets lined with magnificent temples, lavishly decorated mansions, well-planned gardens, and flowing waterways. People of all faiths, creeds, and classes mingled and interacted in the marketplaces and meeting halls, exchanging goods and information in many different languages. For these people, the king allowed the greatest freedom to practice their faiths and trades and his welcoming attitude was adopted by his subjects as well. This helped Vijayanagara become a truly cosmopolitan, bustling centre for trade and commerce.

Krishnadeva himself had a commanding personality. The awed Paes wrote of the king's rigorous everyday routine. He would rise before dawn, drink a quarter pint of sesame oil, and then proceed to exercise, lifting weights and wrestling with strong men. Then, after a bracing horse ride, he would appear in court clothed in finery, where he would enjoy the company of philosophers, writers, and poets. The king was regarded with a mixture of respect and fear. As cheerful as he appeared, he was also known for fits of rage at ingratitude or injustice.

Being of a literary bent of mind, he encouraged scholars and writers. Great works in Tamil, Kannada, and Sanskrit were written during this time, and the learned king is believed to have produced a Telegu work of his own in which he documented his personal ideas on statecraft and efficient administration. It was even rumoured that on many nights, the king would walk around the city in disguise, listening and observing if all was well with his people and what needed improvement.

Krishnadeva Raya was regarded as a godlike being, well in control of all affairs in his kingdom. Centuries later, his bronze image at the Tirupati Venkateshwara temple conveys many subtle messages. He and his queens are pious but also seem to be almost divine. The ruler's pose conveys an impression of power and wealth, hinting at his authority, the grandeur of his court and the strength of the Vijayanagara Empire.

54

Shielding a Battle Horse

Steel horse-head armour, Deccan Sultanate of Golconda, 1617 CE

The illustration on the facing page shows a shaffron—the main part of the armour of a horse that would have been placed on its head, protecting it from the ears down to the muzzle. The two curved bits at the top would have once held steel ear guards. Metal armour for a horse seems rather unusual. And yet, the era seemed to require this special attire.

In the patchwork of multiple kingdoms and sultanates of the Indian subcontinent in medieval times, warfare was the chief means by which to gain territory or assert power. Rulers were not only expected to be great warriors themselves but also to use their resources to recruit, train, and equip large standing armies. An important branch of these armies were horse cavalries, trained for speed in war and communications. And just like the warriors who rode them, war horses were made to wear protective steel and leather plates lined with quilted fabric to defend themselves against the spears and swords of the enemy. What is unique about this piece is the Arabic inscription found at the top edge. It gives us a name and a date for the shaffron! It reads, 'Abu al-Muzaffar Sultan

Muhammad Qutb, sanat 1026'. Abu al-Muzaffar Sultan Muhammad Qutb was the sixth sultan of the Qutb Shahi dynasty of Golconda, in present-day Telangana, and the date given in the Muslim calendar is the equivalent of 1617–18 CE.

With the establishment of the Delhi Sultanate in the thirteenth century CE, things changed in southern India too. Constant raids and attacks from the north weakened previously strong dynasties like the Hoysalas and the Kakatiyas. In their place rose the Bahmani kingdom of the northern Deccan and their arch-rivals further south, the Vijayanagara kingdom. The Bahmani kingdom was an independent Muslim state set up in the early fourteenth century by rebellious nobles of Persian and Turkic origin previously in the service of the Delhi Sultans, while Vijayanagara was ruled by Hindu kings. In the early sixteenth century, the Bahmani kingdom disintegrated into five separate states, later jointly known as the Deccan Sultanates. The Qutb Shahis were one of the five breakaway kingdoms.

It was a time of great churning in the Deccan. The five sultanates not only fought Vijayanagara but also constantly plotted and fought against each other. This is where the battle horses assumed importance.

Although horses were known to have been a part of warfare since as early as the sixth century BCE, it was generally thought that indigenous horses were not of the best quality. Around the early centuries of the

A Shaffron or Metal
Horse-Head Armour

Common Era, Arab traders brought superior Persian and Arabian horses to the ports on the Malabar Coast. From there, Kudarai chetties or horse merchants, transported the steeds to supply the armies of the Cholas, Pandyas, and Hoysalas. We know the Kudarai chetties grew prosperous on this trade from the inscriptions of the time.

In the early fourteenth century, war tactics changed. In the now-frequent wars between the Delhi and Deccan sultanates and the Vijayanagara Empire, swift and effective cavalry became the most important aspect of battle strategy. Imported war horses became the need of the hour. First, Arabs edged out the Kudarai chetties as dealers. The lucrative trade soon attracted other profit-seekers. In the late fifteenth century, the Portuguese, who now controlled parts of the western coast, including Goa, began to supply horses to the Vijayanagara kingdom.

One Portuguese account states that the Raya of Vijayanagara imported up to 13,000 horses a year. Not only did he willingly pay the merchant's exorbitant asking price, but he even paid for horses that had died aboard the ship enroute to India! In his book on statecraft, Krishnadeva Raya of Vijayanagara declares that importing good horses is among the important duties of a king and that horse merchants should be well cared for in his kingdom. Many of the monuments at Vijayanagara feature panels of beautifully carved horses, some of them with Portuguese traders and others with their grooms being presented to important buyers. Foreign travellers wrote in awe of the festive ceremonies at Vijayanagara where beautifully decked horses were paraded wearing expensive silks and saddles studded with precious stones.

These travellers were also mystified as to why Indians could not breed good horses of their own rather than wasting enormous sums of money on imported horses. Some said the climate did not suit horses. Others said the Indians did not know how to feed the horses, indulging them in all sorts of delicacies till the animals became quite fat, lethargic, and unsuited to battle. It was rumoured that the traders deliberately did not allow foreign horse handlers to make their way to India in order to protect their trade monopoly.

The race for good horses was so competitive that it enabled the traders to exploit the rivalry between the kingdoms. By promising exclusive rights over imported horses to both the Vijayanagara Empire and those of the Deccan Sultanate, the Portuguese were able to sign treaties that gave them privileges not only in trade but also helped them acquire large tracts of land along the western coast, which became the foundation of their colonial empire in later years.

Horses were literally worth their weight in gold. The shaffron in the illustration belonged to one such valuable horse, possibly the privileged steed of the Qutb Shahi sultan himself.

55

The Explorer's Final Rest

Marble and sandstone tomb,
Jeronimos Monastery, Lisbon, Portugal,
late nineteenth century CE

What does an ornate tomb faraway in a monastery near Lisbon, Portugal, have to do with the history of India? Take a look at the carved marble figure lying on top in the illustration. His name was Vasco da Gama, Count of Vidigueira, navigator, explorer, and once Viceroy of Estado da India or the State of India! How did a Portuguese nobleman come to have such a title?

It all started in the early fifteenth century when the Portuguese decided they wanted direct access to the profitable trade in the spices of the East. At the time, the overland routes from Asia to Europe were controlled by the Ottoman Empire. The Ottomans charged high taxes on all goods passing through their territories. The Portuguese tried for almost a century to bypass this by finding a sea route from western Europe to India. Although they managed to reach the Cape of Good Hope in present-day South Africa, they could go no further due to their lack of navigational knowledge of the Indian Ocean, and the seas to the east remained daunting and uncharted. Finally, the task of finding the elusive sea route to India fell to a well-known sailor and navigator, Vasco da Gama.

Vasco da Gama's Tomb

Setting out in 1497 with a flotilla of four ships and 170 crewmen, Vasco da Gama rounded the Cape of Good Hope and managed to head up the east coast of Africa to areas previously unknown to most Europeans. The journey was long and dangerous, with storms and hostile encounters along the African coast. Their luck finally turned with a chance meeting at Malindi, in present-day Kenya, with a legendary Kutchi ship pilot named Kanji Malam. Kanji Malam is said to have guided the Portuguese ships across the Indian Ocean. On 20 May 1498, Vasco da Gama and his flotilla landed at a beach near Calicut, now known as Kozhikode in Kerala, on the Malabar Coast.

It was a momentous occasion for the Europeans. However, the locals and curious onlookers were less impressed. The Portuguese had not realized that they had landed in one of the wealthiest and most popular ports of the East, where a great population of merchants and sailors from all over the Indian oceanic region and beyond met and traded. In the streets, there were Chinese, Venetians, Tunisians, Arabs, and Jewish traders from the eastern Mediterranean. The wealthy Zamorin, the ruler of Calicut, was at the heart of a trade network dealing in spices, gold, precious stones, ivory, food grains, and textiles that stretched from China to Persia and beyond to Europe.

The Portuguese were unable to understand the local customs and religious practices and were perplexed that they had nothing of value to offer in trade. When finally granted a royal audience with the Zamorin, Vasco da Gama was more or less laughed out of court when he displayed gifts from the Portuguese king consisting of twelve pieces of striped cloth, four scarlet hoods, six hats, four strings of coral, six wash basins, sugar, two casks of oil, and two of honey!

Having failed miserably to secure a trade contract with the Zamorin, Vasco da Gama and his crew sailed back to Portugal in embarrassment. They took over a year to retrace their route, arriving home with only two ships and fifty-four of their original crew, the rest having perished on the journey.

What happened next changed the course of history in India. The Portuguese, rather than being discouraged, sent out more trade expeditions! In subsequent trips, their ships were heavily armed with naval gunnery. So far, the Indian oceanic trade had been one of peaceful commercial competition, open to traders from all over the world. Now, Portuguese ships came armed for combat, attacking Arab merchant ships and destroying trading stations along the east African coast to set up their own.

On the Malabar Coast, they bombarded the city of Calicut, insisting that the Zamorin expel all the Arab traders. They also signed a treaty with the Raja of Cochin, persuading him to give them land to build a fort and trading factory. In 1510, they managed to grab Goa from the Bijapur Sultanate and later they acquired the ports of Bassein and Diu in Gujarat. This was the Estado da India, to which Vasco da Gama was appointed

Viceroy. The aggressive tactics of the Portuguese to dominate the Indian Ocean trade were the beginning of more than 400 years of European colonialism through commerce and maritime power. They were soon followed by the Dutch, French, and finally the English, each negotiating their own trade treaties and grabbing land in India.

In 1524, Vasco da Gama died in Cochin and was buried in a local church. A few years later, his remains were carried back to Portugal.

The Portuguese finally quit India in 1961, leaving behind a cultural stamp on their former territories and an unusual legacy in India's everyday cuisine by introducing unique ingredients like peanuts, tomatoes, chillies, potatoes, and pineapples that they brought over from the newly explored Americas. Even now, there is a city named Vasco da Gama in Goa, the lasting legacy of the intrepid explorer who now lies entombed in a distant land.

56

The Slave Who Became a Peshwa

Watercolour and gold painting on paper, Delhi, 1620 CE

The portrait of a Deccan nobleman in the illustration on the facing page was painted around 1622 by an artist at the Mughal court named Hashim. The imposing turbaned man with his white shawl, long sword, dagger tucked into his richly embroidered belt, and a dangling green writing case is Malik Ambar. He was an arch enemy of the Mughal Empire. So, it seems rather unusual that the Mughals would bother to paint his portrait. In fact, everything about Malik Ambar was unusual. And his life story is a window into the multicultural world of the Deccan in the sixteenth and seventeenth centuries.

Malik Ambar was born in 1548, far away from Indian shores. Chapu, as he was named, came from the Oromo tribe of Abyssinia, the country we now know as Ethiopia in Africa. As a young boy, Chapu was captured by slave traders, taken away from his homeland, and sold several times before he landed in Baghdad. There, a wealthy merchant bought him at a slave market. Probably sensing that the boy was gifted, the merchant gave

Portrait of Malik Ambar

him a good education, converted him to Islam, and called him Ambar. With this merchant, Ambar, now in his twenties, sailed to the Deccan. There, he was sold to the chief minister or peshwa of the Ahmadnagar Sultanate. At this point, a whole new world opened up for Ambar.

To his great surprise, Ambar found that the peshwa himself was a Habshi, the Arabic term for Abyssinian. Habshis were Africans who came to live in India, arriving as merchants and fishermen as well as slaves. Some of them were also known as Siddi or 'my lord', implying they had an elevated status. Just like Ambar, the peshwa had also begun life as a traded slave from Ethiopia and then worked his way up into a position of great power and wealth. He owned more than a thousand Habshi slaves whom Ambar now joined. However, they were no ordinary slaves meant to toil in households. Instead, they were trained as fighting forces, under the protection and care of their owner. In those unstable times, there was always a demand for well-trained soldiers. It was common practice in the kingdoms of the Deccan to hire African Habshis as they were valued for their fighting skills and their loyalty.

Ambar noticed the Habshis, being cut off from their homeland, had made the Deccan their home, embracing the local culture, customs, and languages. They moved between the courts of the Deccan Sultanate and Vijayanagara, adding to the blend of various foreign groups—the Persians, Arabs, Central Asians, and Turks that made up the multi-ethnic Deccan society at the time.

Ambar discovered something else too. There was no bar to working your way up to the top. And that is exactly what he did. Within a few years of arriving in the Deccan, the peshwa died, and Ambar found himself a free man. Gathering a force of trained Habshis under his leadership, Ambar went back and forth between Bijapur and Ahmadnagar, offering his fighting skills to the local rulers, rapidly gaining a reputation both as a military genius and a man of great administrative ability. It was around now that he earned the title of Malik.

By 1600, Malik Ambar had become important enough in the Ahmadnagar court to be a kingmaker, installing two young princes in succession to the unstable throne. He married his daughter to the young sultan and himself became regent ruler of Ahmadnagar and commander of the forces! When the Mughals in the north began to eye the Deccan kingdoms to add to their expanding empire, it was Malik Ambar who rose to the defence of the sultanates.

Using his skills as both a soldier and a diplomat, he made important alliances. These included alliances with the newly emerging Marathas, the descendants of African sailors who commanded the strategic Janjira fort on the western coast, and a core of fierce Habshi fighters. He used unusual guerrilla warfare tactics and new-fangled artillery to hold off the mighty Mughal armies of Akbar and Jahangir from overrunning the Deccan for several decades. When he was defeated in battle, as he sometimes was, he used clever political means to get the better of his enemies.

In the midst of defending the Deccan, negotiating internal politics at court, and surviving assassination attempts, Malik Ambar found the time to build a new capital, a model city called Khadki, later renamed Aurangabad. Khadki became a base for Maratha nobility and soldiers, including Maloji, the grandfather of Shivaji and a close associate of Malik Ambar.

Powerful as they were, the Mughals were in equal parts frustrated and fascinated by Malik Ambar. Jahangir referred to him rather rudely in his memoirs as 'rebel of black fortune' and 'the crafty Ambar'. But he was obsessed enough to commission a fantasy painting in which he is seen shooting an arrow through the severed head of the Habshi general. But his grudging admiration came out when Malik Ambar died. Jahangir's memoirs admit, 'He had no equal in warfare, in command, in sound judgement, and in administration'! Admiration for Malik Ambar as a respected adversary also reflects in this Mughal-commissioned painting, thought to have been painted on the orders of Emperor Shah Jahan.

The life of Malik Ambar is a testament not just to the considerable African influence in the politics of the Deccan of the time but also to the extraordinary social mobility of those times when talent and ability could take a former slave to the highest positions in the land. Descendants of the Habshis now more commonly known as Siddis, still live in modern Gujarat, Karnataka, and Telegana today.

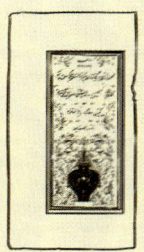

57

The Book of Nine Rasas

Gold on paper manuscript, Deccan Sultanate of Bijapur, early seventeenth century CE

The illustration overleaf is a page from one of the most remarkable books of late medieval India. The book is called *Kitab-i-Nauras* or the *Book of Nine Rasas* featuring fifty-nine devotional songs and seventeen couplets with instructions on the ragas in which they were to be sung. It was written in a language called Dakhni Urdu. On this page, five lines of verse are hand-written in elegant calligraphy that seem to float within clouds. The page is beautifully illuminated or decorated with paintings. From the resplendent red vase springs lush foliage and leafy vines, drawn in finely detailed gold-and-black ink. Closer inspection reveals birds like kingfishers and woodpeckers perched among the flowers. On other surviving pages of the book, scholars have identified eight different species of birds, including waterfowl and herons flitting among the reeds, while fish and ducks swim in the waters, watched carefully by land-bound foxes.

The work was composed at the beginning of the seventeenth century by Ibrahim Adil Shah II, Sultan of Bijapur. Bijapur was one of the five Deccan sultanates, and Ibrahim Adil Shah was known to be a gifted musician. Several years later, this manuscript was made by a master calligrapher

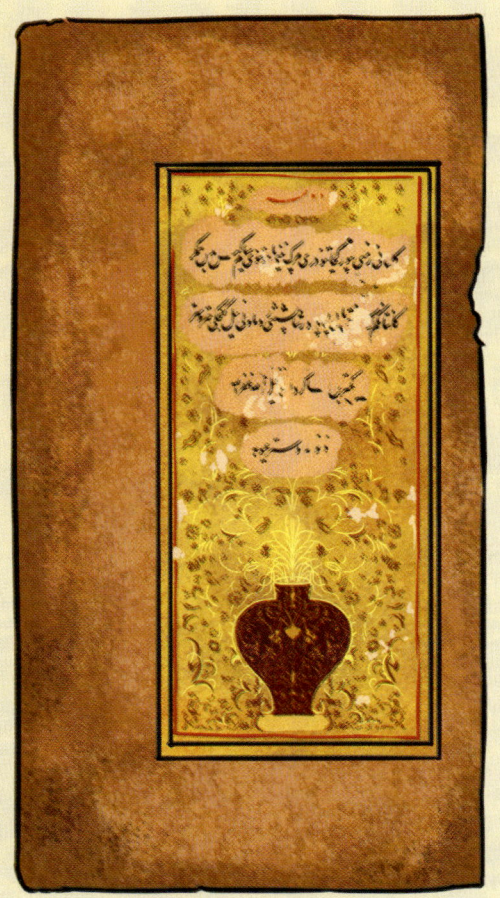

A Page from the Kitab-i-Nauras

named Khalilullah. It was said the sultan was so pleased with it that he named Khalilullah Badshah-i-Qalam, which translates into 'the king of the pen'. As a special reward, the sultan even allowed Khalilullah to sit on his throne for a while!

Apart from the fine artwork, what stands out are the themes of the sultan's compositions. The book opens with invocations to the Hindu goddess Saraswati, the Prophet Muhammad, and a Sufi saint named Gesu Daraz. Further on, there are references to Shiva and Parvati, and the sultan often mentions that he considered Saraswati and Ganapati as his spiritual parents. There are songs in praise of his favourite people, his wife Chand Sultan, his mother Bari Sahib, his pet elephant Atash Khan, and even his tambur (a stringed musical instrument), which he had named Moti Khan! In his songs, the sultan constantly expresses the view that seeking knowledge should be the most important purpose in life.

From *Kitab-i-Nauras*, we learn about the sort of man the sultan was—cultured, learned, and tolerant towards all religions. He spoke several languages, wrote poetry, composed music, and was a keen patron of the arts. During his rule, Bijapur reached the height of its glory, rivalling the Mughals in military power, arts, culture, and wealth.

However, not just the man but also the times in which he lived were reflected in the *Kitab-i-Nauras*.

Since ancient times, the natural resources of the Deccan and its long coastline had been the foundation of kingdoms which were famous the world over for their artistic and cultural achievements. Merchants, scholars, craftspeople, soldiers, and adventurers flocked to these kingdoms, hoping to make their fortunes in their cosmopolitan cities. In the thirteenth century CE, with the establishment of the Delhi Sultanate in northern India, a whole new set of people made their way to the Deccan. The first wave of Central Asian Turks trickled down from the north, with the constant raids of the new Muslim rulers on southern kingdoms. Then, when rebellious nobles decided to defy the Tughlaqs and make the northern Deccan their permanent home, they founded the first Muslim kingdom of the Deccan—the Bahmani kingdom.

All these people brought with them the culture and manners of the Persian and Arab worlds. By the time the Bahmani kingdom broke into five different sultanates in the early sixteenth century, the kingdoms were directly recruiting their administrators, soldiers, artisans, and architects from the Persian world. This was not without its problems as local Deccan-born Muslims who had moved from the north in previous generations often resented the new, Persian-speaking Westerners who were given favourable treatment in these sultanates. Nevertheless, there was a great influx of new ideas and artistic styles, crossing over into the Vijayanagara kingdom and influencing their court manners, dressing style, and architecture.

The Deccan at this time was a place of cultural and ethnic diversity. The courts were packed with Maratha and Telegu warlords, brahmin ministers and accountants, Persian artists, Central Asian architects, African soldiers, European merchants, and holy men of all faiths. Architecture, crafts, music, art, and dress combined traditions with ease. Even languages blended.

It is against this backdrop that Sultan Ibrahim Adil Shah II came to write his book in Dakhni Urdu, a language that merged Persian with words from Dehalvi, also known as Old Urdu, Telegu, Kannada, and Marathi. This is also why the sultan, a Sunni Muslim, could reveal the influence of Hindu traditions on him by beginning his work with an invocation to the Hindu goddess of learning, Saraswati. He was even fondly referred to by his subjects as Jagadguru Badshah, which roughly translated, means the ruler who is also a spiritual master of the world.

In one extraordinary verse, the sultan declares, 'There are different languages; but there is one emotional appeal. Be he a Brahmin or a Turk, He is only fortunate on whom, The Goddess of Learning [Saraswati] smiles, Ibrahim says, the world seeks knowledge. Be focused on the Word, on the guru, on meditation'. The *Kitab-i-Nauras* is considered one of the finest representations of a time when differing beliefs, practices, cultures, and languages blended by emphasizing their underlying unity.

58

Banner of the Devout

Brass processional standard,
Deccan Sultanate of Golconda,
late seventeenth to early eighteenth century CE

An intricately made object, the Alam processional banner seen in the illustration on the next page is a beaten brass disc encircled by a pair of dragons with intertwined tails. Rows of tiny holes run up their scaly backs. Punched out of the centre in beautiful calligraphy are the words 'Allah, Mohammad, Ali'. The same words are engraved around the circle.

Around the late seventeenth century, in the kingdom of Golconda in present-day Telangana, the Alam banner would have been shone to a mirror finish, mounted on a sturdy flag pole, and carried at the head of a procession to mark the tenth day of Muharram, known as Ashura. Muslims, particularly Shia Muslims, observe Muharram as a period of mourning for the deaths of Imam Hussain—grandson of the Prophet Mohammad—his family members, and a band of his followers who died at the Battle of Karbala in 680 CE in present-day Iraq. Alam banners are derived from the battle standards of that fateful battle and are symbols of martyrdom in Islam.

From the earliest days of Islam, there were two sub-groups of the religion who came to be known as the Shias and the Sunnis. Both groups share the central beliefs of Islam. They differ in a few ways, central among which is the notion of who the true successor of Prophet Mohammad should have been. Sunnis believe that since Prophet Mohammad did not declare a successor, they should elect the most capable person as leader, known as the Caliph. Shias believe that the Prophet had designated his cousin and son-in-law, Hazrat Ali, as the first in a line of hereditary imams from the Prophet's family to lead the community after him. The Shias regard Imam Hussain as the true successor of Prophet Mohammad.

The Qutb Shahis, who ruled the northern Deccan Sultanate of Golconda from the sixteenth to the late seventeenth century CE, were of Persian origin and popularized the practices of Shia Islam in India, especially in the Deccan. Muharram was an important part of their religious calendar, a month in which almost all regular activities came to a halt. There was no music, dancing, or eating meat during that month. Everyone dressed in black, and no celebrations were allowed. On the tenth day of the month, the Alam banners were decorated with silks and jewels, some of them weighing over 100 kilograms each. They were carried in slow, solemn processions to the Badshahi Ashurkhana, which was set up by the sultan. At this beautifully decorated hall near the Charminar, in present-day Hyderabad, people gathered to pray and mourn the death of Imam Hussain and his companions with tears and lamentation. People of all faiths, including Hindus, gathered there to catch a glimpse of the Alam banners, touching them with reverence and seeking blessings.

Islam had entered India almost immediately after the death of Prophet Mohammad in the early seventh century CE. It came with Arab traders to the Malabar Coast and with the conquest of Sind in the north-west by an Arab general. It became more widespread with the advent of the Turkic and Afghan rulers of the Delhi Sultanate and made its way to the

south in the fourteenth century with the Bahmani Sultanate, the first Muslim dynasty of the Deccan.

In India, Islamic law has had to adapt itself to the populations of Hindus, Jains, Buddhists, and Christians who do not follow the religion. And those who accepted the new religion adapted its practices to local traditions of language, social customs, and architecture. Interestingly, the terms 'Hindu' and 'Muslim' to define different religious communities were unknown until at least the fourteenth century. It was more common to identify people by their religious sects or their places of origin. For instance, the community that came to be called Hindus was referred to as Shaivas, Vaishnavas, or Bhagavatas. Others identified with their professions or castes. As for those who later came to be known as Muslims—although they were all followers of Islam—they were not considered one consolidated group but were instead distinguished as smaller groups who were identified by their places of origin. Turks were called Turushkas, Parashikas were people from Persia (present-day Iran), Afghans were sometimes called Shakas, and those from Central Asia were termed either Tajikas or, generally, Yavanas, meaning those who came from the west.

Then there were those who decided to question formal religion, concentrating instead on individual devotion to a Supreme God or Bhakti. Within Islam, one such group known as the Sufis believed that salvation could come not by following dogmatic rules but through personal devotion to God and compassion for fellow humans. By the eleventh century CE, ascetic Sufi teachers established large followings of their own, based around a khanqah or hospice. Here, people from all walks of life, including royalty and those from different religions, would flock to listen to the words of the shaikh or spiritual master, sing devotional songs, receive blessings, or partake in acts of charity. The shaikhs were said to have spiritual powers to heal and their tombs often became places of pilgrimage.

The Chishtis were among the most influential of the Sufi orders. They came from Afghanistan around the twelfth century CE. One of the most famous pirs or spiritual leaders of this order, Shaikh Nizamuddin Auliya, established his khanqah in Delhi, which attracts large crowds to this day. In the fourteenth century, a Chishti shaikh, scholar, and mystic known as Khwaja Bande Nawaz Gesu Daraz moved south to Gulbarga, modern-day Kalaburagi in Karnataka, where he was welcomed by the Bahmani sultan. When he died, his tomb became one of the most popular Sufi dargahs in India. A huge, annual Urs or death anniversary is observed there, which is a great fusion of cultures involving people of all religions.

At the Badshahi Ashurkhana in Hyderabad, the tradition of displaying rows of beautiful Alam banners during Muharram continues to this day, viewed and venerated by people of all faiths.

59

Kalamkari Goes Global

Painted and dyed cotton cloth, Coromandel Coast, early eighteenth century CE

Can a piece of cloth shape the course of world history? We can certainly say this about the piece of textile shown in the illustration here. It is a length of Indian chintz cotton dated to the early eighteenth century CE that originated on the Coromandel Coast—the south-eastern coastline of India. The term chintz is derived from the Hindi word *chhint* meaning spotted or speckled, and the name was given to cloth with small, spotted or coloured floral designs. This piece was part of a consignment made for export to Europe. However, long before it made its journey there, India was already the world's largest producer of fine cotton textiles, renowned for excellent quality, superb printing technique, and vibrant colours.

The art of painting and dyeing cloth goes back to ancient times in India, as evident from the fragment of dyed cloth that was discovered in the 4000-year-old Harappan civilization. Cave paintings, such as those at Ajanta and temple murals from the Vijayanagara era show costumes made with different techniques of dyeing, printing, and painting on fabric.

Kalamkari Textile

The piece in this illustration is an example of the painted textile art of Kalamkari. Kalamkari literally means artwork done with a pen. In the seventeenth century, under the patronage of the Qutb Shahi rulers of Golconda, the artists were called kalamkaars, with the name originating in the Farsi language: *kalam* (pen) and *kar* (work).

Kalamkari work involved a complex process of drawing and dyeing. The design was first sketched out or block printed in black outline on the cloth. Colours were then applied in stages, using wax to resist dye on those areas to be coloured in later. The colour palette of reds, blues, pinks, yellows, and blues came from fruits, flowers, barks, and roots, each treated separately as the fabric went through many complex processes. These included washing the cloth in running water, de-starching, dyeing, soaking in buffalo milk, boiling, bleaching with a cow-dung solution, and finally drying on sand. Indian artisans knew the secrets of dyeing cotton with brilliant colours using techniques that were not known or practiced anywhere else in the world.

The strong links between Persia and the Qutb Shahis of Golconda led to a steady demand for Kalamkari work from Persia and the Middle East. Thus, Kalamkari artists began to feature Persian-influenced geometric patterns, flora and fauna, interlacing patterns of leaves and creepers, the tree of life, and scenes from court life.

Meanwhile, Kalamkari and other fine textiles, including patolas, ikats, and bandhanis, had already made their way to Southeast Asia as early as the ninth century CE, to Sumatra, the Malay peninsula, and Java. The colourful prints, catering to local tastes in design and colour, were high-value items, often used as currency, stored as heirlooms, and coveted by royalty as status symbols.

In the mid-fifteenth century, due to the disruption in overland trade between Europe and Asia, the Portuguese, prospecting for spices, managed to discover an ocean route to India. By early seventeenth century, the British and Dutch East India Companies too began to follow the same sea route to the East. Now, they did something rather crafty. Noting the high demand for Indian textiles in Southeast Asia, they began to buy textiles in India at cheap rates. They bartered these for the rare spices of the Malay islands which they then took back to Europe, making huge profits from the trade.

Soon, traders set off a frenzy when they began to carry Indian textiles directly back to Europe. The light fabrics and beautifully coloured prints were such a hit that almost everybody, from royalty to commoner, was dressed in Indian Kalamkari or chintz as it came to be known in the West. Home furnishings like curtains and bedcovers in chintz were all the rage. The demand grew exponentially and, as a result, the designs were customized for the European market, with floral themes including roses and tulips, depictions of holy saints, and people in European clothes.

The tide soon turned, though. Unable to cope with the competition, cloth makers in Britain and France forced their governments to protect their interests. In the late seventeenth century, Indian chintz was completely banned in France, while in the eighteenth century, Britain enforced a partial ban. In fact, in France, rules were so strict that you could be arrested for merely wearing a patterned cloth! Spurred on by the unending demand for these textiles, innovators in England began to look for ways to imitate Indian textiles. Machines like the spinning jenny and steam engine changed cotton weaving to a cheaper, mechanized process, sparking the beginning of the Industrial Revolution. New cotton plantations in North America spurred the trade in slaves from West Africa to carry out the hard plantation work.

All this had a devastating impact on Indian artisans as the demand for their exquisite, but more expensive, textiles fell drastically. However, Indian motifs and designs had by now spread all over the world, leaving a lasting impact, despite the bans.

So, every time you see a small, repeating floral pattern or hear English words of Indian origin like calico, pyjama, gingham, bandana, dungaree, and khaki, remember that they are evidence of the huge Indian influence on Europe and America. They show that Indian textiles like this one were once the centre of the first global trade network.

60

A Fine Piece of Bidri Ware

Zinc alloy hookah base with silver and brass Bidri inlay work, Deccan region, early eighteenth century CE

A beautiful brass and silver-inlaid piece, the object shown in the illustration comes from the early eighteenth-century Deccan and has several stories attached to it. It was once the base pot of a hookah, which is a three-piece contraption made to smoke tobacco. The tobacco leaf is first heated with coal in the base of the pot to the point of vapour, the resulting smoke then passes through a small urn filled with water to cool it down and, finally, the user draws the smoke through a long flexible pipe, with an attached mouthpiece. Delicate floral inlay work runs diagonally along the base of this particular hookah pot, glowing against the polished black background. The alternating lines of Persian calligraphy are humorous verses that describe the pleasures of smoking a hookah! According to a stamp on the base, the hookah once belonged to someone called Shaikh Ahmad.

The pot is a fine example of Bidri ware, which is a form of inlay art. Said to have originated in Persian and Turkish crafts, inlay art was brought to India by the waves of artists and artisans who flocked from these lands seeking employment in the Islamic Deccan courts in fifteenth century CE. When Sultan Ahmad Shah of the Bahmani Sultanate decided to set up a new capital in Bidar, in present-day northern Karnataka, he had a Persian master craftsman brought in to decorate the fort and the brand-new palaces, mosques, pavilions, tombs, and mausoleums. The intricate florals, brightly coloured tile work, geometric patterns, and delicate mother-of-pearl inlay work on black basalt stone on these buildings inspired the local craftspeople. In turn, the local artisans replicated these designs on inlaid metal ware such as basins, jugs, trays, boxes, and hookah bases. This new craft came to be known as Bidri ware, named after Bidar, the beautiful new capital city of the Bahamani Sultanate.

Bidri ware is still made today using a painstaking multi-step process that begins with casting the metal—a mixture of zinc, copper, and lead—in a mould of the desired shape. Once the piece is ready, designs are etched onto its surface with a sharp tool. The designs range from *ashrafi ki booti* or five-pointed leaves, *teen patti ki booti* or three-pointed leaves, and *mahi pusht* or fish scales, to *kairis* or mango-shaped motifs. The artisan then fills the etched design with silver or gold wire called *tarkashi* or thin sheets known as *taihnishan*. The Persian terms used in this art-form indicate the origins of the craft.

However, hidden in the next stage is a surprise! The piece is dipped in a special solution of copper sulphate and soil to give it that distinctive black background that makes the silver metallic design stand

Hookah Base with Bidri Inlay Work

out in contrast. The secret, it is said, is in the soil. This soil is taken from a particular area inside Bidar Fort, a shadowed area with not much sunlight and many distinctive minerals that turn the metal totally black. Craftspeople are known to taste the soil before use to check for its suitability! Bidar was thus able to stamp its unique identity on an ancient craft that originated in Persia but is now uniquely Indian.

Bidri ware first became popular among the Deccan nobility. As exquisitely crafted pieces made their way up north, the Mughals were fascinated by their delicate beauty Hookah bases were among the most popular articles of Bidri ware.

Hookahs, however, require tobacco, which comes from a plant that is not native to India. This is where the cosmopolitan courts of the Deccan factor in. Tobacco was first brought from the Americas to India and introduced to the court of Bijapur by Portuguese traders towards the end of the sixteenth century. It became so popular and adapted to the climate so well that it soon emerged as a major cash crop in the northern Deccan, generating huge tax revenues for the state.

A hakim or local doctor from Bijapur, in modern Karnataka, is said to have invented the hookah, using water to reduce the harmful effects of smoking tobacco.

Early in the seventeenth century, the Mughal emperor Akbar sent his envoy, a nobleman named Asad Beg, to the court of Bijapur. Sultan Ibrahim Adil Shah of Bijapur plied the ambassador with many gifts, including a beautiful pouch filled with the finest tobacco of the land. Asad Beg relates a fascinating account of how, upon his return, he persuaded the emperor Akbar to try out a hookah for the first time, despite the deep disapproval of his doctor! Soon after, unheeding of the dire warnings of hakims and an outright ban by the Emperor Jahangir due to the 'disturbance tobacco brings about in most temperaments . . .', hookah smoking became a fashionable activity of leisure among the nobles, increasing the demand for elaborately decorated Bidri-ware hookahs. Soon, the trend filtered down to ordinary people who used more modest hookahs made of clay. Paintings of the time feature noble men and women enjoying this activity using elaborate Bidri-ware hookah bases. The piece in this illustration was possibly commissioned by one such aristocratic smoker.

61

An Unlikely Family Gathering

Ink, gold, and watercolour painting, northern India, 1707–1712 CE

The illustration on the facing page is a family portrait, painted in the Mughal miniature style, sometime between 1707 and 1712 CE. We can spot the first six rulers of the Mughal Empire or the Great Mughals (as they popularly came to be known) and their forefathers. Although featured together in the painting, they were all born at different times in a time span of over 300 years, between the fourteenth and early eighteenth centuries CE. So, while they belonged to the same family, some of them had never even met each other! Then why are they shown posing together? In this miniature painting, what we are really looking at is how the Mughals *wanted* the world to see them.

The Mughals first entered India as a small, highly mobile, conquering force under Zahir-ud-din Muhammad, better known as Babur or 'the Tiger'. Babur was the ruler of Ferghana, an area that is now in Uzbekistan in Central Asia. He was a descendant of Timur, the fierce Turkic ruler who almost destroyed Delhi during the reign of the Tughlaq dynasty. Babur wanted nothing more than to recapture Samarkand, once the beautiful capital of his ancestors' vast kingdom. Despite many attempts, some of them successful, Babur could not hold on to Samarkand and ended up taking Afghanistan instead. From there, it was just a short hop across the River Indus to the legendary kingdoms of India. In 1526, Babur's forces quickly overwhelmed the disunited Lodi sultans with swift battle tactics and new artillery technology, including guns and cannons, grabbing Punjab, Delhi, and Agra. Unlike many others who had come from Central Asia before him and returned to their homeland once they had had their fill of India's bountiful wealth, Babur made the unusual decision to stay. This was the beginning of the Mughal era, and Babur was the first of the Great Mughals.

Now that they were in new territory, the Mughals had to show they meant business. Babur and his successors—Humayun, Akbar, Jahangir,

The First Six Rulers of the Mughal Dynasty from Babur to Aurangzeb, with Their Ancestor, Timur

Shah Jahan, and Aurangzeb—continued on a spree of conquests and alliances. They drew into their empire lands that lay both east and west of their existing kingdom until almost all of northern and western India, and eventually the Deccan was under their rule. They were generous to some rulers, allowing them to keep their titles and lands and appointing them to senior positions at the Mughal court. Others were drawn even closer through the ties of marriage. As the decades went by and the Mughal Empire became one of the strongest and richest of the age, everyone forgot that the Mughals had once come from faraway Central Asia. The Mughals wanted to emphasize their right to rule over their large population of diverse subjects who belonged to many different ethnicities and religions. For this they needed a unifying symbol, and who better than their formidable ancestor, Timur, to serve as the central figure!

The Mughals descended from two great lines of rulers. On Babur's mother's side, they were descendants of Genghis Khan, the Mongol ruler who conquered China and Central Asia. The name Mughal is the Indo-Persian form of 'Mongol'. However, since they were descendants on Babur's father's side from Timur, who once ruled a vast kingdom from Turkey to Iran, the Mughals preferred to call themselves Timurid or related to Timur. Babur styled his language and court manners after the Timurids, being rather dismissive about his Mongol side.

In this painting, we see a haloed Timur sitting in the centre. The third, fourth, and fifth figures seated on his right are Babur, Akbar, and Shah Jahan. On his left, the third, fourth, and fifth figures are Humayun, Jahangir, and Aurangzeb. The four figures closest to Timur are Babur's father, grandfather, great-grandfather, and great-great-grandfather! Experts tell us that this painted family tree represents continuity. After almost two hundred years of ruling India, the Mughals wanted to remind the world that their royal ancestry entitled them to rule the Indian subcontinent that they had won as worthy descendants of Timur.

62

Sher Shah's Silver Legacy

Silver coin, northern India, 1542 CE

In 1540, an ordinary but ambitious Afghan soldier—who had once served in the Mughal army—briefly halted the rising fortunes of the mighty Mughals in India. His name was Sher Shah Suri, and he managed to chase Babur's son and successor, Humayun, out of India and into exile in Persia. He then took over the reins of the entire Mughal kingdom, stretching from Baluch, present-day Baluchistan in Pakistan, to Bengal. However, just five years later, Sher Shah died in an accident. Not long after, Humayun came stomping back to India with the support of Shah Tahmasp of Persia and wiped-out Sher Shah's quarrelling descendants.

In the few years that he was in power, Sher Shah managed to set up an impressive government machinery—revamped the political, revenue, and military departments; improved security for ordinary citizens; modernized roads; and even established a system of dak chowkies. Dak chowkies were a forerunner to the modern postal system, established in order to keep in touch with news from all over the kingdom. However, one of his greatest achievements was the object in the illustration—a humble silver coin. Since coin currency was common by the sixteenth century, you may wonder why this one was special. To find the answer, we will have to go a back a bit in time.

A very long time ago, before money was invented, people used the barter system to get what they needed. Life was simpler back then, and it was easy to exchange a bag of grain for cattle or a clay pot for fresh fish. As people began to produce more things, this system of exchange became more complicated. For instance, a jeweller would have found himself hungry if the grain merchant did not *need* his gold pendant. That's how money came to be invented. The principle on which money or currency is based is simple—people have to agree on its value. For example, if someone is paid a certain amount of money for a goat, they can then exchange the money for a good metal axe. The seller of the axe can then buy themselves a bag of grain to feed their family. This was how early monetary systems operated. Ancient people used all sorts of objects as money. Cowrie shells, rings, bracelets, lumps of gold, and even chocolate—according to accounts about the Mayan civilization!

Metal coins first appeared more than 2700 years ago in ancient Turkey where the sea-faring people of Lydia invented flat coins made of a naturally occurring combination of gold and silver, called electrum, with stamped designs. Before long, the Greeks and then the Romans were doing the same. Coin designs developed and became more sophisticated, with images of gods and goddesses and even the faces of emperors, which were supposed to bring good luck to the user.

The earliest metal coins found in India so far date back to the sixth century BCE, to the time of the ancient republics or Mahajanapadas. The people of the time were great traders. It is thought that their merchants fabricated Karshapanas or flat pieces of copper and silver of a standard weight punched with geometric designs or symbols. In the third century CE, the Mauryas were issuing silver coins called *rupyarupa*. Does the word sound familiar? *Rupya* is Sanskrit for wrought or shaped silver, and *rupa* means form or image. This is the origin of the word rupiya, which is now familiar in India as the common name for the basic unit of currency.

In the early centuries of the Common Era, the Indo-Greek rulers of north-western India and, later, the Kushanas from Central Asia infused a new level of sophistication into coin design. Realistic portraits of kings, queens, and gods adorned their beautiful coins. And with the advent of the Guptas in the third century CE, gold coins were minted with unique portraits of their kings and queens. Sometimes they look business-like, heading out to battle with axes and bows. On other coins, their cultural side is on display, and they are shown playing musical instruments or performing important rituals.

Early Muslim rulers used copper and silver coins, often blending Islamic calligraphy with Indian motifs. The maverick fourteenth-century Sultan Muhammad bin Tughlaq experimented disastrously with representative money. He used brass coins of low value to represent gold and silver coins. There was an outpouring of forgeries at the time and the system had to be reversed, at great loss to the treasury.

However, the most important introduction to Indian currency was this silver coin of Sher Shah Suri. Dating back to 1542, it weighed precisely

Sher Shah Suri's Silver Coin

11.4 grams and was made up of mostly pure silver. The rupiya, as it was called, was meant to equal forty copper pieces or *paisas*. Sher Shah's rupiya was so successful that the Mughals adopted it on their return to India as did the British. They later called it the rupee, which is the name of India's currency to this day. It is interesting to note that the rupee is also the name of the currency not just of India but that of several other countries of the region, including Nepal, Pakistan, Mauritius, the Maldives, the Seychelles, Sri Lanka, and Indonesia.

63

The Mughal Diaries

Illuminated manuscript with watercolour and gold on paper, northern India, c. 1590–1595 CE

The Mughals loved to record things. Everything about their lives was written down in great detail—lists of battles; hard-earned conquests; important appointments of nobles at court; the administration of their extremely large empire; building plans for grand palaces and forts; names of exotic imported plants to fill fabulous gardens; details of daily royal family life (including lavish wedding celebrations and birthday parties); shopping lists for everything from horses and arms to precious jewellery; the resulting hefty bills. No detail was left out.

Since the rulers themselves were busy ruling, they appointed trusted scholars and scribes to do the actual writing for them. These learned men took their jobs very seriously. They produced thick manuscripts filled with beautiful calligraphy, or ornamental handwriting, that mirrored Islamic scriptures. The pages were decorated by professional artists and often overlaid with pure gold foil. In other words, the chronicles, as scholars call them, were works of art in their own right.

The illustration on the facing page is a leaf from one such book called the *Akbarnama*. It was commissioned by Emperor Akbar in the year 1589 and entrusted to his friend Abu'l Fazl. Akbar was impressed by Abu'l not just due to his great scholarship in history and philosophy but also because he was an independent thinker who expressed himself fearlessly. Just the kind of person Akbar wanted to write a detailed account of his life and times. 'Write with the pen of sincerity the account of the glorious events and of our dominions-increasing victories,' the emperor instructed Abu'l.

For thirteen years, Abu'l did just that. He wrote so much that the *Akbarnama* went into three volumes. The first two were a detailed, almost day-to-day description of Akbar's reign, which focused on significant events like battles, conquests, alliances, courtly, and family life. The third volume, known as the *Ain-i-Akbari*, was different. Akbar needed information to help him govern his empire more efficiently. For this, Abu'l systematically gathered information from a vast array of sources including official records, ancient maps, documents, and even oral stories from the elderly.

All this data went into a manual on the workings of the empire including information about imperial orders, the physical appearance of certain provinces, the organization of the imperial court and armies, various kinds of state taxes, and even the culture and customs of the many different kinds of people who lived within the Mughal Empire. In Abu'l's words, '. . . I spent much labour and research in collecting the records and narratives . . . and I was a long time interrogating the servants of the state and old members of the illustrious family. I examined both . . . old men and active minded . . . young ones and reduced their statements to writing.' Abu'l took no chances, revising the manuscript at least five times, checking and re-checking for mistakes or inaccuracies. It is estimated that the information in the *Akbarnama* would fill about 4000 printed pages in a modern book!

Ever since Babur, the first of the great Mughal emperors, who had written his own memoirs, each of the Mughal emperors followed suit and commissioned such histories for themselves. Shah Jahan had his *Badshahnama*; Jahangir had the *Tuzk-i-Jahangiri*; and Aurangzeb, the *Alamgir-nama*. Akbar was so keen on these diaries that he even requested his aunt Gulbadan Begum, the daughter of Babur, to write an account of her half-brother, the emperor Humayun. The result was an engaging book called the *Humayun-nama* that was filled with her observations of not just the Mughal court but also family relations and, most unusually, anecdotes from the usually very private royal harem!

These books were produced in special, well-funded workshops known as kitabkhanas where paper makers, calligraphers, miniature artists, and scribes gathered. Once the calligrapher had filled the handmade-paper pages with fluid writing, the letters were decorated or 'illuminated'

with gold foil and brilliantly coloured floral designs. Blank spaces were left between the chapters for painters to fill with miniature depictions of the events being described. Each completed manuscript often had more than a hundred paintings. The prepared pages were bound carefully by skilled book-binders and set within ornamental covers. Each of these books were considered a precious object in itself, carefully preserved in the kitabkhana and brought out with the utmost care on special

A Page from the Akbarnama

occasions to be read and admired by a chosen few, usually family members and trusted courtiers of the Mughal emperors.

As these handsomely produced chronicles were funded by emperors, they naturally featured flattering depictions of the rulers and their reigns. However, today, books like the *Akbarnama* are considered valuable for another reason. This book particularly is a rare treasure trove of information about the lives of ordinary people in Mughal times. We hear of merchants, labourers, pilgrims, and forest dwellers, and how even the humblest of citizens were affected by the ideas and grand plans of the emperor.

64

The Search for Universal Peace

Miniature painting on paper, northern India, 1605 CE

In the miniature painting shown in the illustration, the Mughal Emperor Akbar is holding court at his famous Ibadat Khana or House of Worship at Fatehpur Sikri. Our eyes are drawn to the two rather sombrely dressed figures on the left. Look where the two men in black are seated. In the strict protocol of the time, only courtiers of the highest status or honoured guests were allowed to sit so close to the emperor. So, we must conclude that these two were people of some importance. They are, in fact, priests of the Jesuit mission, a Christian order from Europe. One of them is Father Rudolf Acquaviva, the leader of the mission, as we discover from his name written at the top of the painting. His companion is Brother Francisco Henriques. How were the two Christian missionaries, who had arrived only recently, able to gain an audience with one of the world's most powerful Muslim monarchs of the time? And what did they have to discuss with the emperor?

You could say that it all began with Akbar's curiosity. Despite his privileged royal upbringing with the best of tutors, young Akbar never really learned to read and write. Perhaps it was an undiagnosed learning disability of some kind, but being a shrewd judge of character, he managed to surround himself with wise advisors. Aides read out books to him so he never lacked in learning. Military commanders trained the young man in the arts of warfare and strategy. The highly intelligent boy learnt to understand the world through keen observation and interaction with people from all walks of life. Everyone remarked on his insatiable curiosity and deep desire to know more.

During Akbar's reign, through relentless wars and clever alliances, he was able to expand the Mughal Empire across a vast swathe of land from what are now Afghanistan, Gujarat, and Rajasthan right across to Bengal and present-day Odisha. As the power and prestige of the Mughal Empire increased, the court featured a diverse array of noblemen from all over the world. There were Persians, Turks, Tajiks, and Abyssinians. Powerful warlords came from Iran, Syria, Russia, Egypt, and Arabia. This elite group also included Rajputs, Deccanis, and Indian Muslims, known as Shaikhzadas, and Hindu Khatris and Kayasthas working as administrators or accountants. Akbar himself married a Rajput princess, the daughter of the Raja of Amber.

Akbar keenly observed the different social and religious practices of his diverse subjects. Apart from Hindus, Muslims, Jains, and Zoroastrians, there were smaller groups of mystical thinkers like the Sufi and Bhakti saints and wandering ascetics of various schools of thought. Feeling the need for first-hand information, the curious emperor began to regularly sneak out of the royal palace in disguise! He mingled with common folk in bazaars and street squares, listening in on their discussions and conversations. Apart from verifying that his ministers were doing a good job of administering the people, it was also a way of understanding what was needed from him as ruler of a vast empire with people drawn from many different ways of life.

Akbar Grants an Audience to Jesuit
Missionaries at the Ibadat Khana

In 1571, construction began on his new capital, Fatehpur Sikri, near Agra, the home of a prominent order of Sufi saints. Muslim ulema, learned Brahmanas, Jain saints, Zoroastrian priests, mystics, and thinkers were invited to hold free discussions on all kinds of religious questions at the

Ibadat Khana. Fierce debates raged among them, each trying to convert the audience to their own way of thinking.

And that is how the two Jesuits featured in this painting. At the end of the fifteenth century, when Portuguese traders appeared on the western coast of India, they brought along Christian missionaries with them. Akbar, ever eager to hear about new ways of thinking, invited some of them to Fatehpur Sikri in 1580. Delighted at the opportunity to convert one of the most powerful emperors in the world, the two padres hurried over. There, they talked freely of their religion among all those gathered at the Ibadat Khana. Akbar enjoyed their company, as is evident by their place of honour at court. He allowed them to tutor his children and accompany him during his battle campaigns. Somewhat to their bafflement, although the emperor listened carefully to what they had to say, he showed no signs of converting to their religion!

By this time, Akbar had made an important decision of his own. He found that although the common essence of all religions was peace and compassion, clergy and scholars often emphasized rules and dogma, creating tensions and disharmony among the people. Akbar chose, instead, an idea he called sulh-i-kul or universal peace, as the basis of his governance. Universal peace, according to Akbar, would not discriminate on the basis of religion but instead would treat all equally with justice and tolerance. It was a unifying idea for a vast and diverse empire. In this miniature painting of the Jesuit priests talking to Akbar, we glimpse one such moment of clarity in which Akbar encouraged discourse with people of different faiths in his quest for this unifying idea of universal peace.

65

Armour for a Maharana

Chain-mail suit with helmet, Udaipur, Rajasthan, late sixteenth century CE

At the City Palace Museum in Udaipur, there is a special gallery that displays a suit of chain mail along with a helmet, lethal-looking spears, swords, and a shield. These formed the battle gear of the sixteenth-century king, Maharana Pratap of Mewar, one of India's most fearless warriors. The illustration depicts this suit of armour as it would have been worn by the maharana. Chain-mail suits were made with linked metal rings that formed a dense, flexible mesh, often reinforced with smaller bits of plate armour. That way, the wearer could prevent injury during battle while still moving unhindered by stiff plate armour. Maharana Pratap's legendary horse, Chetak, rode out with his own set of equine chain-mail armour.

The suit comes with its own legends. It is believed that the maharana was seven-and-a-half-foot tall and that his armour weighed over seventy kilograms. It is also said that he carried two swords weighing over 200 kilograms and his spear alone weighed eighty kilograms. It seems rather unlikely that he could have done much fighting, being weighed down with all that heavy stuff until you realize that this is how people imagined him!

As a towering hero who fought for over a quarter of a century, standing up to the all-powerful Mughals, while many of his Rajput brethren had blended themselves into the Mughal system. He was the ideal king, the Rajput hero that bards composed songs about, singing tales of his valour, nobility, and loyalty.

From around the eighth century CE onwards, the area that is now mainly in Rajasthan was divided into a number of kingdoms ruled by various Rajput clans, with names like Chauhan, Tomara, and Sisodia. Scholars believe the clans had originally descended from different backgrounds, but they all came to follow a common ethos of brave warriors who were proud of their martial traditions of death before dishonour and their devotion to their motherland. A few centuries later, with the arrival of Muslim rulers—the Turks, Afghans, and then the Mughals—the Rajputs were faced with a challenge. They were often in conflict with the newcomers who came with better weapons and battle tactics. By Mughal times, most Rajput kingdoms had been accommodated within the Mughal system, either by conquest or alliances of cooperation, including marriage.

Mewar was an exception. Steadily defiant against domination, Mewar held out as an independent state until the time of Akbar. Despite the best efforts of the Mughal emperor, Mewar turned down all offers of political or marriage alliances. This irked Akbar because Mewar was a prosperous region, strategically situated on the route to Gujarat, where his major ports were located. In the winter of 1568 CE, at the end of a brutal five-month siege, Akbar managed to capture the stronghold of the Mewar kingdom, the great fort of Chittor. The Mewar rana escaped and set up a new capital at Udaipur. Four years later, when Maharana Pratap took over the throne of Mewar, Akbar sent emissaries once again, asking him to see sense and become a Mughal vassal. The maharana flatly refused resulting in a great battle fought in the narrow mountain pass of Haldighati in 1576 CE.

The Mughals triumphed, but the maharana vanished into the dense forests of the Aravalli hills, along with his family and some of his soldiers. Maharana Pratap was now forced to lead the rough life of a guerrilla fighter. He and his family slept under trees and in caves, eating frugal food wherever they could find it. There were dangers lurking everywhere, and the fear of being captured by the frustrated Mughal army was ever present.

However, personal comfort was the last thing on their minds when there was a kingdom to be won back. Moving from place to place and using mobile troops to continually harass the Mughal garrisons at various forts, Maharana Pratap played the waiting game and found an unexpected ally. The forest-dwelling Bhil tribespeople came to his aid. Legends speak of the Bhils saving the royal children, carrying them to safety in baskets. They protected the Rajputs, found them food and shelter, and even joined the Mewar army as deadly archers.

A few years later, when Akbar's attention was diverted by rebellions in the north-west, the maharana struck. After gaining back many of the Mewar forts, he was able to build a new capital and even set up court. He encouraged his people to cultivate the neglected and war-ravaged land but advised them to escape to the hills temporarily if the Mughals attacked.

By the time he died in a hunting accident in 1597, Maharana Pratap had gained back most of western Mewar from the Mughals. The Coat of Arms of the House of Mewar features a Bhil archer standing with a Rajput. This is a tribute from a great warrior to those who fought by his side to defend their homeland of Mewar.

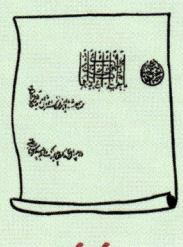

66

Royal Order of the Padshah Begum

Ink on paper manuscript, northern India, early seventeenth century CE

A *farman* is a royal executive order from a royal court. During Mughal times, direct orders often went out from court on important matters. Farmans were the emperor's instructions, stamped clearly with an elaborate royal signature and seal. Since they came directly from the emperor himself, they were intended to be the last word, the law. The one depicted in the illustration is from the time of Emperor Jahangir. However, there is something rather unusual about it. Instead of Jahangir's name and seal, it bears those of his queen, Nur Jahan! A Mughal queen issuing an executive order in her name was a most extraordinary occurrence. Nur Jahan, though, was a most extraordinary woman.

Born Mehr-un-Nisa in Kandahar, Afghanistan, Nur Jahan's parents were impoverished Persian nobility. Fleeing oppression in their own country, they arrived at the Mughal court of Akbar, hoping to make a better life for themselves. Once Mehr-un-Nisa's father had established himself within the ranks of Mughal nobility, her upbringing was like that of most

other ladies of high status at the time. She was educated in the arts and philosophy, wrote poetry, learnt how to ride horses, wield a sword, and shoot. By the age of sixteen, the beautiful and accomplished Mehr was married to a Persian nobleman. By her early thirties, she was widowed.

She and her young daughter were brought to the Mughal harem at Agra to live under the protection of Akbar's senior wife. It was here that Mehr's talents began to be noticed. She began to design beautiful clothes for the Mughal women, using intricate embroidery on brocades and muslins, attaching lace and gold threads, and setting design trends in *odhnis* or veils and *peshwaz* or gowns. She designed jewellery and even produced a luxurious attar or perfume, distilled from roses. Not long after, Mehr caught the eye of Emperor Jahangir and, in 1611, became his twentieth wife. Mehr-un-Nisa was now the Empress Nur Jahan.

At a time when women were rarely educated and even the most high-ranking Mughal princesses were expected to keep a discreet presence behind purdah, Nur Jahan began to chart her own, unique course. First, she established herself as co-ruler with her husband by sending out farmans in her name. In the one shown in the illustration, the square stamp declares, 'Command of her most Sublime and Elevated Majesty Nur Jahan Padshah Begum'. She was no mere royal spouse; she was the Padshah Begum, Female Emperor! By 1617, silver coins circulated with her name opposite that of Jahangir's. Nur Jahan shocked the court by appearing by his side in public on the palace balcony or *jharoka*, to greet the public. She bought trading ships, making deals with foreign traders to export embroidered cloth and indigo.

What was Jahangir's response to these bold moves?

We can assume that it would have been wholehearted approval. Although court documents do not mention Nur Jahan very often, Jahangir himself talks admiringly of his wife in his memoirs. Clearly, she was a loving and supportive companion, administering to his needs with great care, supervising his food and medicines, and making sure he did not overindulge in alcohol. She advised him on matters of state and even accompanied him on hunts. The empress was a crack shot who was said to have once shot four tigers with six shots while perched on the back of a swaying elephant! She is featured in a painting dressed in masculine hunting attire, loading her own musket. Courtiers, visiting diplomats, and officials noted Nur Jahan's special status in the Mughal court.

Nur Jahan's artistic flair showed in her designs for public buildings like mosques, *sarais* or rest houses for travellers, and ornamental gardens. The marble-inlayed, Persian-style tomb she built for her father at Agra, known as the tomb of Itimad-ud-daula, was said to have been the inspiration for Shah Jahan's Taj Mahal. Nur Jahan gave generously to charity. She looked after orphans, particularly girls, and it is said, designed the Nur Mahali, a special, affordable, wedding dress made for girls from poorer families.

She was also a woman of action. Towards the end of his life, when Jahangir was weakening in power and health, he was kidnapped by a disgruntled noble. Nur Jahan personally rode to his rescue, commanding troops from the back of an elephant, shooting deadly arrows at her enemies.

Over time, Nur Jahan's story began to be erased from history. Perhaps disapproving chroniclers wished to downplay her role as a woman who was an active ruler. However, she lived on in the popular imagination, among the poor and oppressed to whose lives she had made a difference. And she lived in these scattered objects—coins, paintings, and farmans that historians have used to put together a picture of a remarkable woman. Perhaps there are many other such women whose histories are waiting to be similarly discovered.

67

Patron of the Arts

Nephrite jade and watered steel dagger, northern India, c. 1640 CE

In the seventeenth century, the Mughal Empire was at its most powerful, and the court at its most opulent. If you peer very closely at a miniature painting from this time, you may see the emperor, his sons, or other important noblemen wearing a dagger with a carved hilt tucked into their cummerbund or belt. The one depicted in the illustration is a particularly fine example of a Mughal ceremonial dagger.

This dagger was made around 1640 and had a curving metal blade. Its hilt was fashioned into an exquisitely realistic likeness of a nilgai—the blue bull, which is one of the largest antelope species found in India. Even the colour of the stone, a deep blue-green, matches the natural colour of a nilgai! The hilt is made of a rare stone known as nephrite jade that was imported at great expense from China. The jade was so hard that it could not be carved like normal stone. Instead, it had to be carefully scraped into shape, using drills with tiny diamond heads. It required great skill to handle the jade. It is very likely that this dagger would have been expensive to produce, and it must have been a rare artefact.

The Mughals were originally from Central Asia, appearing on the north-western borders of India in 1526 and then deciding to stay on. Between the first six rulers, sometimes called the Great Mughals, they set up one of the longest ruling dynasties in India, which was finally forced to call it quits by the British in 1858. At first, it was all about conquests to expand an empire. Then, finding the need to connect with the diverse population they found themselves ruling, the Mughals cleverly set up alliances, inter-community marriages, and cultural interactions that eventually fashioned one of the greatest empires of its time. Despite their busy empire-building activities, the Mughals always found time for art. So, the Mughal Empire was not just powerful and wealthy but also a cultural and artistic hub.

Mughal Ceremonial Dagger with Carved Nilgai Hilt

The Mughals built forts, palaces, tombs, and soaring mosques in Agra, Delhi, and Lahore, as well as exquisitely planned gardens in Kashmir. They commissioned books full of miniature art, fine jewellery studded with exquisite precious stones, and luxury objects like the fabled Peacock Throne with its legendary emerald pillars. Mughal royalty had refined taste with the added advantage of unlimited wealth. The best architects, planners, calligraphers, craftspeople, and artists from around the world flocked to their dazzling courts, hoping to make an impression on the

Mughal art enthusiasts and gain employment. The result was a period of great cultural and artistic interaction.

Persian masters supervised Hindu and Muslim artists, blending styles in the Mughal art workshops. Architects incorporated Central Asian, Persian, and Hindu-style elements into forts and palaces. Persian jewellers used the skills of traditional Hindu goldsmiths to craft inlaid pieces of outstanding beauty. And in the translation bureaus of the kitabkhanas, the Ramayana and *Harivamsa* were translated into illustrated Persian editions.

Among the Great Mughals, Jahangir was especially known as a generous patron of the arts. Jahangir was particularly fascinated by the natural world. Artists accompanied him on royal hunting expeditions and even on war campaigns, observing and furiously sketching details of all the flora and fauna of the Indian countryside. They were granted special access to the royal zoo, where they painted exotic animals like zebras, which had been presented to the emperor by foreign merchants. When the Europeans arrived with examples of their own botanical sketches, Jahangir had his artists study them and use their painting techniques of realism. The result was an outpouring of superbly detailed botanical studies of Indian plants and flowers in miniature art—a trend that eventually found its way to the carved marble flowers of the Taj Mahal.

It was during his reign that a multi-talented Persian poet named Sa'ida-ye Gilani arrived in India, seeking work. Apart from his poetry writing, Sa'ida was a goldsmith and calligrapher with special knowledge in cutting and engraving precious stones. Naturally, he was immediately employed at the royal *karkhana* or workshop, fashioning translucent jade wine cups, gold-inlaid jade pendants, and dagger hilts. Even by the standards of the immensely wealthy Mughals, these were very precious objects. A carved dagger of this standard would have been something only the emperor could afford. He, in turn, would have given them as exclusive gifts to his sons or particularly favoured nobles who had pleased him in some way. If they appeared wearing this at court, it was a sure sign that they were close to the emperor.

It is not certain that this particular dagger was a work of the famous Persian poet. It may have been made later. We do know, however, that a work of such great beauty represented the greatest artistic skills of the day, a demonstration of the deep cultural and artistic intermingling prevalent during Mughal times.

68

The Tribal Way of Life

Carved wooden door, the Baiga or Gond tribe, modern but represents a way of life in the fourteenth to fifteenth century CE

The carved panels of the heavy wooden doors shown in the illustration on the next page feature scenes from the everyday life of a group of people often referred to as a tribe. If you look carefully, you will notice many different activities depicted on it.

On these panels, we can see men returning from a successful hunt, people carrying food and water or performing rituals, men on horseback, and others being pulled along on an elaborately made cart. Women are dancing outside decorated mud huts with thatched roofs. While both men and women are simply dressed, they don elaborate hairdos and plenty of jewellery. There are trees and floral decorations too, and, along the frame, all manner of creatures—snakes, lizards, scorpions, and tortoises—can be seen slithering, crawling, or walking. It is a picture of a lively community, one that clearly enjoys a close relationship with nature.

Elaborately Carved Door from a Tribal Community Building

Such elaborate doors would have once secured important houses in the villages of the Gonds or Baigas of central India, perhaps those of the chief or of community buildings known as ghotuls.

Who were these people, and where are their descendants?

By the seventh century CE, as ambitious regional monarchs continued to carve out large chunks of territory into kingdoms for themselves, the subcontinent began to go through great political upheavals. Naturally, these brought about social and economic changes too. While many people still lived in villages, continuing old traditions of farming and craft-making, others flocked to towns and cities where they took up a number of different professions. What they had in common was that they now lived according to strict social rules, either laid down by Brahmanas in the caste system or by the customs of Muslim rulers who arrived in the following centuries. Social differences based on caste, noble birth, or wealth increased.

There were some groups that did not follow any of these rules. They had lived, since very ancient times, in the mountains, forested hills, deserts, and coasts, spanning from the Himalayas to the Northeast, down to the south and the islands of the Indian Ocean. They lived in isolation from the rest of the world, following their own ancient ways of life, closely connected to nature. They worshipped clan deities and nature spirits and spoke languages of their own. They were particular that their resources were shared equally among all clan members. These groups are usually called tribes. Some are recognized today under names such as indigenous people, Adivasis, or original inhabitants of the land. The everyday lives of many of these tribes would have looked very much like the pictures carved on the wooden door in the illustration.

Many of these groups, like the Gaddis in the Himalayas, were nomadic pastoralists and shepherds. Others, like the Naga tribes in the Northeast, were shifting cultivators. In western India, the Bhils were hunter-gatherers, and the Banjaras in southern India were nomadic traders. Although they didn't mingle with settled people, they did come into contact with them at markets and fairs where they exchanged goods like forest produce, milk products, or cattle. But as land-hungry settlers increased in number, they began to encroach on tribal lands. Tribes that had occupied forests or hills for centuries suddenly found their livelihood and customs threatened. In these clashes, the tribal people found their way of life changing rapidly.

Some of them gave up on their old ways and merged with the settlers. Others retreated further into the hills and forests, becoming even more reclusive. And some, like the Gonds, did something more surprising. They challenged the intruders.

The Gonds were among the oldest and largest of Indian tribes, occupying a vast area of the hilly forests in present-day Telangana, Madhya Pradesh, Maharashtra, and Chhattisgarh. Starting from the thirteenth century, their lands and valuable forest resources became desirable to both the Rajputs of western India and the Mughals from the north. Because of their rich resources, some groups of Gonds became more powerful than others by associating with outsiders. With time, these powerful groups turned from being self-contained, forest-dwelling hunter-gatherers and pastoralists to rulers of kingdoms like Garha Mandla, Deogarh, and Chanda!

Rather than going back to their early traditions, the Gond rajas took on the ideas of their non-tribal adversaries They converted to Hinduism or Islam, intermarried with Rajputs, and took on new social customs and religious practices. They granted land to Brahmanas, creating unequal social classes where once they had all been equal. Then, to enhance revenue, they cleared their most precious resource—the forests—for agriculture and irrigation. All of which meant that by the eighteenth century, when the Marathas and, later, the British, annexed Gond territory and wiped out the Gond rajas, the social and religious customs of the Gond people had already changed forever.

Today, the tribal populations of various parts of India still struggle with problems of poverty, lack of access to essential resources and services, like healthcare and education, while mainstream communities continue to put pressure on them to part with their precious resources and lands.

69

Nimble Galivats

Sketch by Thomas Buttersworth, marine painter of the East India Company, England, c. early nineteenth century CE

Towards the end of the seventeenth century, the once-invincible Mughal Empire was starting to look a little shaky. Although at this time Emperor Aurangzeb was ruling over the largest empire ever seen on the Indian subcontinent, it was also true that it had become unwieldy and hard to govern. By the time of his death in 1707, Aurangzeb had used up much of the money in the royal coffers to fund his attempt to conquer the Deccan. His successors found it increasingly difficult to control powerful governors from grabbing territory for themselves. To add to their woes, even local chieftains, big zamindars, and other rebel groups now began to challenge their once unquestioned authority. Independent regional kingdoms came up in northern India under the Rajputs, Sikhs, and Jats.

Perhaps the biggest of their challengers came from the west, the area that is now around Pune, in Maharashtra. The Marathas were led by Shivaji Bhonsale, a supremely clever military commander. Shivaji was aware that he did not have the troops or the equipment to confront the well-trained Mughal army in an open battle. Instead, his highly dexterous army was trained to fight using guerrilla tactics. Lightning-quick cavalry would suddenly cut off supply lines, confusing the massive, heavily armed, and slow-moving Mughal force. With their superior knowledge of the local terrain, the Marathas would lure the enemy into traps, where they could be ambushed and routed. To the frustration of the Mughal commanders, the Marathas would vanish as quickly as they had emerged, disappearing into one of their series of strategic hill forts, camouflaged among the heights of the Western Ghats.

Apart from his nimble army and his invincible hill forts, Shivaji had one more secret weapon. He had a formidable navy! The Konkan coastline, the strategic heartland of the emerging Maratha Empire, was crawling with enemies. The aggressive Portuguese traders who controlled the Arabian Sea were recently joined by the English. The Siddis—soldiers and sailors of African descent—dominated parts of the western coast of India, including the important fort of Janjira. Although they sometimes joined the Mughals, most of the time they were a law unto themselves, threatening Maratha control of the coastline. There were also plenty of pirates and brigands waiting in the waters to attack and loot any stragglers on the seas.

Shivaji realized early on that his new kingdom would need to be protected from sea attacks. Around 1657, he purchased twenty galivats. These were small, swift ships with triangular sails powered by oarsmen. You can see them in the illustration on the facing page. The sketch, originally made during the days of East India Company depicting events of the later seventeenth century CE, is currently the front piece of an early nineteenth-century book in England. It shows Shivaji's galivats attacking the much larger English ships with gusto! Shivaji hired experienced Portuguese, Arab, and Siddi sailors to command his troops from the seafaring communities of Konkanis and Kolis who lived along the coast. These were fishermen with traditional skills in navigation and deep knowledge of the coastline who had now honed their skills in order to fight at sea. And fight they did!

In 1679, Shivaji annexed the island of Khanderi, off the coast of present-day Mumbai, and built a fort there. A combined English–Siddi force blockaded the fort, trying to dislodge the Marathas. Five months later, the combined force signed a peace accord with the Marathas and quietly sailed away. Shivaji had done it again. But how?

The Maratha galivats were clearly no match for the huge English and Portuguese frigates with long-range guns. The game was, once again, all about tactics. The small size of the galivats was used by the Marathas to their advantage by sneaking up on the broadside of the foreign ships, firing into them, and then sailing swiftly back along the coastline, disappearing into narrow creeks where they could not be followed. Galivats rarely ventured into the open seas, where they would have been at a disadvantage against large vessels.

Shivaji's successors continued what he had started by expanding the navy and adding ghurabs, a modified galley-type ship with sails. In

Maratha Galivats Attacking English Ships

1699, Kanhoji Angre was appointed sarkhel or admiral of the Maratha fleet. Kanhoji set up a series of forts along the coast, protecting the Maratha traders from pirates and compelling foreign traders to buy licences to enter Maratha waters. Any failure to pay was immediately punished by capturing the foreign ships and holding the crew to ransom. Kanhoji defeated the English, the Portuguese, and the Dutch and fended off several joint attacks on his forts. By 1710, the admiral was in control of the entire western coast, from Surat to Goa, with over 100 ships under his command. So terrifying was his reputation that the English had to spend more than 50,000 pounds a year on armed guards for their ships! He died undefeated in 1729, a legend in his lifetime.

Shivaji was one of the first Indian rulers who had the foresight to use a navy for political ends, keeping his enemies busy at sea while building his kingdom on land. It was a strategy that clearly worked because, by the middle of the eighteenth century, the Marathas were overlords of a vast region that stretched all the way from Lahore to Tanjore!

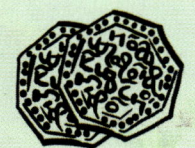

70

Coins from the East

Octagonal silver Ahom coin, Assam, 1670 CE

Let us look at some more coins that help us explore Indian history. This time, we examine one in the rare octagonal shape depicted in the illustration on the next page. It tells of a group of people called the Ahoms who migrated to India in 1228 CE, led by Sukaphaa, a prince from Mong Mao in what is now China. Chao Lung, or Great Lord, as he was also known, crossed the Patkai mountains with around 9000 clansmen, rampaging down the Brahmaputra valley into what is now Assam. Sukaphaa saw that the thickly forested but fertile river valley was a good place to settle in. Using a combination of warfare and intermarrying with the local tribes, the Ahoms set up a kingdom that was to last for the next 600 years!

The stability of the Ahom kingdom was based on a strong administrative system. The Ahoms brought with them new techniques of irrigated wet rice cultivation. Large areas of the richly silted land were cleared to grow rice. Instead of taxes, each village was bound to send one man out of three to the king's service. Some of these men were put to work building dams, irrigation channels, and other public works, while others had to join the army.

The king was appointed by a council of ministers, the patra mantris. They would keep a close eye on his activities and if he showed signs of incompetence, they would not hesitate to throw him out and take over the state's affairs themselves.

The Ahom kingdom soon became a prosperous land with a well-organized administration and a sophisticated culture that encouraged poets and scholars. It was said that every household stored at least a years' worth of food supplies.

All this prosperity naturally began to attract the attention of those living nearby. Traders from Bengal began to make their way to the borderlands where they would exchange coins for goods like ivory, lac, muga silk, bell-metal objects, and gold from the Ahoms. Later, when the Mughals came along, there was a high demand for elephants, wood, and musk from the Ahoms. Jean-Baptiste Tavernier, a seventeenth century French gem merchant who travelled extensively in the Indian subcontinent during the time of Mughal emperors Shah Jahan and Aurangzeb, wrote in his book *Travels in India*, 'The kingdom of Assam is one of the best countries in Asia, for it produces all the necessities of life, and there is no need to go for anything to the neighbouring states'.

By now, the Ahoms found that they were at an advantage. Being located on a busy trade route between Tibet and what is now the China-Myanmar border, they became prosperous traders, bringing in rock salt, gold, horses, silks, and yak tails in exchange for cotton, lac, fish, and rice. All this trade meant the Ahoms were forced to change from using simple cowrie shells as currency to these sophisticated octagonal silver coins. The distinct shape is said to be based on the number eight being sacred to the Ahoms with many of their temples being octagonal in plan as well. This element adds a unique quality to the Ahom coins because, across history, coins have mostly been circular in shape.

Much of what we know of the Ahoms is based on the names and inscriptions on these coins.

At first, the Ahoms used the Tai language, worshipped Ban Phi or spirit gods, and buried their dead in maidams or hill-like burial mounds, surrounded by their possessions for the afterlife. At Charaideo and Rangpur, now in the Sivasagar district, the remains of these burial mounds and their beautiful earthquake-proof seven-storied palaces, fortifications, large tanks, and even an amphitheatre can still be visited. With changing times and the expansion of their kingdom, they began to adopt Hindu gods, particularly Vishnu, Indra, Shiva, and Shakti, building temples dedicated to them. Their language changed too. By the middle of the sixteenth century, they were more familiar with Sanskrit and Assamese than Tai-Ahom.

In the incredible six centuries of its existence, the Ahom kingdom faced plenty of invading armies, keen to take over a region with such rich resources and thriving trade. They were strong enough to hold off the armies of the Delhi Sultanate and even challenge the Mughals who, despite fighting seventeen major battles, never really managed to subjugate them! In 1662, a deeply frustrated Aurangzeb sent his fiercest general, Mir Jumla to the Northeast, with instructions not to return until he had conquered the stubborn Ahoms. Mir Jumla finally had some success, capturing Gargaon, the Ahom capital, and plenty of booty consisting mostly of elephants, gold, and rice. But the Mughals could not hold on for long. The Ahoms struck back. In 1671, under the command of their legendary General Lachit Borphukan, they took advantage of the torrential rainfall of Assam, the marshy terrain, and their deep knowledge of the River Brahmaputra to inflict a crushing naval defeat on the mighty Mughal army at the Battle of Saraighat. The Ahom kingdom remained proud and independent until it was finally annexed by the British East India Company in 1826.

71

Nader Shah's Battle Axe

Metal axe with gold relief inscriptions and floral designs, Delhi, 1739 CE

The richly worked battle axe in the illustration once belonged to one of the deadliest invaders ever to ride into the Indian subcontinent. Both sides of the blade and the socket are thickly plated with gold and are engraved with inscriptions from the Holy Quran. The octagonal handle is delicately worked with beautiful designs in floral and creeper motifs. And just so no one had any doubt as to who owned this impressive weapon, among the flowing gold inscriptions in Persian is a name and the title, 'Sahib-i-Qiran Nader'.

'The lord of the auspicious conjunction', Nader Shah was the ruler of Persia. But what was he doing in India?

By the early eighteenth century, there were already signs that things were not looking so good for the once-mighty Mughal Empire. After the death of Aurangzeb in 1707, his successors were a series of either weak or incompetent princes, constantly bickering or fighting with each other to grab the throne. In 1719, when Muhammad Shah became emperor, the Mughals were still ruling over a vast and rich empire with the magnificent city of Delhi as its capital. All that was about to change.

Emperor Muhammad Shah was popularly known as 'Rangila' or the 'Colourful'. Rangila liked to have fun. He spent most of his time organizing lavish parties, watching elephant fights, or training his pet hawks, and spending vast amounts of money on artists, musicians, and poets. He did not notice that his governors in Bengal and the Deccan were rebelling and setting up independent courts; or that the Marathas, Sikhs, and Jats were chipping away at Mughal territory. He did not hear the rumours that the frontiers of his empire were insecure and that the new Persian ruler had his eye on the enormous wealth of the Mughal treasuries.

Nader Shah was a ruthless warrior who had risen through the ranks of the Persian army through sheer military talent and had recently crowned himself the Shah of Persia. Through the centuries, the fabled wealth of the Mughal treasuries in India had always attracted invaders hoping to make a quick fortune. Now, Nader had heard from his spies that the once invincible kingdom was slowly crumbling. He decided to make his way to Delhi without further ado.

In March 1739, Nader Shah's forces took the ill-prepared Mughal forces by surprise. They appeared suddenly at Karnal, near Delhi, and handed the much larger army a resounding defeat. In public, the two rulers appeared to be quite civil with each other, but in reality, Rangila and his family were hostages of the Persians and Rangila was forced to invite his Persian 'guest' into his home in the Red Fort at Delhi.

The sudden appearance of the Persians caused a fair amount of tension in the city. Every small incident had the potential to spark a fire. So it happened, some Persian soldiers were involved in an argument with merchants at the grain market. Things turned violent and, in a frenzy of mob violence, more than 900 Persians were killed.

The next morning, a fuming Nader Shah emerged from the Red Fort in his battle dress. He was bent on revenge. Within hours, the magnificent city of Delhi, the pride of the Mughals for over three centuries, was reduced to rubble. Over 30,000 citizens were massacred until, it is said, it seemed as though it was raining blood. Persian soldiers looted every house, stripping gold, silver, precious stones, and pearls from the rich houses of Delhi. Nader only called off his troops when a Mughal governor begged for mercy and promised to pay 100 crore rupees.

Fifty-seven days later, Nader headed back to Persia. His baggage train consisted of more than 700 elephants, 4000 camels, and countless horse carts, barely able to pull along the entire wealth of the Mughal treasuries and of the people of Delhi. Somewhere in this unimaginably gigantic mass of loot was the famed gem-encrusted Peacock throne topped with a diamond so huge that Nader is said to have exclaimed in shock when he first saw it, 'Koh-i-Noor', or the 'mountain of light'.

Nadir Shah's Battle Axe

The city of Delhi never recovered. Neither did the Mughal Empire. Although they rebuilt the city and the Mughals ruled for over a century more, they were a shadow of their former selves. No one could quite take them seriously any more as the undisputed rulers of most of the Indian subcontinent. Regional powers began to assert themselves. Others, like the newly arrived traders from Europe, were awaiting their turn greedily. Finally, they saw their chance to step in. There was power and wealth to be gained at the expense of a crumbling empire.

Nader Shah had made his mark, and his time-ravaged battle axe is testament to that.

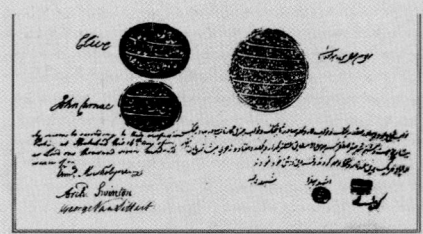

72

A Merchant Company Takes Over

Manuscript, Prayagraj, Uttar Pradesh, 1765 CE

Could a mere piece of paper bring an empire of monumental power to an end? This empire had possessed unimaginable wealth and territories that had covered almost an entire subcontinent, and had achieved some of the most dazzling artistic expressions that the world has ever seen. Could this document then change the fortunes of one of the richest civilizations in the world, handing over its charge to a profit-hungry private corporation? A corporation which then proceeded to drain this rich empire of all its resources accumulated over centuries? Unbelievable as it sounds, the paper scroll in the illustration did just that!

This document is known rather grandly as the Treaty of Allahabad. But the truth is that when it was signed on 12 August 1765, Mughal Emperor Shah Alam really had no choice. He was putting his stamp on a document that had been dictated by an Englishman named Robert Clive, who was the representative of the United Company of Merchants of England trading in the East Indies, otherwise known as the English East India Company (EIC). The young Mughal emperor, reportedly sitting on

a silk-lined armchair, perched on a dining table in Clive's tent to give the impression of majesty, handed over the Diwani of three of the richest provinces in the Mughal Empire to the British trading company. Mughal officials were dismissed, and British traders were now the official tax collectors of Bengal, Bihar, and present-day Odisha. With over twenty million people to tax and the plentiful resources of these provinces, the EIC were looking at bringing in annual revenues of the equivalent of over 300 million pounds in today's money into its coffers! The event was so significant that it was later commemorated in a rather more majestic fashion by an English painter. You see his painting in the illustration here, where the original humble tent is now depicted as a royal palace and the covered armchair on a table is a silken Mughal throne.

It was a turning point in Indian history—a document that transformed a trading company into a colonial power.

How did a bunch of merchants pull off such a victory?

The English East India Company was set up in 1600 CE as a private trading corporation seeking fine textiles, indigo, tea, and spices from the East, goods that were in huge demand to be sold at great profit in England. India was one of the richest countries in the world at the time, a major manufacturing hub of fine textiles and the centre of global trade in spices.

In 1608, when the first EIC ships docked in Surat, in present-day Gujarat, the British merchants found that they faced stiff competition from the French, Dutch, and Portuguese merchant companies that had arrived in India before them. The EIC decided to up their game by approaching the Mughal court, humbly requesting trade and tax concessions at the grand court of the Mughal Emperor Jahangir. These were granted, but the desperate hunt for profits continued. Careful to work within Mughal rules, the EIC now armed itself, fortifying its warehouses and recruiting a private army with which it battled the European trade rivals. Using a combination of threats and bribes, the EIC coerced local officials into affording it more privileges.

This aggression paid off because, by 1651, the EIC owned warehouses at Surat, Masulipatnam, and Bengal and trading posts at Bombay (Mumbai), Madras (Chennai), and on the banks of the River Hooghly, an area which later became Calcutta (Kolkata).

In the mid-eighteenth century, the once-invincible Mughal Empire was showing signs of gradually collapsing. Powerful regional governors were striking out independently. The EIC decided this would be a good time to grab yet more profits.

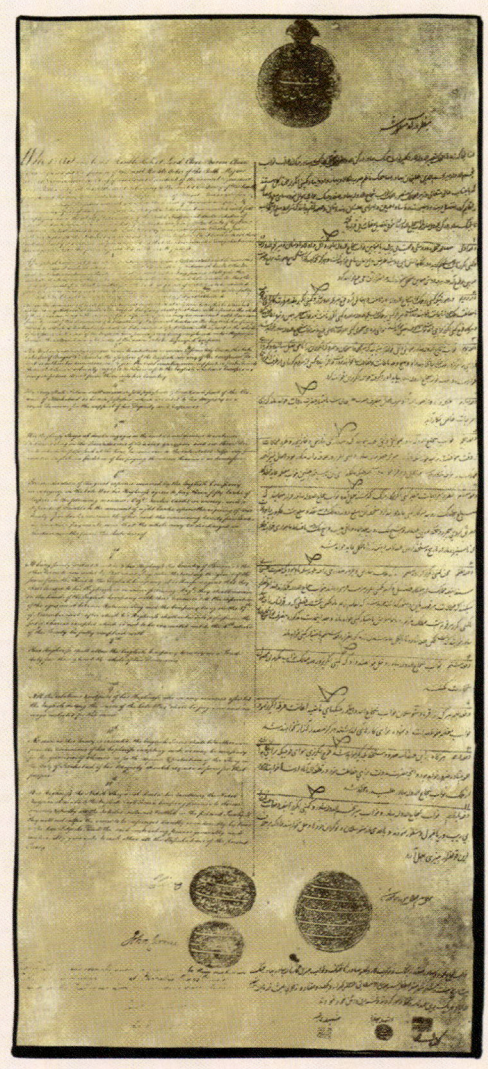

When the Nawab of Bengal refused to grant the EIC further concessions and forbade it from setting up fortifications, the merchants were confident enough to interfere in the nawab's political affairs. First, the EIC tried to dethrone the inconvenient Nawab Siraj-ud-Daulah and replace him with a puppet of its choosing. When that did not work, the EIC declared war.

The Treaty of Allahabad

Manipulating and allying with various factions at regional courts, the EIC waged a series of full-fledged battles. In the winter of 1764, it defeated the combined force of the Bengal, Awadh, and Mughal armies at Buxar on the banks of the River Ganga, in present-day Bihar. A weakened and isolated Mughal emperor was forced to hand over the Diwani of Bengal and other eastern provinces to the EIC in exchange for an annual fee. Robert Clive became Governor of Bengal. And in a bizarre twist, the EIC which, until now, had been bringing in shiploads of gold and silver to pay for the goods it bought in India, started using the revenues of Bengal to buy what it needed!

With its new-found power, the EIC now turned from seeking commercial profits to grabbing large chunks of Indian territory. Where it could not conquer, the EIC used its trademark combination of armed threats and political pressure.

Hundred and fifty years after its first ships docked at Surat, a private corporation of British merchants was effectively ruling almost the entire Indian subcontinent. India was on its way to being colonized, its wealth sailing away to Britain on EIC ships. And to think that all of this had begun with the mere stamp of an overwhelmed Mughal emperor on a document now known as the Treaty of Allahabad.

73

Visuals of
Eighteenth-Century India

Hand-coloured aquatint print by Thomas Daniell, Kolkata, West Bengal, 1788 CE

If you live in Calcutta (or Kolkata, as it is now known), or if you have ever visited the city, you may be rather surprised by the artwork on the next page. It is an aquatint, a hand-coloured etched print that looks like a water-colour painting, called 'The New Buildings at Chouringhee'. It depicts what is now one of the busiest roads in the city, Chowringhee Road, as it appeared in 1787.

At the time, the city of Calcutta did not exist. All that existed were three large villages and a fort which the English East India Company (EIC) had built for itself. Having recently annexed large parts of Bengal and Bihar, the British now decided they needed more than just a fort in which to live. They started moving out, taking over large tracts of land, moving the locals out of the way to outlying areas. They began planning a well-laid-out city for themselves with public buildings and grand mansions situated along broad streets. The aquatint forms part of a set of twelve called *Views of Calcutta*, featuring various parts of the newly developing city.

The set was made by an unusual duo. Thomas Daniell was a struggling landscape painter in Britain when he decided to try his luck in faraway India, where, it was rumoured, there were fabulous fortunes to be made. His idea was to travel through these unknown territories, painting the local landscapes. Back home, he knew he would have a captive market for his art. It was a time before the invention of photography, which was only introduced to the world in 1839. Victorian Britain waited eagerly to see first-hand views of the 'exotic' Orient.

When Thomas and his sixteen-year-old nephew and assistant, William, arrived in Calcutta in 1786, they got the timing just right. The EIC was rapidly establishing a foothold in the country. The Company already controlled Bengal, large parts of the Ganga basin, and parts of southern India. It had established forts and trading centres in the three presidencies

'The New Buildings at Chouringhee', Hand-Coloured Aquatint by Thomas Daniell

of Bengal, Madras, and Bombay. The Daniells knew they could travel with a certain amount of security.

Their first set of prints, *Views of Calcutta*, made over the course of a two-year stay there, sold out almost immediately. The pair now had the funds to travel to the interiors of India. Hiring a boat and accompanied by a staff of over forty, they equipped themselves with palanquins, tents, and all manner of art supplies and set sail down the River Ganga. They travelled through Kanpur and Delhi, and then abandoning the boat, trekked into the hills of Garhwal. Along the way, they made pencil sketches, water colours, and aquatints of landscapes, temples, forts, pastoral scenes, and some of the first artistic views of the Himalayas.

Travel was slow in those days, and many of the areas the Daniells journeyed through were dangerous and somewhat desolate. Yet, in the eight years they spent in India, the intrepid artists also managed to travel down south to the newly acquired territories of the Mysore kingdom, Madras, and Sri Lanka. They sketched temples at Tanjore and Madurai, abandoned forts at Trichy, and the stunning landscapes of the Thamirabarani river valley in present-day Tamil Nadu. They painted people too—village maidens, noblemen, and maharajas. They also painted verdant nature vignettes with freely roaming wild animals.

For their final tour, the Daniells headed for the western coast where, even as they waited in Bombay for a ship to return to Britain, they managed to paint sites like the Kanheri and the Elephanta caves.

Back home, the Daniells started the process of converting the hundreds of rough sketches and paintings they had carried back into aquatints and oil paintings. Their aquatints were hand painted and so finely produced that they are often regarded as very close to photographs. They produced a limited-edition book of 144 prints called *Oriental Scenery* which went on to become wildly popular despite being very expensive. The Daniells were now both rich and famous. The Orient, as depicted in the Daniells' works, fired the imagination of the Victorian Britons, influencing art, literature, and architecture, even inspiring intellectuals to delve into the study of Indian languages and scriptures.

Scholars today believe that the Daniells emphasized the 'exotic' aspect of their art to pander to their eager audience back home. However, there is little doubt that their work is an unsurpassed visual record of the Indian subcontinent in the eighteenth century, at a time of sweeping changes that would have repercussions for centuries to come. The Thomas Daniell collection, including *Views of Calcutta*, is now considered to be a rare documentation of India's geographical and cultural heritage. Of course, with time and rapid modern development, these landscapes have changed beyond recognition.

74

Tipu's Tiger

Wooden mechanical toy with organ keyboard, Mysore, Karnataka, late eighteenth century CE

On 4 May 1799, Tipu Sultan, the ruler of the state of Mysore (now Mysuru) in southern India, died defending his fortress capital, Srirangapatnam, against the army of the English East India Company (EIC). The EIC had been defeated in three previous wars against the state of Mysore. This time, as they stormed through the breached defences of the fortress, the triumphant Company troops set about looting and burning the city and palace. Precious objects from the treasury were stolen and distributed among the EIC soldiers. Tipu's golden throne was broken to pieces and later sent to the EIC's directors in England. And oddly, among all the valuable loot carried out from the fortress that day, there was a toy!

The toy, illustrated on the next page, was found in the music room of Tipu's palace. An almost life-sized wooden automaton or mechanical toy, it is a spectacularly striped tiger that seems to be mauling a European soldier dressed in uniform. Concealed inside the tiger's body is a metal and ivory organ that is operated by a crank handle. When the crank handle is turned, the organ makes sounds reminiscent of a tiger growling, drowning out the wailing cries of its desperate victim as he flails his left

Tipu's Tiger, a Wooden Mechanical Toy

arm up and down. The English called it 'Tippoo's Tiger' and carted it off to the EIC headquarters in London.

Why did they consider a toy important enough to take all the way to Britain?

Tipu Sultan was known as the Tiger of Mysore. The tiger was his royal symbol, used liberally across art, architecture, and battle paraphernalia during his reign to proclaim his power. His personal flag had the image of a tiger on it and his weapons had jewelled tiger heads and stripes as decoration. Tipu minted tiger-striped coins and even had an elite armed force known as Tiger Sepoys dressed in tiger-striped uniforms.

Apart from all these symbols, he was also known as a fierce and capable opponent of the rapidly expanding power of the EIC. Unlike many other rulers of the time, Tipu had realized that the English trading company was interested in more than just trade. The EIC was, in fact, a dangerous force which was operating with the ulterior motive of conquering all of India under the guise of promoting trade. Tipu even tried to warn the other rulers about their true motive. He wrote to the Nizam of Hyderabad, 'Know you not the custom of the English? Wherever they fix their talons they contrive little by little to work themselves into the whole management of affairs'.

The English found Tipu and his father, Haider Ali, annoying. Much to their frustration, the kingdom of Mysore was well administered and prosperous, with flourishing agriculture, trade, and irrigation works. The EIC was unable to elbow its way into Tipu's territory or use the kingdom's ports for export. The usual EIC tactics of waging war against those who threatened its profits were also not working this time.

Both Haider and Tipu were clever and aggressive warriors that the English were unable to defeat despite fighting three wars against them. Tipu was also innovative, making sure the Mysore army was a disciplined force, well trained by French officers, and equipped with state-of-the-art weapons. The French were, traditionally, trade rivals of the English in the east and jostling them for influence in Europe. They were happy to ally with Tipu since he was a formidable enemy of the English. Tipu's army was among the first in the world to use weaponized metal rocket artillery, launching them from the backs of camels, shocking the English forces, and causing them much damage on the battlefield. Tipu set up diplomatic relations with the Ottoman Empire and with France. It is believed that he even wrote to Napoleon Bonaparte, inviting him to visit India and help him get rid of the English!

All that ended with the fall of Srirangapatnam.

With its expanding power in India, a determined EIC turned up at Srirangapatnam a fourth time with its largest army ever. However, it found the going tough. The fortress was designed to resist the most modern arms and every advanced battle tactic of the day. When it finally fell, a month after the siege began, there were rumours of betrayal by some key Mysore nobles, with whom the EIC had colluded.

The English were ecstatic. Finally, their most powerful enemy was vanquished. India was theirs. Back in England, there were public celebrations. Magazine articles gloated about the victory, jubilant plays were performed, and triumphant paintings were put on display, portraying to the English public that a terrible tyrant had been finally defeated.

The mechanical toy tiger was put on display at the East India Company museum in London. The piece was intended to show the public how nasty and tyrannical Indian rulers were and especially how Tipu deeply hated the English. This was a key piece of the propaganda machinery that a company of traders needed in order to justify their actions of taking over a faraway country.

75

The Sutlej Six Pounder

Bronze 6-pounder cannon,
Lahore, Pakistan, 1838 CE

The Sikh Horse Artillery Light 6-pounder cannon that you see in the illustration on the next page, apart from being a lethal weapon of war in its time, is something of a work of art. The glittering bronze barrel features a carved tiger head, birds, florals, foliage, and has hooks curved into elephant trunks. It is attached to a mahogany wood gun carriage designed to be pulled by horses with beautiful brass and copper inlay work, ornamented wheel hubs, seats, and buckets. The Sutlej Gun, as it came to be known, is thought to have been produced in the famous Lahore gun foundry of Maharaja Ranjit Singh around 1838. It was well known that the Maharaja was passionate about artillery. And there was a good reason for it.

With the declining fortunes of the Mughal Empire, the area between the Rivers Indus and Yamuna, much of what is now Punjab, rapidly became a place of contest. The Sikhs, followers of the fifteenth-century religious leader Guru Nanak, had by now been converted into a political and military force. They ruled in several independent states known as *misls* until a young leader named Ranjit Singh captured the city of Lahore in 1799

and soon afterwards united the misls and declared himself the maharaja of all Punjab. It was the beginning of the Sikh Empire. Maharaja Ranjit Singh was a powerful ruler, rapidly expanding the Sikh kingdom from the River Sutlej to Kashmir, as far north as the Khyber Pass and holding off the Afghans who kept coming on raids across the pass. To the east of the Sutlej, however, there was an obstacle.

The English East India Company (EIC) was in control with its well-trained and well-equipped army. The two sides came to a sensible agreement, a treaty of friendship, where the English recognized the maharaja and vowed not to interfere in his affairs. After all, the Sikh kingdom was a useful buffer for them against the Afghans. The Sikhs, in turn, promised not to expand their kingdom east of the River Sutlej. It was a strategic agreement that suited both sides.

But Maharaja Ranjit Singh was a canny ruler. Observing the EIC armies, he realized that to maintain this balance, the Sikh kingdom needed a centrally controlled, modern army. What he had inherited was a scattered force of horse-mounted cavalry units from the various misls and ill-trained infantry using outmoded arms and tactics. The maharaja's first move was to hire experienced European soldiers to help train his armies. Several French veterans who had served in Napoleon Bonaparte's army were looking for employment in the East at the time. The maharaja hired these officers, tasking them with training and modernizing an elite force known as the Fauj-i-Khas. The Fauj-i-Khas, equipped with modern arms, bright red uniforms, and put through French-style drill training, made a name for itself for its discipline and firing form. They formed the elite vanguard of a new, cohesive Sikh army.

The maharaja did not stop there. Realizing that he could not always depend on the English for arms, he set up a foundry at Lahore to cast cannons and a smithy for the manufacture of gunpowder and shot. Artillery manufacture was the maharaja's pet project, one that he personally oversaw. Engineers from the Sikh kingdom were sent to the EIC workshops, liberally copying the technology they observed there. Diplomatic gifts of heavy guns presented by the Company to the maharaja were also dissected and copied.

Soon there were foundries in Amritsar, Multan, and Peshawar. These were supervised by Claude Auguste Court, the French officer in charge of the Fauj-i-Khas artillery wing and Sardar Lahina Singh Majithia, a prominent noble at the Lahore court who was also a skilled ordnance technician. In a few years, they produced pieces of exceptional quality, rivalling those of the European armies.

Maharaja Ranjit Singh ruled for thirty-eight years. When he died, the Sikh army had over 5000 gunners and more than 500 pieces of modern artillery, including horse-drawn cannons that were quick-moving and effective on the battlefield, making up a truly formidable force.

Unfortunately, within ten years of the maharaja's death, infighting within the Sikh kingdom encouraged an increasingly aggressive East India Company. The EIC completely forgot their 'treaty of friendship', initiated two wars, and finally annexed the Sikh kingdom as Company territory. In 1845, this Sutlej Gun was captured by the British forces during the course of the First Anglo-Sikh War. It was presented as a trophy by the Company directors to the Governor-General of India and shipped off to England where it is displayed at the Queen's Own Royal West Kent Regiment Museum at Maidstone today, still speaking of the exceptional technical and artistic skills of the foundries of the Sikh kingdom and the vision of a maharaja.

76

Santhal Hul

Illustration from the *Illustrated London News*,
London, England, 1856 CE

On 23 February 1856, this sketch appeared in the *Illustrated London News*, a popular weekly news magazine in England. The image is violent and shocking, depicting a group of Santhal men being mowed down by gunfire which they face, quite hopelessly it seems, with rudimentary weapons like knives, bows, and arrows. It depicts the Santhal Rebellion, an uprising that took place in the Santhal Parganas in present-day Jharkhand between June 1855 and January 1856.

The origins of the rebellion goes back more than fifty years, to the time when the Santhals, an Adivasi people, were lured to the foothills of the Rajmahal hills from their original homelands in western Bengal and present-day Odisha. The British government of the time needed to expand agriculture in the virgin forests of these hills. They needed more land and agricultural labour to produce cash crops like indigo and opium which they could export for huge profits.

The Santhals had laboured for many years under exploitative landlords, traders, and moneylenders and were looking for a place where they could settle and be free to practice their own unique way of life. So, they were pleased to be given a large portion of land to do just this. They named it Damin-i-Koh, literally, skirts of the hills. They worked hard, clearing the dense forests and cultivating rice and commercial crops. By 1851, some estimate that there were as many as 82,000 Santhals living in the area.

Then trouble arrived. Merchants and traders from the plains flocked to the area. They realized it was easy to exploit the simplicity and honesty of the Santhals.

An English bureaucrat, William Wilson Hunter, wrote in his book, *Annals of Rural Bengal*, of their outrageous cheating:

'The Santhal country came to be regarded as a country where a fortune was to be made, no matter by what means, so that it was made rapidly . . . hucksters settled upon various pretences, and in a few years grew into

A Sketch of the Santhal Rebellion in the Illustrated London News, 1856

men of fortune. They cheated the poor Santhal in every transaction. The forester brought his jars of clarified butter for sale; the [merchants] measured it in vessels with false bottoms; the husbandman came to exchange his rice for soil, oil, cloth, and gun-powder; the merchants used heavy weights in ascertaining the quantity of grain and light ones in weighing out the articles given in return.'

Moneylenders or mahajans, who gave them small advances to buy seeds for new crops, charged high rates of interest. When the Santhals could not repay the loan, they seized the harvests, their land, their huts, and even the ornaments the women wore. Entire families were reduced to bonded labourers. Zamindars managed to gain control over large tracts of Santhal land, charged high taxes and forced the once independent Santhals to work as labour on their plantations. The British government also charged high taxes and generally ignored appeals for help from the Santhals.

Pushed to the brink, the Santhals realized they had to do something about the *dikus*, as they called the outsiders who would not let them live in peace.

On 30 June 1855, at the village of Bhagnadihi in present-day Jharkhand, the brothers Sidhu and Kanhu Murmu, along with their brothers Chand and Bahirab and sisters Phulo and Jano made a declaration to a large gathering of Santhals. They were starting a *Hul*, a movement for liberation, telling the dikus and the white men to leave their land forever or face armed resistance. Secret messages in the form of *dharwak*, folded leaves of the sal tree, were sent from village to village. The Hul began.

Armed with only bows and arrows, the Santhals attacked the properties of the dikus. Moneylenders' and zamindars' houses were burnt down, their cattle looted. Police and army contingents sent to quell the rebellion were met with fierce resistance.

For six months, the Santhals fought. Bows and arrows faced artillery gunfire. More than 15,000 Santhals are believed to have died, their villages burnt down, and survivors dragged off to jail. British officers later wrote admiring accounts of the Santhal's courage. But given their meagre resources, it was only a matter of time before the movement was brutally put down.

The Santhal Hul took place almost two years before the 1857 uprising. It was a revolt against all forms of exploitation, not just against colonial injustice. The Hul was an inspiration to other Adivasi groups with similar problems. Today, it is remembered by the Santhals and other Adivasis and commemorated every year as they still fight the battle against forces that threaten to snatch their lands and destroy their way of life.

77

A Sepoy Remembers

Memoir, Awadh, Uttar Pradesh, 1861 CE

In 1861, Subedar Sitaram Pandey, recently retired from the 12th Punjab Infantry, wrote an extraordinary memoir. It was written in his mother tongue of Awadhi, a dialect of Hindi spoken in what is now eastern Uttar Pradesh. The book was an account of the forty-eight years Sitaram Pandey had served in the Bengal Army of the English East India Company. Unfortunately, the original manuscript in Awadhi is lost to us. But the English version, translated by Sitaram's commanding officer, Lieutenant Colonel James T Norgate, survived in the book we have today.

There are many accounts of those years but Sitaram's work, *From Sepoy to Subedar, Being the Life and Adventures of Subedar Sita Ram, a Native Officer of the Bengal Army Written and Related by Himself* is unique. It is the personal account of the life of an ordinary soldier, giving us a rare glimpse into the experiences and thoughts of ordinary people who lived through those turbulent times.

From the mid-eighteenth century, as the once mighty Mughal Empire was falling apart, a private trading corporation called the English East India Company (EIC) saw an opportunity. Quite forgetting that they had

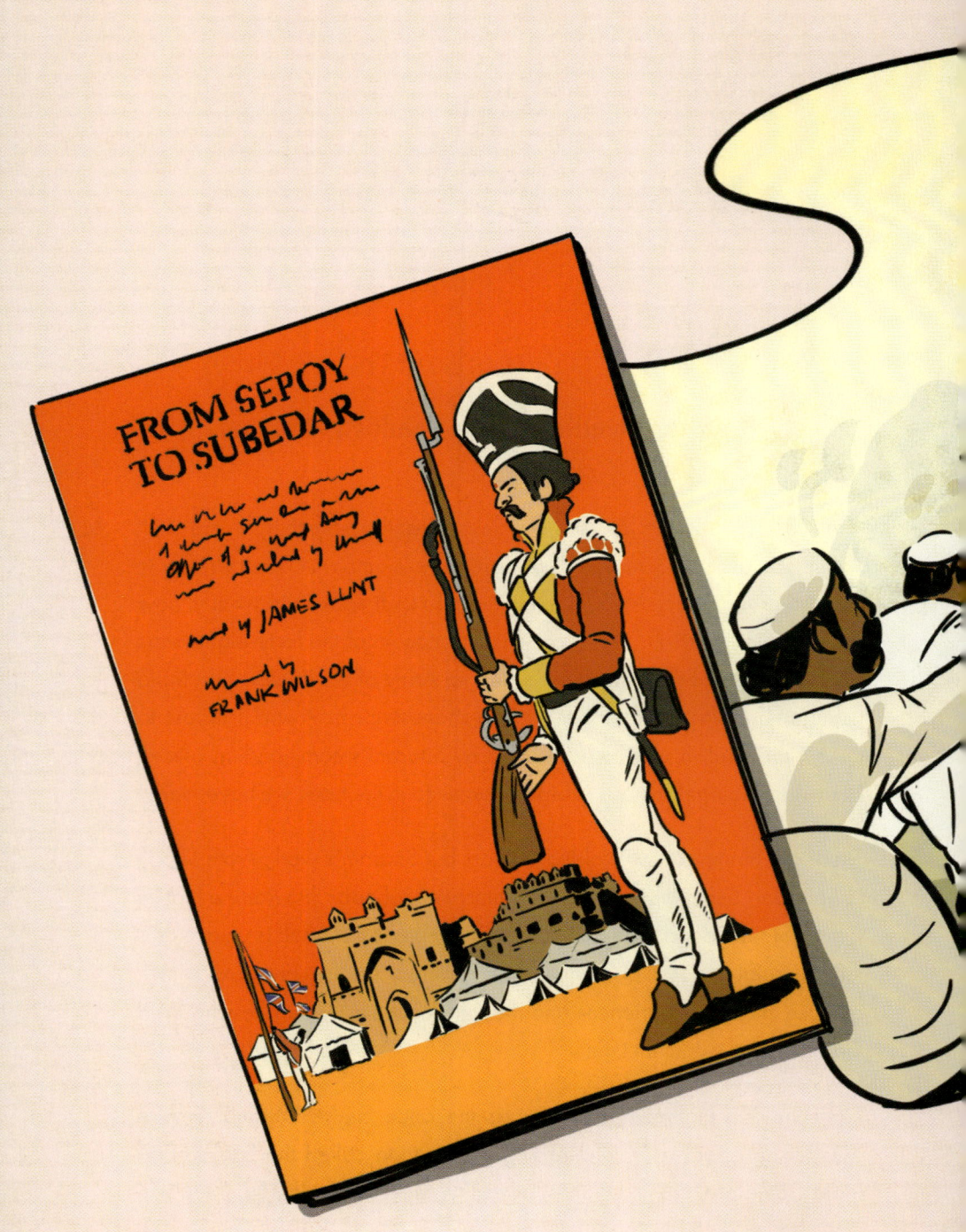

originally come to trade, they not only grabbed huge profits by fending off European trade rivals, they also began interfering in the political affairs of Indian rulers to seize vast territories for themselves. By the mid-1850s, almost two-thirds of the Indian subcontinent was being ruled by the EIC!

Company directors ran their administration from London. But in India, they needed local help. They set up an army with European officers and Indian soldiers called *sipahis* or sepoys, who were then trained in European-style war and weaponry.

Seventeen-year-old Sitaram was recruited into the Bengal Native Army in 1812. In his action-packed career of almost five decades, he managed to survive getting shot at close range, almost being blown up in an explosion, and being sold into slavery in Kabul! Back home, he faced other troubles like losing his caste for crossing River Indus and getting thrown out of his village. But of all his experiences, Sitaram recalls one in greatest detail: the great Revolt of 1857.

In the years of their rule, the EIC stirred up much hostility throughout India. Many Company officials were arrogant and high handed, and some were extremely corrupt. Nawabs and rajas were elbowed aside ruthlessly, their armies disbanded and their revenues diverted into EIC coffers. Their lands were confiscated with flimsy excuses like 'misgovernance' and 'no legal heir' and they were forced to rely on pensions from the Company. Zamindars and peasants were reeling from the high taxes they were forced to pay. Many felt the Christian missionaries had come with the sole purpose of destroying their social and religious customs. All of this led to resentment bubbling everywhere.

But the sepoys really started it all. The sepoys of the EIC army were already chafing at their poor working conditions and low pay. Sitaram writes of how the newer British officers were often rude and insulted their sepoys. Many were suspicious of the sahibs who seemed intent on making them lose their social standing by forcing them to break caste taboos like crossing oceans and mixed caste dining. By 1856, rumours began to circulate across northern India that the flour supplied to the army was being mixed with ground animal bones. Another rumour was that the cartridges for the new Enfield rifle that had to be torn open with their teeth before loading were greased with cow and pig fat, both considered taboo for Hindu and Muslim soldiers alike.

Sitaram, hearing outraged talk in the barracks, tried to warn his British officers that trouble was brewing. They dismissed his fears, telling him the excitement would die down.

In May 1857, a wave of mutinies spread across northern India, from Meerut to Delhi, then Aligarh, Kanpur, and Lucknow. In what appeared to be well-coordinated actions, entire regiments of Company soldiers broke out of their lines, grabbed arms, attacked European officers, and set fire to government buildings. The mutinying soldiers were joined by local peasants, zamindars, rajas, and nawabs until it became a great popular uprising against a common enemy. Their message was clear: 'Firangis, leave India!'

Two years and a great deal of bloodshed and brutality later, the EIC managed to regain control. Shocked at these events, the British government stepped in and took over direct governance of India. A few years later, the East India Company was dissolved.

Sitaram remained loyal to the Company, not wanting to betray those who had employed him for many years. Imprisoned and nearly shot by rebel soldiers, he was finally rescued by the EIC Army. Only to face the grief of finding his son among captured mutineers at Lucknow, due to be shot by his own firing squad. Although some scholars question the authenticity of the book, others feel From Sepoy to Subedar is a valuable first-person account of one of the most momentous events in the history of India.

78

The Great Theodolite

Land surveyor's telescope, Dehradun, Uttarakhand, early nineteenth century

At the Survey of India headquarters in Dehradun, a strange-looking device sits in quiet retirement. Not many are aware that this object once formed the heart of what one historian called 'one of the most stupendous tasks in the history of science'. This is Lambton's Great Theodolite—a land surveyor's telescope that you see in the illustration. The 'stupendous task' it was involved in was mapping the terrain of the entire Indian subcontinent, a job that eventually went on to give scientists proof that the Earth was shaped like a grapefruit, that the highest mountains in the world were not the Andes in South America but the Himalayas on the subcontinent, and that the highest point on Earth was a mountain named Chomolungma that came to be known as Mount Everest!

The idea of a land survey dates back to the eighteenth century when the English East India Company (EIC) went from being a trading corporation to actively conquering and ruling large parts of India. At this time, they urgently required maps. These were required mostly for military use, so they could plan their battle strategy or to identify unfamiliar lands. Later, as they conquered more territory, they needed accurate maps to

William Lambton's Great Theodolite

administer the country, plan their revenue collection, and build canals and railways. For this reason, they established the Survey of India, tasked with exploring, surveying, and mapping the subcontinent. In 1799, an English army officer named Colonel William Lambton proposed a remarkable plan. He wanted to conduct a geographical survey of the Indian peninsula using the method of triangulation.

Triangulation is a mathematical method where a line between two points, or a baseline, is first measured. Then a third reference point is marked some distance away, forming a triangle with the ends of the baseline. Using the methods of trigonometry, the interior angles of this triangle can then determine the lengths of the other two sides and, hence, the distance of the third reference point. It sounds simple enough on a piece of paper but, doing this on actual land is a herculean task.

On 10 April 1802, Colonel Lambton formally started the Great Trigonometrical Survey of India. Finding an accurate baseline was the key to his project. Between a flag pole on Marina Beach, Madras (now Chennai), and the grandstand of the Madras Race course, a 12.1 kilometre line was so painstakingly measured that it took almost fifty-seven days to complete! From here, Lambton identified a hill at a distance, and using the three mutually visible reference points, he formed the first triangle. Using the Great Theodolite, he measured the interior angles of the triangle to calculate the distance and height of this hill. Each of the sides of the triangle then became the baselines for two other triangulations. Thus, a chain of triangles was built up from the Coromandel Coast across to the Western Ghats, and the coordinates carefully mapped.

At that time, it was already known that the Earth was not a perfect sphere. It was known that the planet bulged at the Equator and flattened out at the North Pole and South Pole. However, the degree to which it was flattened was not accurately known. In order to convert the distances measured on the spherical Earth to its exact coordinates of latitude and longitude, this curve had to be factored in. Colonel Lambton decided to measure a series of close triangles along the central meridian of longitude in India. In 1808, the Survey began at Kanyakumari, finally ending in the Himalayas in 1847. The corrections for the Earth's shape were then worked into the triangles using spherical geometry.

The mammoth survey took over forty years, cost many lives, and almost bankrupted the EIC. The survey officers, mathematicians, porters, carpenters, and messengers faced immense physical hardships, having to walk for months through dense forests teeming with wild animals, enduring illnesses, blistering heat, freezing cold, and the occasional hostile ruler.

Twelve skilled porters undertook the task of carrying the Great Theodolite, which weighed more than 500 kilograms, as a bumpy bullock cart could have damaged the precisely calibrated instrument. When they lacked a suitable hill or vantage point to use for triangulation, the team had to make do with temple or mosque minarets. This came with its own risks. Once, the heavy theodolite came crashing down from a temple gopuram and smashed to pieces. Lambton spent six weeks secluded in his tent, fixing it bit by bit.

Eventually, with an astounding 423,276 kilometres of triangulation, the Survey minutely mapped more than 2500 kilometres of India. Tragically, Lambton died during the course of the survey. He did not live to see the day in 1852 when one of the greatest scientific expeditions ever undertaken made an amazing discovery. For weeks, the team had observed a Himalayan peak known as Chomolungma from six different stations. It was Radhanath Sikdar, an Indian mathematical whiz and Chief Computer of the Survey, who realized the significance of the data they were reading. Legend has it that he walked into the office of the Director General to declare, 'Sir, we have discovered the highest mountain in the world!' Chomolungma was re-named after George Everest, the man who had succeeded Lambton as superintendent of the survey and later was the Surveyor-General of India. The Great Theodolite eventually retired to Dehradun, having played a major role in defining India's geography as we know it today.

79

Mountain of Light

Diamond, Golconda Mines, Telangana, probably millions of years old, but we pick up the story in 1849 CE

The Koh-i-Noor diamond, perhaps the world's most famous gemstone, forms the centrepiece of a jewelled crown that today belongs to the British royal family. It is on public display within a closely guarded cabinet in the Jewel House of the Tower of London. The Koh-i-Noor is not considered the biggest or even the best diamond ever found. And yet, hidden within the gently glinting 105 carats is an astounding story. It is a story that began a very long time ago in ancient India and still resonates with almost every Indian today.

Millions of years ago, diamonds erupted from the bowels of the earth. They flowed out with the molten lava that eventually solidified into the Deccan plateau. For over 4000 years, people in southern India had been sifting the gravel of river beds where diamonds were commonly found. The crystals were often tiny with the occasional rare and precious large stone. They were valued not just for their beauty but also for their indestructible hardness and a certain mysterious power. Ancient Indian texts described diamonds with a mixture of awe and fear, cautioning

The Koh-i-Noor Diamond Set in Maharaja Ranjit Singh's Amulet

those who wore them to obtain them honestly or be prepared to be cursed.

Rulers and noblemen in the southern kingdoms were famed for their lavish displays of bejewelled attire. Often, they wore more gemstones than clothes. It is from one of these southern courts, possibly the twelfth century CE Kakatiya court at Warangal in present-day Telangana, that rumours of an exceptionally huge diamond, some say even larger than a hen's egg, first began. There was talk in the sixteenth century, during the early days of the Mughal Empire, of just such a gemstone that was added to Babur's collection, 'gifted' by a conquered raja. And again, there were rumours that this exceptional diamond was lost or had somehow left India and was in the collection of the Shah of Persia. But in the absence of historical records, there was no way of verifying these stories. That is until the appearance of Nader Shah at the gates of Delhi in 1739.

The once powerful Mughals watched helplessly as the Persian warlord stripped one of the richest cities in the world of all its accumulated wealth. Somewhere in the caravan of loot that made its way back to Persia with Nader Shah was the fabulous Peacock Throne, reported to have cost twice as much as the Taj Mahal. Perched on the canopy of the gem-encrusted creation was an emerald and ruby peacock with a huge diamond on its head. When Nader Shah saw it, he is said to have exclaimed, 'Koh-i-Noor' or 'mountain of light' and that it what this diamond has been called ever since. We know this because a Persian historian wrote about the event, the first real historical reference to the diamond as the Koh-i-Noor.

Back in Persia, Nader Shah did something quite unexpected. He prised out the two biggest stones in the Peacock throne: the massive Timur ruby and the Koh-i-Noor diamond. He had them fashioned into an amulet and wore them on his arm! He seemed to be showing the world that owning these precious and almost mystical objects gave him the right to rule. The Koh-i-Noor now began to be seen as a symbol of power.

Not long after Nader Shah's violent death, the Afghan Durrani rulers got hold of the diamond. When the Durranis fell on dark days, there were rumours that the stone was cursed.

Despite the speculation, there was someone else who wanted the diamond—Maharaja Ranjit Singh, the man who had united Punjab into a strong and independent Sikh kingdom.

In 1813, the Afghan ruler Shah Shuja Durrani, handed it over to the maharaja in gratitude for saving his life. The normally modestly dressed maharaja started wearing the Koh-i-Noor, now separated from the Timur ruby, as an amulet. Maharaja Ranjit Singh saw the Koh-i-Noor as a gift to himself for all the hard work he had done to unite the Sikh kingdoms, expel the Afghans, and take over from where the Mughals left off. He was now all powerful.

The British too seemed to look upon the Koh-i-Noor as a symbol of power, the crown jewel of India. After the death of Maharaja Ranjit Singh, when the English East India Company annexed Punjab in 1849, they ensured the diamond was handed over to them by the unsuspecting child king

Duleep Singh. The ambitious Governor-General Lord Dalhousie, then sent it as a gift to Queen Victoria of England. The significance of the diamond was clear to the British as Lord Dalhousie wrote to a friend, '. . . the Koh-i-Noor has become a sort of historical emblem of the conquest of India.'

By now, the diamond was a legend that had caught the world's imagination.

Of all the treasures taken unjustly from India, the Koh-i-Noor arouses the most passion, even today. And so, the allure of the great stone continues.

80

The Colour of Protest

Blue indigo dye block, West Bengal, late nineteenth century CE

Can a colour influence the course of a nation's history? In the illustration on the facing page is a block of the natural dye known as indigo. And strange though it seems, the production of indigo was one of the issues that sparked the beginning of the Indian independence movement!

Indigo is a particularly rich and vibrant natural blue dye that is extracted from the leaves of a plant of the genus *Indigofera,* related to the bean family. The use of the dye was known since very ancient times in several parts of the world including Peru, Egypt, West Africa, Mesopotamia, and India.

India was a major producer of indigo, exporting the dye to the ancient Greeks and Romans where it was a much sought-after luxury. Clothes of a deep blue colour were considered a status symbol and the name 'Indigo' comes from the Greek term *Indikon,* which means 'from India'. Among her many thriving business enterprises, the sixteenth-century queen Nur Jahan, wife of the Mughal Emperor Jahangir, was well known for her indigo exports to Europe. The demand for Indian indigo remained

high until the seventeenth century when there was competition from the Americas and the Caribbean Islands.

However, by the end of the eighteenth century, there was a crisis. Britain's Industrial Revolution was well under way, producing huge quantities of mill cotton cloth which required indigo dyes. At about the same time, the indigo plantations in the Americas and the Caribbean Islands suddenly collapsed. By now, with much of India under the control of the English East India Company, the British turned to fertile Bengal for their indigo supplies. Numerous indigo factories sprung up overnight, many of them set up by retired Company officials and others from Britain eager for the high profits of indigo production.

But someone had to grow the indigo plants. Under a system known as ryoti, they forced *ryots* or peasant farmers, to grow indigo on a certain portion of their lands, often the most fertile areas which were traditionally reserved for food crops. Ryots were given cash loans at very high interest for production and paid a pittance for the produce. Meanwhile, the planters made huge profits back home. In addition to this burden, the ryots had to pay the zamindars rent since they did not own the land they cultivated. The next year, the ryots were, once again, forced to sign a contract to cultivate indigo. This meant they could never manage to pay off their debts, which often ran into generations. If they defied the British planters, their food crops would be burnt down or their cattle seized. The defaulting farmers and their families were beaten or even evicted.

The indigo planters were notorious for their greed and cruelty, showing no mercy to the ryots who fell into a cycle of extreme poverty and starvation. It was said at the time that 'not a chest of indigo reached England without being stained with human blood.'

Finally, in 1859, a most unusual revolt took place. The oppressed ryots simply refused to cultivate indigo any more! They rejected the planters' contracts. When the planters' rent collectors turned up with lathi-wielding toughs to collect their money, to their shock, they were attacked by thousands of ryots brandishing makeshift weapons, bows and arrows, knives and swords, and even women armed with pots and pans. The angry ryots proceeded to burn down factories, and the situation became so serious that the army was called in to protect the planters. An alarmed government set up an Indigo Commission that declared the ryots had the right to refuse indigo cultivation in Bengal. The ryots had finally triumphed.

But the story of indigo did not end there. The British planters merely shifted their factories to Bihar. There, they continued the same oppressive practices that had instigated the Blue Mutiny, as it was later called.

Quite soon after Mahatma Gandhi returned to India from South Africa, he was persuaded to visit Champaran in Bihar to see the plight of the indigo farmers there. Gandhi travelled there in 1917 and saw firsthand, the suffering and brutal exploitation of the poor peasants. He began to gather evidence for a formal report. When the authorities served him notice to leave the district or go to jail, Gandhi knew what to do. He decided to listen to his inner conscience and face a jail sentence. The authorities were taken aback. But, observing the crowds of restive farmers who had gathered around him in support, they anticipated trouble and nervously withdrew the notice.

Gandhi's visit galvanized the government to set up the Champaran Agrarian Enquiry Committee. Six months later, most of the exploitative laws and excess taxes on the indigo-growing ryots were abolished. It is said that the Champaran satyagraha had a profound influence on Gandhi and that it was the start of the transformation of Mohandas Gandhi to Mahatma Gandhi, the leader.

This was Gandhi's first demonstration of his unique form of non-violent resistance in India. Satyagraha or 'holding on to truth' was to become his sole 'weapon' against the British Empire in the fight for freedom. The indigo growers' success was a symbol to the rest of the country that they could also stand up against the British and fight for freedom.

81

The Puffing Fairy Queen

Steam locomotive manufactured in England, shipped to India in 1855 CE

In this illustration, meet the beautiful Fairy Queen in all her green and shiny brass splendour. She was made in 1855 by the British locomotive manufacturers Kitson, Thompson, and Hewitson and despatched by ship to Calcutta (Kolkata). On arrival, she was given the rather ordinary name of EIR-22 or Eastern Indian Railway-22 and put to work. She pulled mail trains in Bengal and worked as a troop train during the Revolt of 1857.

Hardworking and versatile, she became a favourite of the EIR and was given the name Fairy Queen. Although she retired from active duty in 1909, the Fairy Queen was so popular that almost ninety years later, to the delight of steam engine enthusiasts, she was restored to full working order. Currently, the Fairy Queen works on a limited route between Delhi and Alwar, Rajasthan. She pulls a two-bogey train, chugging along at a sedate forty kilometres per hour with frequent coal and water breaks. Not too bad considering she is over 160 years old and one of the oldest working steam locomotives in the world!

Of all the changes the English East India Company (EIC) brought to India, perhaps none transformed the Indian subcontinent as much as the railways. As with most other schemes of the EIC, the railways were introduced purely for their own benefit, for '. . . the commerce, government, and military control of the country'. Railways were undeveloped even in Britain at the time. But the EIC was keen to introduce trains since India did not have a large network of roads or waterways.

The railways were going to be convenient and quick, transporting raw materials like coal, iron ore, and cotton from the countryside to ports where they could be shipped for use in British factories. They would also bring cheap and plentiful labour from the countryside to the newly developing cities. Troops could be moved quickly across the country and administrators could move around with relative ease. There was a sense of urgency in the planning and laying of railway tracks.

On 16 April 1853, the first passenger train chugged out from Bombay, pulled along by three steam locomotives named Sahib, Sind, and Sultan, making the short journey to Thane in record time with 400 passengers on board. The EIC was triumphant. But they were also cautious. Being such a strategic asset, the railways did not employ Indians, making sure all the important jobs went to only the British and later to the Eurasians.

Soon, the entire countryside was criss-crossed with railway lines. Dense forests were uprooted, hillsides dissected, and rivers bridged. It was hard and dangerous work with many thousands of railway workmen dying of disease, heat, and wild animal attacks. At first, terrified villagers ran from the sight of these steam-belching metal monsters, convinced they were sent to destroy their homes and eat their livestock! But soon, a strange thing began to happen.

People all over the country realized that those metal beasts made them quite mobile. Journeys across the vast subcontinent that had previously taken months could now be accomplished in days. People began to travel for employment and trade. New technologies began to trickle into the most remote areas. Agricultural and other produce were transported cheaply and quickly, while new jobs cropped up in industry and mining. Market towns and new cities began to grow around railway terminals. Ideas began to travel too, with newspapers and books now delivered across the country in bulk. Women and people of lower castes who had traditionally not been able to move out of their homes, were now able to travel, making a social impact.

Even as these changes took place, Indians noticed how poorly they were being treated on the trains. Crammed into third-class compartments with no food or sanitation facilities while Europeans had exclusive facilities for themselves, there was a growing anger against the colonial powers. Many stories of the leaders of the independence movement are inextricably linked with their travels across India and their ideas for uniting the country against the colonial powers. Mahatma Gandhi, in particular, is associated with his iconic rail journeys across the length and breadth of the country, addressing crowds at railway platforms, rushing to events and protests or offering support to agitating workers and those affected by natural calamities.

Today, the Indian railway network is the fourth largest in the world, after the US, China, and Russia. There are 20,000 trains that carry a record-breaking twenty-five million passengers and 2.8 million tonnes of freight *every day!* The railways have assisted in transforming the Indian economy in a way that the colonials never allowed or intended it to do.

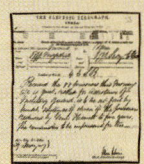

82

News on the Wire

Paper telegram, Meerut, Uttar Pradesh, 1857 CE

Just over 150 years ago, in a time without the internet, instant messaging, or even telephones, the quickest method of communication was through small pieces of paper—like the ones you can see in the illustration—bearing cryptic, hand-written messages. It was known as a telegram. The one in the centre of the illustration was sent on 9 May 1857, from Meerut to Agra, alerting the British administration of some Indian soldiers of the English East India Company (EIC) army who had rebelled, flatly refusing to use a new set of controversial cartridges. The rebel soldiers were imprisoned. 'All is quiet,' says the message reassuringly. The next day, the Revolt of 1857 broke out.

It was later said that the British Empire in India was saved during that turbulent period only because of the telegram. One relieved British administrator in colonial India, Sir Robert Montgomery, was quoted as saying, 'The Electric Telegraph has saved India.'

What was this powerful object?

A telegraph was a machine used to send out messages using electrical pulses that travelled long distances through a series of interconnected

SECRET CIPHER
TELEGRAM

Desp. 1600 17 Aug.
Recd. 1220 18 Aug.

THE ELECTRIC TELEGRAPH.

INDIA.

(OPENED TO THE PUBLIC ON THE 1ST FEBRUARY 1855.)

Messages, (not exceeding 16 words,) can be sent at any distance not exceeding 400 Miles, at a charge of 1 Rupee.

Ditto	Ditto	Ditto	800	"	"	2 Rupees.
Ditto	Ditto	Ditto	1,200	"	"	3 "
Ditto	Ditto	Ditto	1,600	"	"	4 "

No charge for delivery within half-a-mile of the Office; a charge of 4 annas a mile for all distances beyond that.

The following Message from *Meerut* To To *Agra*

Name and Address : *Offg. Magistrate*

Name and Address : *Offg. Secy. to Govt.*

Number of Words: 43

Received the 85 prisoners this Morning. All is quiet. Asked for Assistance of Military Guard, is to be at Jail by Sunset. Sentence of eleven of the prisoners reduced by Genl. Hewitt to five years. The remainder to be imprisoned for ten —

Agra, Elec. Tel. Office.
the 9 of May 1857.

No inquiry respecting this Message can be attended to without the production of this paper.

Head Assistant in charge.

SPACE FOR STAMPS.

SAVE SAFELY
for the FUTURE
Buy
NATIONAL SAVINGS CERTIFICATES
Rs.10 becomes Rs.15 in 12 yrs.

The ACCURACY of telegrams is not guaranteed; the Sender and Receiver must arrange delivery errors or delays. The receipt granted for the telegram should be enclosed with...

INDIAN POSTS AND TELEGRAPHS

Class	Amount	No.	Date
	Rs.		

Office of Origin

Service

Code

If this telegram is to be classed EXPRESS write the Class here. — Express.

Special Instructions
(See Clause XV, Post and Telegraph Guide.)

TO Name *Ganeshdass*
Address
Telegraph Office *Sivagganj (Pabna)*

Send	paper	Calcutta	Nitahari
Nalini-mohan	Chaha	9A Gunglee	Lane
Calcutta	immediately	don't	

wires. An operator at one end tapped a switch, sending long or short pulses, each one representing a different letter of the alphabet in what came to be known as the Morse code. The faraway receiver, operating a similar machine, deciphered the travelling pulses into ordinary language, writing the message on a piece of paper. The message had to be short and precise, as the code was unwieldy to work out. The paper or telegram was then carried by specially appointed postmen who rode, ran, or walked to deliver the urgent news to the recipient. The telegram was the text message of its era, an awe-inspiringly fast way to communicate over long distances.

Large empires with far flung outposts have always needed to set up efficient communications. Even in very ancient times, rulers spent enormous amounts of money on roads, postal systems, and horse-mounted couriers because good communications meant better control over the kingdom. In the mid-nineteenth century, the EIC was ruling areas of India almost as large as the Mughal Empire. To better administer their vast colony, they introduced the railways and extended the postal system to cover even the remotest villages. And then the telegraph was invented.

It was Lord Dalhousie, Governor-General of India in 1848, who was intent on introducing the new technology to India. Roping in an army surgeon and part-time inventor named William O'Shaughnessy, they began the process of laying telegraph lines between the major Indian cities in 1853. A year later, government reports and orders that earlier took over a month between Calcutta (Kolkata) and Bombay (Mumbai), were relayed by telegraph in one day! And with newly laid submarine cables, instructions from the EIC headquarters in London reached India in six hours instead of six months.

By 1856, over 7000 kilometres of telegraph wire were laid. This was fortunate for the British because the very next year, the Revolt broke out.

As mutineers attacked British posts across north India, telegraph signals went back and forth, establishing vital communication between the beleaguered EIC forces in Lucknow, Kanpur, and Delhi. The British were able to plan strategy and order reinforcements with great speed.

Warning telegrams went out from the staff of the Delhi telegraph office to Ambala in Punjab. One famous message read, 'Cantonment in a state of siege. Mutineers from Meerut 3rd Light Cavalry; numbers not known . . . cut off communication with Meerut; taken possession of the Bridge of Boats . . . Several officers killed and wounded. City in a state of considerable excitement. Troops sent down, but nothing certain yet. Further information will be forwarded'. Forewarned, European officers in Punjab were able to quickly disarm their units before news of the rebellion reached native soldiers, thus preventing any violence.

The telegraph had indeed saved India. For the British, that is. And they were grateful enough to have it commemorated on a twenty-foot granite column known as the Mutiny Telegraph Memorial. It still stands in Delhi today, honouring the services of the Delhi telegraph office staff that sent timely warning of impending disaster.

The British felt they were now firmly established in India. By 1900, there were about 5000 telegraph offices around India. But the telegraph system had an unexpected consequence. Indians began to use it to access information from around the world. They shared ideas on freedom and injustice, organized political meetings, and mobilized mass protests across the country. Jailed leaders of political parties directed action through telegrams to regional offices. And often, protestors attacked telegraph lines to disrupt government communications. Previously isolated cultural and linguistic groups across India made strong links, seeing themselves as united and belonging to one nation, rising together against colonial rule. Those pieces of paper were, in fact, the beginning of the end of British rule.

Until the 1980s, telegrams remained the fastest mode of communication in India, the bearer of urgent news, both good and bad, to millions of Indians. With the arrival of the internet and smartphones, telegrams became obsolete. The last telegram in India was sent five minutes before midnight on 14 July 2013.

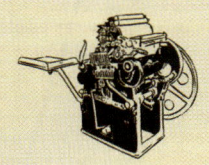

83

Spreading the Word

Printing press, later model of one that came to India in 1556, Goa

In the illustration on the next page, there is an old-fashioned printing press now preserved in the State Museum of Goa. It tells the story of an invention that revolutionized India.

The printing press is a mechanical device that uses ink to transfer words and images on to paper. In the early versions, raised ceramic, wooden, or metal letters were arranged on wooden plates to form words and sentences. They were then brushed with ink, and a sheet of paper was pressed on to the prepared page. This would produce a sharply printed image on the paper. Since the letters were movable, they were called movable type and they would have to be constantly rearranged to form new pages.

Movable type and paper were first invented in China where they were used to print currency and official documents as early as the eleventh century. In the fifteenth century, a German goldsmith and inventor named Johannes Gutenberg introduced mechanical movable type printing to Europe.

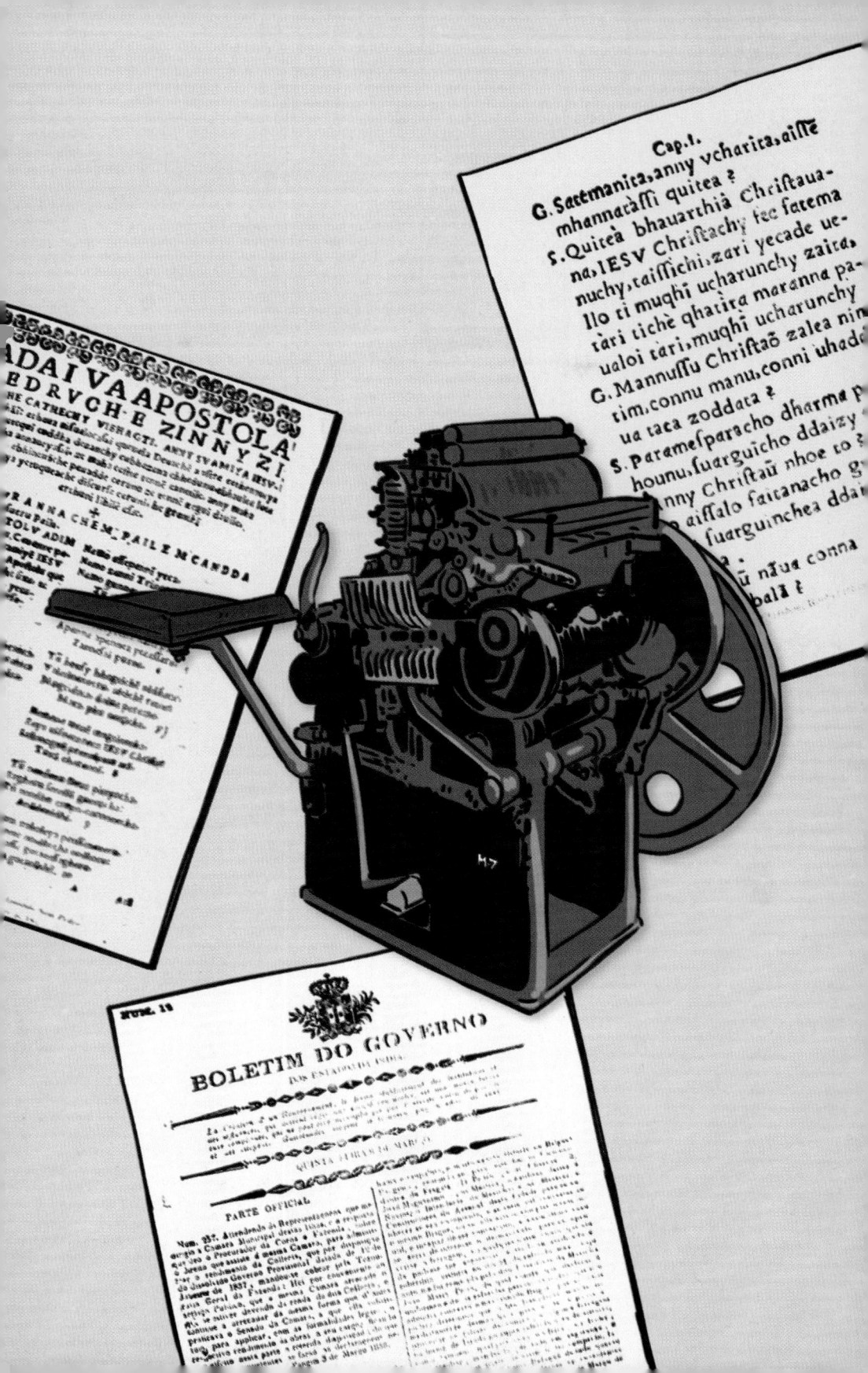

Gutenberg's printing press is considered one of the most important inventions in human history. This is because, until now, books were being copied by hand. This slow and painstaking process made books both rare and expensive, something only the elite could afford. The printing press, on the other hand, could print up to 250 pages per hour. This meant that books, news pamphlets, and other texts could be mass produced, making them cheaper and more accessible to the middle class. Information and news spread more easily, and literacy rates went up. Religious reformation and the scientific revolution in Europe were both the result of the rapid spread of information through the printed word.

The printing press found its way to India in a rather unexpected way. In 1556, a Portuguese ship docked at Goa, capital of the Portuguese State of India. On board were a few Jesuit missionaries bound for the kingdom of Abyssinia, modern-day Ethiopia. To aid their activities, they carried with them a wooden printing press, complete with movable types. Meanwhile, news arrived that the Abyssinian ruler had suddenly changed his mind and no longer wanted to welcome the missionaries to his kingdom. The printing press was unloaded and carried from the docks to the College of St Paul. There, João de Bustamante, a Spanish printing technician who had travelled with the machine, installed it with the help of an unnamed Indian assistant.

Until the mid-eighteenth century, publishing in India was mainly the effort of Christian missionaries with a view to propagating Christianity. They created metal types for Indian scripts and printed religious pamphlets, translations of the Bible, dictionaries and grammar books in Tamil, Konkani, Marathi, Malayalam, Telegu, and Bengali.

The British realized the importance of publishing much later. From the early nineteenth century, the East India Company (EIC) decided to give Western education and the English language a push in India. According to their plans, Western education was important to 'enlighten' Indians, improve their moral character, make them more honest, and create a class of English-educated Indians who would serve the cause of the empire loyally! English books, journals, and newspapers were published to cater to this modern education.

But the result was the opposite of what was intended.

Like in Europe, books in India had once been restricted to the very wealthy. Hand-written manuscripts in Sanskrit, Arabic, and Persian with elaborate illustrations were commissioned by royalty and the well-to-do. Palm-leaf manuscripts with religious literature could only be read by scholars. Even in schools, students did not read from books. Instead, gurus dictated memorized verses that the children wrote down, thus becoming literate without reading a single book!

With the appearance of newspapers and journals, many of them published by Indians, educated people now had access to ideas from around the world. They read of ideas like liberty, equality, freedom, and nationalism. Printing reduced the cost of books, making them accessible to a wider reading public, including women. Many questioned social evils like sati, child marriage, and caste discrimination. Across the country, readers of these new publications became aware of their belonging to a nation that was ruled by an oppressive colonial power.

Nationalists and social reformers expressed their ideas in newspapers like Raja Rammohun Roy's *Sambad Kaumudi* in Bengali and *Mirat-ul-Akhbar* in Persian. Newspapers like *Kesari*, *Mathrubhumi*, and *Amrita Bazar Patrika* highlighted colonial tyranny and demanded freedom from colonial rule. Journalists and newspaper editors like Bal Gangadhar Tilak and G. Subramania Iyer were at the forefront of the freedom movement. Mahatma Gandhi edited several newspapers, including *Harijan*, *Young India*, and *Navajivan*, where his ideas were read by grassroots workers.

When the colonial government panicked and imposed censorship, the printers got creative, running secret underground presses that continued to print handbills and posters, distributing them through a network of couriers.

The printing press that had been brought to India with the intention of imposing colonial ideas had, instead, created a weapon against colonial rule.

84

The Symbol of Bharat Mata

Watercolour painting by Abanindranath Tagore, Kolkata, 1905 CE

Here is an odd question: When were countries invented?

A country or a nation is a group or several groups of people who live within a defined geographical space with borders that are sovereign. They often have common histories, cultures, or languages, as well as common goals. They decide for themselves how to run their lives and what their future should look like. In the world we live in, a country is an important part of a person's identity. You will hear people proudly declare that they are Indian or Malaysian, or French. So, it certainly feels like countries have always existed.

But here is a surprising fact. The concept of countries or nations is quite recent. Nations as we know them are only a little over 200 years old. Until the middle of the eighteenth century, people all over the world lived within small or big kingdoms, estates, or even just homesteads ruled by chieftains. They identified themselves by their clans, castes, or professions. If you asked them where they came from, they would

probably have given the name of their village or city. The idea of a country did not exist!

At the end of the eighteenth century, the French Revolution brought about a radical idea. A monarch could be replaced by a group of ordinary citizens. People no longer wanted to be told what to do by any individual or privileged group, such as royalty or the church. Common people could join together, consult with each other, and take their own decisions on how to live. The idea quickly spread throughout Europe. In areas that we now know as Germany and Italy, dozens of small, independent states with common heritage decided it would be smarter to join together into larger, self-ruled nations. Increasing literacy, education, and the printed word also helped spread this new idea of nationalism. These new nations began to define themselves by how unique they were and how different their traditions and customs were from others. Thus, national pride was born.

Something similar happened in the Indian subcontinent towards the end of the nineteenth century as a response to British colonial rule. Indian freedom fighters tried to unify the people against a common oppressor. But it was a hard task. Town dwellers, peasants, plantation labourers, educated businessmen, and forest tribesmen—each group had a different experience of colonial rule. People spoke different languages and belonged to various ethnic groups, many of them seemed to have nothing in common. None of them knew each other personally. How were they to be united under the idea of a single nation with the common cause of freedom?

They needed something to *show* them that they belonged together— shared symbols of their culture like folklore, songs, history, or art. This is where the image of Bharat Mata, or Mother India, came in.

In 1882, the Bengali poet Bankim Chandra Chatterjee, in his novel *Anandmath*, referred to the land of India as 'mata' or mother. In 1905,

'Bharat Mata', Watercolour Painting by
Abanindranath Tagore

as a response to the outpouring of anger over the British partition of the Bengal province—which divided Hindus and Muslims who had lived together peacefully for centuries—the artist Abanindranath Tagore painted the lady in the illustration, calling her 'Bharat Mata'.

Bharat Mata is simply dressed, and in her four hands she holds a book, sheaves of paddy, a piece of white cloth, and a rudraksha mala. Something about her serene look, her offering of food, clothing, and wise words, and the fact that she looks like a protective goddess struck an immediate, emotional chord among the people. It was a visual representation of the country, a symbol of India for people to identify with.

Sister Nivedita, the Irish teacher, social activist, and disciple of Swami Vivekananda, declared, '. . . the picture is an appeal, in the Indian language, to the Indian heart . . . I would reprint it, if I could, by tens of thousands and scatter it broadcast over the land, till there was not a peasant's cottage or a craftsman's hut between Kedar Nath and Cape Comorin, that had not this presentment of Bharat-Mata somewhere on its walls.'

And soon, that is just what happened. The figure became an object of reverence. Various forms of Bharat Mata were printed and painted, appearing on posters and banners from the Central Provinces to Punjab to Madras, becoming a rallying point for freedom fighters. Through shared respect, people across the country saw they also shared a bond. Despite their differences, there was a new-found sense of belonging to a motherland and a motive to fight for a common cause. The image of Bharat Mata was a powerful unifying symbol of nationalism and, some believe, a step towards the creation of a country called India.

85

The First Tiranga

First Indian tricolour flag, Pune, Maharashtra, 1907 CE

On 22 August 1907 at the International Socialist Conference in Stuttgart, Germany, a firebrand Indian freedom fighter named Bhikaji Cama stood up and unfurled the flag in the illustration. 'Behold, the flag of independent India is born! It has been made sacred by the blood of young Indians who sacrificed their lives in its honour. In the name of this flag, I appeal to lovers of freedom all over the world to support this struggle,' she declared. It was the first time that the Indian tricolour had been displayed abroad and a thousand delegates from across the globe are said to have stood to salute it. With her passionate appeal, Bhikaji Cama drew the world's attention to India's suffering under an oppressive British rule, gaining support for the cause of Indian independence.

The flag she unfurled, however, looks different from what we know today as our Tiranga or tricolour. The flag had three horizontal stripes of green, saffron, and red from top to bottom. The top green stripe had eight half-open lotuses, representing the eight Indian provinces under British rule. The middle stripe of saffron had the words 'Vande Mataram' written in Devnagari script. The bottom red strip had the moon and the

Bhikaji Cama's Flag of Independent India

sun, representing Islam and Hinduism, the two major religions of India at the time. An Indian delegate to the conference, Indulal Yagnik, later smuggled the flag back into India. Avoiding British authorities who would have confiscated and destroyed it, Yagnik took it to Pune, Maharashtra, where it is still displayed at the Maratha and Kesari Library.

Since ancient times, Indians have always respected *dhvajas* or flags. Usually a piece of cloth bearing designs and attached to a pole or staff, flags were carried into battle, associated with dynasties, hoisted outside forts and sacred places, and honoured with rituals. In modern times, a flag came to represent a nation, a symbol that the people could rally around with courage, defending it as they would defend their country.

Early Indian nationalists were impressed with the French tricolour flag, which was a symbol of the French Revolution and the rallying point of their slogan, 'Liberty, Equality, and Fraternity.' They realized that the cause for Indian freedom could well do with a flag of its own.

In the early 1900s, an Irish disciple of Swami Vivekananda, known as Sister Nivedita, came up with a design. It was a red square with 108 yellow lamps along the border and the vajra, the weapon of Lord Indra, and a symbol of strength, in the centre. The words 'Vande Mataram' was inscribed on either side of the vajra in Bengali.

On 7 August 1906, at a huge rally in Calcutta, a tricolour flag was hoisted. It was the first anniversary of the declaration of the partition of Bengal, a controversial move by the British government that was met with widespread protests. The flag, said to have been inspired by the French tricolour, had green, yellow, and red stripes. There were eight half-open lotuses on the top stripe, a white sun and crescent moon on the bottom stripe, and the words 'Vande Mataram' inscribed in blue on the middle yellow stripe. It came to be known as the Vande Mataram or the Calcutta flag. In fact, Bhikaji Cama's famous flag was based on this design.

Flag hoisting now became rallying points for independence rallies. The British government took note, threatened by the symbolic power of these unofficial flags. People were arrested and jailed for merely carrying them and they had to be made and transported in secret.

After Bhikaji Cama's dramatic flag reveal in Stuttgart, flags took on even more meaning, varying with the twists and turns of the freedom movement itself. In 1917, the Home Rule Flag appeared with a British Union Jack in the upper left corner, signifying the demand for Dominion Status for India, which would mean freedom but under the supervision of the British Empire. The idea was not popular, and the flag was shelved. Mahatma Gandhi wanted the spinning wheel or charkha in the centre of the flag.

It was Pingali Venkayya, a freedom fighter and Gandhian, who designed what came to be called the Swaraj flag, with red, green, and white stripes and a charkha at the centre. The red represented the Hindus, the green the Muslims, and the white all the other communities in the country living together in harmony while the charkha depicted progress. The Swaraj flag accompanied many significant events of the freedom struggle. Netaji Subhas Chandra Bose adopted it for the Indian National Army with a springing tiger in place of the charkha.

Prominent leaders became involved in designing the flag, trying to incorporate colours and symbols that would represent all communities. But, by 1947, India had changed. Indians no longer wanted the colours to represent particular communities or faiths. They wanted a flag that represented a united, cohesive nation that honoured all citizens. In July of the same year, the new tricolour was adopted by the Constituent Assembly. The chosen flag had three broad stripes. A saffron stripe at the top represented courage and sacrifice, white in the middle depicted peace and truth, green at the bottom showed fertility, growth, and auspiciousness, while the central blue wheel, from the lion capital of Emperor Ashoka's edict pillar, represented movement and progress. India's flag symbolized her character, her independence, and the synthesis of all the communities that lived within her borders.

86

A Poet and His Prize

Nobel Prize medal for Literature, Shantiniketan, Bengal, 1913 CE

This Nobel Prize medal, illustrated on the facing page, has caused a huge furore twice over.

The first time was when it was awarded. On 16 November 1913, Rabindranath Tagore, possibly India's most influential literary figure, received a telegram. The message was in typical cryptic telegram-style language: 'SWEDISH ACADEMY AWARDED YOU NOBEL PRIZE LITERATURE WIRE ACCEPTATION SWEDISH MINISTER.'

It was unbelievable news! Tagore had won the Nobel Prize for Literature for his book *Gitanjali*, a collection of poems. There was an outpouring of joy and celebration all over India. He was the first Asian to win this most prestigious of awards and the first non-European to be awarded the prize for literature.

The second time, the medal was in the news for the wrong reasons. On 24 March 2004, it was stolen from its special vault at the Vishwa Bharati University in Shantiniketan, Bengal. This time, there

Rabindranath Tagore Won the Nobel Prize for Literature for His Book Gitanjali *in 1913*

was nationwide outrage. Who would steal one of the nation's most treasured objects?

Much of the outrage had to do with the towering personality of Rabindranath Tagore and his enormous influence on the literature and intellectual life of India. He was born in 1861 into a wealthy, scholarly family in Bengal. His early, formal education at school was not particularly successful, as the young Tagore hated the stifling atmosphere of the classroom. He preferred, instead, to read widely in the family library, travel through the countryside, observe everyday life among the common people, enjoy the changing seasons, star gaze, and conduct home-made scientific experiments. As he searched for knowledge from all kinds of sources, his creativity poured into his writing. Since the age of eight, when he wrote his first poem, hundreds more poems, essays, plays, songs, children's stories, and verse in both Bengali and English, flowed from his pen.

In his work, Tagore constantly questioned orthodox beliefs and fearlessly challenged those social and political views which he believed were irrational. He wrote strong pieces against the terrible condition of peasants and divisions based on religious beliefs. He opposed the caste system and the oppression of women. Above all, he asked his fellow countrymen and women to open their minds and free themselves from traditions based on blind belief by using reason and a scientific outlook.

By the early twentieth century, Tagore was a renowned intellectual figure. His innovative literary ideas and brilliant language profoundly influenced the Bengali world, changing its language, literature, culture, arts, and even history, forever. It was not long before the rest of India heard of his genius through translations of his work. His reputation soon spread to the world through leading literary figures of the day like the English poet W.B. Yeats. He was invited on lecture tours to Britain, Europe, and the United States of America, where he addressed packed halls of spellbound audiences who sometimes regarded him as a sage from the East. In later years, he met Albert Einstein and Bertrand Russell and was invited to South America, a journey that took months in those days.

In India, Tagore had a great influence on many leaders of the freedom movement, including Mahatma Gandhi, Subhas Chandra Bose, and Jawaharlal Nehru. They discussed topics like truth, freedom, and democracy, often disagreeing but always respecting others' views.

But there were critics too, as many questioned his patriotism. Going against the popular notions of loyalty to one's nation, Tagore believed in individual freedom and a 'world family' where national borders dissolved and humanity came together to share their best ideas for common good. In one of his most famous poems, he writes his most fervent wish for his country:

'Where the mind is without fear and the head is held high,

Where knowledge is free,

Where the world has not been broken up into fragments by narrow domestic walls,

Into that heaven of freedom, my father, let my country awake.'

Believing that the foundation of progress lies in education, Tagore started an inclusive, co-educational school called Vishwa Bharati at Shantiniketan in present-day West Bengal. Here, children still study in an atmosphere akin to what Tagore knew as a child. They are free to read, to explore, to question, and to express their opinions. They study in beautiful natural surroundings, work with their hands like craftsmen or peasants, and are encouraged to play, dance, and sing.

A unique reminder of Tagore's genius is the fact that the national anthems of two countries, 'Amar Sonar Bangla' of Bangladesh and 'Jana Gana Mana' of India, are both his works.

The lost Nobel medal has not been found yet. Currently, in its place are two replicas sent by the Nobel Foundation. Rabindranath Tagore's impact on India's thought, though, remains irreplaceable.

87

The Taste of Civil Disobedience

Salt, a symbol of national protest countrywide, 1930 CE onwards

When Mahatma Gandhi chose salt as the symbol of the Civil Disobedience movement, many were bewildered. Why salt, they asked? Surely, there were other, more important issues they could focus on. Gandhi, of course, had his reasons.

In January 1930, as calls for Purna Swaraj or complete independence for India from British rule grew louder, Mahatma Gandhi sent a letter to the Viceroy, Lord Irwin. The letter listed eleven important demands from the British government on behalf of the people of India. And a subtle message from Gandhi that if these demands were not met, the Congress Party would launch a Civil Disobedience movement, in which people would actively break unjust laws. Lord Irwin was unmoved and did not even bother to reply. On 11 March, with no reaction from the British government, Gandhi swung into action.

Among the demands sent to the Viceroy was the rather mild-sounding request to abolish the tax on salt. To everyone's surprise, it was on this that Gandhi focused. He gave notice that he was about to break the salt law by leading a march to the seaside to gather salt himself. Some were amused at the idea of challenging the mighty British Empire with a kitchen condiment. One newspaper remarked, 'It is difficult not to laugh . . .' Others, like the Viceroy, dismissed the idea as 'Mr Gandhi's crazy scheme of upsetting the government with a pinch of salt.'

But salt was Gandhi's masterstroke.

The British government had a monopoly on the sale and production of salt. Anyone who tried to manufacture or sell salt was considered a criminal and could be sent to jail. This meant that even the very poor were forced to buy salt from government shops, which was taxed at fourteen times its value. 'Salt officers' were posted along the coastal salt pans to prevent local people from collecting natural sea salt for their personal use. And, in a particularly wicked move, mounds of unsold natural salt were deliberately destroyed.

Being the most basic necessity of any household, this law affected everyone, causing widespread resentment among both the rich and the poor. 'Next to air and water,' Gandhi said, 'salt is perhaps the greatest necessity of life.'

The salt tax was a symbol of British injustice, and the idea of defying the salt law resonated with people from all walks of life across India.

On 12 March 1930, Gandhi began walking from his ashram in Sabarmati, Gujarat, towards the coastal town of Dandi. He was accompanied on the 386-kilometre journey by a group of handpicked volunteers. As they walked, crowds came out to greet them, many waiting for hours to catch a glimpse of the frail-looking figure leading the march with his trademark bamboo stick. They cheered the walkers, showered them with flower petals and coins and offered food and water. Gandhi stopped to speak to them, telling them of *Swaraj* or self-rule and *satyagraha*, how to use

the force of truth rather than violence to shame the enemy into defeat. Excitement and hope filled the air as people began to realize that they had the power to take action against injustice.

Twenty-four days later, the marchers reached Dandi. Gandhi stood on the beach, scooped up a handful of the natural salt crystals and held them out for all to see. 'With this, I'm shaking the foundations of the British Empire,' he declared.

Meanwhile, news of Gandhi's actions had spread. In extraordinary scenes across the country, people gathered along the coasts, panning for natural salt and selling it in packets. They raided government salt works, calmly braving brutal beatings and arrests. In all, over five million people broke the salt laws. Meanwhile, peasants, tradesmen, lawyers, and teachers refused to pay taxes and resigned from their jobs to join the movement. Forest people and tribals defied laws that prevented them from using their own forests.

In a key moment of the independence movement, women from all social backgrounds came out in huge numbers to join the protests. Many of them were stepping out of the domestic space for the first time. Encouraged by the example of leaders like Kamaladevi Chattopadhyay and Sarojini Naidu, they sold packets of 'illegal' salt in the markets, picketed foreign liquor and cloth shops, were beaten, arrested, and jailed.

The foreign press covered the events, telling readers all over the world of the gut-wrenching scenes they witnessed in India of unarmed, non-violent protesters fighting a mighty empire with a simple kitchen condiment. In the months following the Salt March, the British imprisoned over 60,000 protesters, including all the major Congress leaders and Mahatma Gandhi.

However, now the entire country was united in a common cause to attain Swaraj. And for the first time, the British government recognized that they were up against a moral force that they would find hard to defeat.

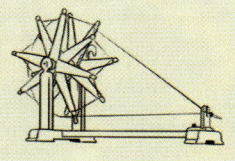

88

Spinning Ideas of Independence

Charkha, countrywide, 1920s CE onwards

One of the most iconic images of the Indian freedom movement is a black-and-white photograph of Mahatma Gandhi taken in 1946 by the American photographer Margaret Bourke-White. In the photo, Gandhi is seen sitting on a mat, reading. In the foreground, dominating the picture, is a charkha or spinning wheel. Widely regarded as one of the most influential photographs of all time, we see the leader deep in thought with his charkha by his side.

The charkha is an ancient device used to spin yarn that was then woven into cloth. In India, it was once a common sight, particularly among village women who spun thread to be used by weavers. It was Gandhi who turned this everyday device into a powerful symbol of the Indian independence movement.

When Gandhi returned to India from South Africa in 1915, the freedom struggle was already well under way. The Indian National Congress party was active with branches all across the country. The Swadeshi movement in which people vowed to buy Indian-made goods and actively boycott foreign goods had enthusiastic support from the middle class.

After his return, Gandhi spent a year travelling around India, trying to better understand his country and its people. He was pained by the widespread poverty and desperation of the peasants and workers. They formed the great majority of India's population and yet, they remained exploited and powerless under oppressive colonial rule. Gandhi knew that without their active participation, the independence movement would never be strong enough, which meant there would be no real freedom for India.

At the end of his travels, Gandhi understood what he had to do. His first move was to change the way he dressed. He gave up his Western suits and began to wear a simple, homespun short dhoti and shawl. It was one way to communicate with the common people. They, in turn, could now identify with a leader who looked like them. Gandhi then began to speak up on behalf of the voiceless masses, intervening when they were denied justice and convincing them that they could indeed change their destinies and that they had a valuable role to play in national events. Through his simple acts, Gandhi managed to make a big impact, bringing peasants, farmers, workers, and artisans into the fold of the freedom movement.

It was while transforming Indian nationalism into a mass movement that Gandhi found a tool for India's social and economic revival in the ancient device of the charkha.

At this time, a flood of cheap mill-made British textiles had ruined India's traditional handloom sector, throwing thousands of skilled weavers out of work. Farmers forced to grow cash crops, such as cotton and indigo, to fuel the cloth mills of Britain, were reduced to poverty and starvation. For Gandhi, a rediscovery of the age-old tradition of hand-spinning yarn and wearing khadi, the coarse homespun cloth made from this yarn, was not just a way out of poverty but also a revival of dignity of labour, sustainability, and the ideal of swadeshi or self-sufficiency. Only swadeshi could lead to swaraj or freedom.

He believed that the nation could be changed through the simple act of spinning. 'The Indian people,' he wrote, 'would only be free from European domination, both politically and economically, when the masses take to spinning, weaving, and wearing homespun cloth, khadi.'

Gandhi suggested that everyone spin for at least half an hour every day. For the poor, spinning yarn would help them achieve financial independence. For others, it was an act of non-violent protest, a challenge to British authority. Spinning yarn on the charkha became an act of meditation. It became a compulsory activity for Congress members who, from 1922, wore only khadi. Often, a certain length of spun thread was required to qualify for a party post! The members also taught spinning to the common people and spread the word about boycotting foreign cloth.

Hand-spun and hand-woven khadi were the new badges of nationalism. The charkha was now the symbol of the national movement, uniting

Mahatma Gandhi Spinning Thread on His Charkha

people across India from all walks of life. It even featured on a flag designed by freedom fighter Pingali Venkayya, eventually called the Swaraj flag, officially adopted by the Indian National Congress in 1931.

Gandhi tried tirelessly to promote khadi as the fabric of India. However, not everyone was happy. Some found it too coarse to wear, while others wanted different clothes to make political statements. Bhimrao Ambedkar, for instance, never gave up wearing his Western-style suits as a protest against the caste discrimination based on clothes that the Dalits had faced for centuries. Yet others simply could not afford the price of khadi which was higher compared to cheaper mass-produced mill cloth.

Today, the charkha that once united a nation is rarely seen. But the most enduring depiction of the Indian independence movement remains that of Mahatma Gandhi with his charkha.

89

Painting an Identity

Oil on canvas by Raja Ravi Varma, Vadodara, Gujarat, 1896 CE

When the Hindu goddess of learning, Saraswati, is mentioned, chances are that almost everyone will visualize her as she is here in the painting depicted on the next page, from the collection of the Maharaja Fateh Singh Museum at Vadodara, Gujarat. A beautiful, serene lady in a silken saree, adorned with glittering jewels, playing a veena with a peacock by her side, set against a backdrop of natural beauty. How did we learn to visualize the goddess like this? Who gave her this image?

It was Raja Ravi Varma, a late nineteenth-century artist, who first changed the imagery of the gods and goddesses into the style in which we see them today. He was born in 1848 into a family that was closely connected with the royal family of Travancore in Kerala. As a child, he showed a great talent for art and was taken to the royal court to learn from the masters there. But the artists at court were not too keen to teach the young Ravi Varma. So he learnt by observation. He watched as a visiting Dutch painter mixed and blended oil colours, using light

Raja Ravi Varma's Painting of Goddess Saraswati

and shadows on his painting to enhance and shape figures, giving them depth. He observed the Indian artists painting finely detailed works with rich colours, highlighting costume and jewellery details.

Ravi Varma started painting in his own unique style, combining Western techniques of realism with Indian themes and iconography. In a most original style, he depicted Hindu gods and goddesses, not as supernatural beings but as humans in a realistic form. He painted in great detail with light, shadow, and textures, enhancing their calm expressions, their rich costumes and jewellery. These true-to-life figures were unlike anything people had seen before.

Raja Ravi Varma's art captured the imagination of people all over India. Soon, he was in demand everywhere to paint portraits of aristocratic families and royalty. Accompanied by his brother, Raja Raja Varma, an artist in his own right, Ravi Varma travelled extensively across the country using the newly introduced railways, to showcase his talent, secure commissions from nobles and royalty, and research details for his art in the farthest corners. Among his greatest patrons were the Gaekwads of Baroda.

Apart from portraits of nobility and gods and goddesses, Ravi Varma painted scenes from the epics and Indian mythology. Among his most famous works were scenes from the Ramayana, Harishchandra, Nala and Damayanti, and portraits of Lakshmi and Saraswati. In 1890, when some of these paintings were exhibited to the public in Baroda, they created a sensation. For the first time ever, people saw beloved characters from mythology and the epics portrayed in this realistic fashion. With their human forms and expressive faces, the common people found the gods were suddenly approachable and not tucked away in the deep sanctum or within the high walls of a temple. And yet, their rich costumes, serene expressions, and celestial backgrounds ensured they retained their divine air.

Towards the end of the nineteenth century, India was changing quickly. Until this time, India had been a series of separate regional powers. But now, with new industries, cities were emerging with a rapidly growing middle-class population that came from all parts of the subcontinent. At the same time, nationalist leaders and thinkers of the day were trying to unite Indians, emphasizing their common identity in their quest for freedom from colonial rule. Raja Ravi Varma's art seemed to depict just such an Indian identity, one that cut across barriers of region, class, and caste. Since his original art was too expensive for the common people, there was a sudden demand for cheap copies of his works.

To meet this demand, Raja Ravi Varma set up his own lithographic printing press in 1894 at Ghatkopar, near Mumbai. There, multiple prints of his popular works were made and sold at affordable prices. Framed pictures of Ravi Varma's works began to appear everywhere across India, in household puja rooms, offices, cafes, and shops. Most popular among them were his depictions of Lakshmi, Saraswati, Shakuntala, and scenes from the epics. Raja Ravi Varma's art had created a pan-Indian style, a new visual language. People began to see their gods and heroes just as Ravi Varma had painted them!

They were so popular that, soon, plenty of illegal copies appeared which led to the press making losses. The Ravi Varma Fine Art Lithographic Press was finally sold to a German printing technician, but by then his art had moved to calendars, political posters, advertisements, biscuit tins, and even matchbox covers. In 1913, a young photographer named D.G. Phalke who had trained in Ravi Varma's press went on to make India's first feature film, *Raja Harishchandra*, where the imagery was said to be based on Ravi Varma's art. In fact, much of the depiction of Indian mythology today in films, television serials, and even comics is based on the style of Raja Ravi Varma, India's first modern artist.

90

Letter from an Indian Soldier

Translation of a letter sent from France to Hyderabad, Telangana, 1916 CE

On 5 July 1916, Daya Ram, a soldier of the 2nd Lancers, a cavalry regiment of the British Indian Army, wrote a letter from France to his friend Subedar Mahomed Khan of the 24th Punjabi Regiment in Hyderabad, India. The original letter was in Urdu and has not survived. But what we have here is the censored translation. Official censorship of letters was a standard practice in the army, particularly during war when there was a danger that a soldier might give away secret information such as the location of troops, battle strategy, or the morale of the soldiers, should the letter fall into enemy hands.

Daya Ram's regiment was stationed in France during the First World War (1914–1918), so called because this was the first time that war had engulfed many nations at once. Britain, France, Belgium, Russia, and later the USA were on one side, known as the Allies, and were fighting against Germany, Austria-Hungary, Bulgaria, and the Ottoman Empire, known as the Central Powers.

Much of the fiercest fighting was on the western front of the war in France and Belgium, using trench warfare. Both sides dug deep trenches within their territories, stretching for miles across the countryside. These were occupied by armed soldiers, making it difficult for either side to advance. If they so much as peeped over the edge of the trench, they were likely to be shot by enemy gunfire. If the enemy did not kill them, disease would, as the soldiers spent months in the narrow, muddy trenches, eating cold food in horribly unhygienic conditions. In this dangerous situation, with almost no medical aid, entire units were wiped out in a matter of days. Despite more than 2500 kilometres of trenches, for almost the entire war, neither side gained ground. In his letter, Daya Ram describes the situation.

'On the 18th, I went into the trenches and came back all safe on the 29th. The fight is very severe. The fire of bombs descends all night long, and the rain of machine guns never stops. I live in a dug-out . . . Everybody sleeps, eats, and drinks underground . . . I am alive up to date through your kindness, but God knows what will happen. There is great discomfort in the trenches and the lice swarm on the men.'

What was an Indian soldier doing in the trenches in faraway France?

When war broke out, entire divisions of the British Indian army were shipped out to Europe, North and East Africa, and Mesopotamia to fight on the side of the Allies. These army men had been mainly recruited from poor agricultural families of northern India, particularly Punjab, the North-West Frontier, and what is present-day Uttar Pradesh. A salary of Rs. 11 per month was attractive for a poor or landless peasant at the time. In their five to seven years of service, the sepoys would develop a strong bond of loyalty to the army and particularly, their regiment. In addition, they would manage to send money to their families back in the village.

Now, because the empire demanded it, for the first time, Indian troops went overseas. Forces were also sent from the princely states of Mysore,

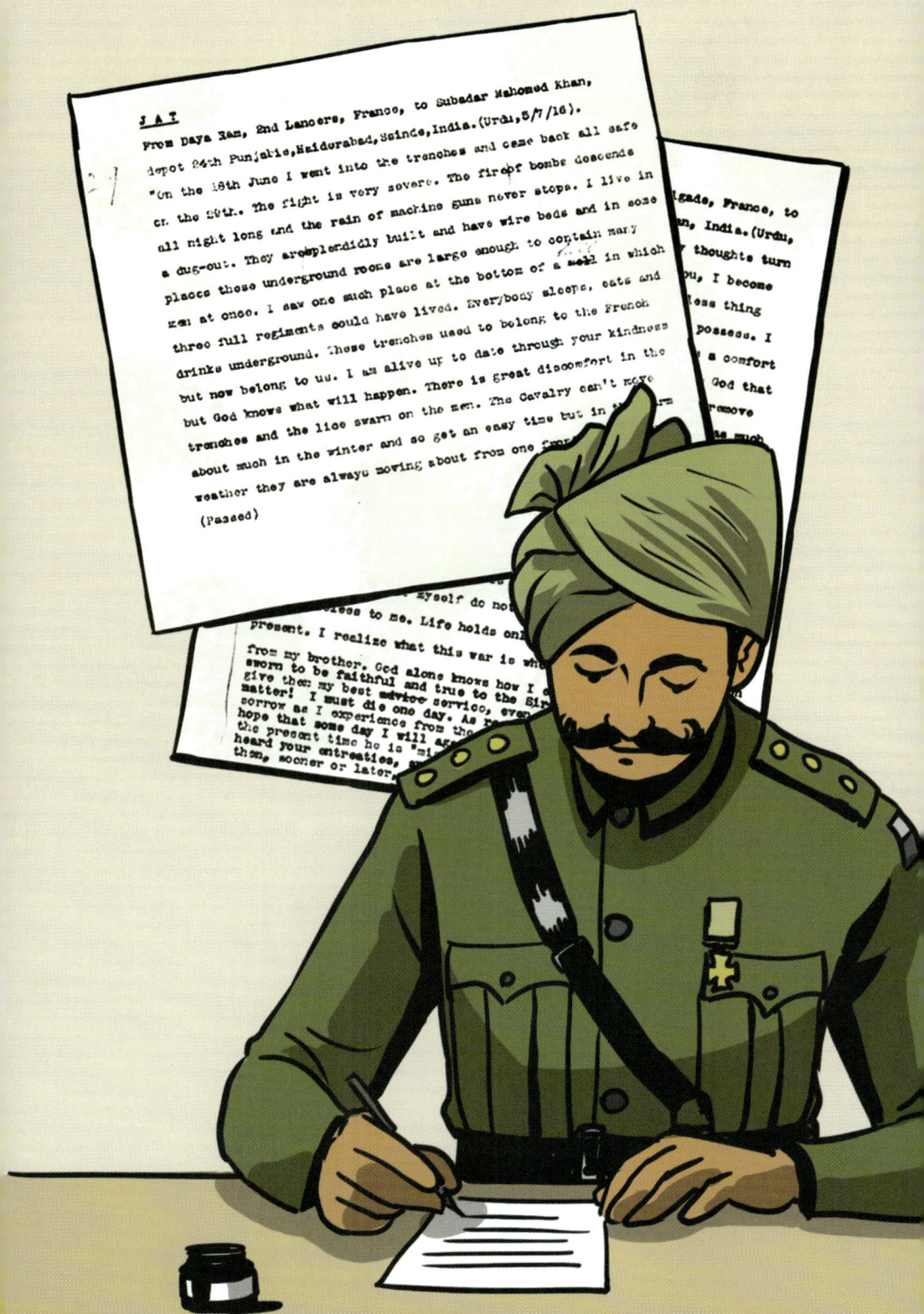

Jodhpur, and Hyderabad. There, in strange, often cold lands, ill clad, underequipped, homesick, and unsure why they were fighting so far from home, the Indian soldiers saw themselves as doing their professional duty, fighting out of loyalty to their country and emperor, but also to bring honour or *izzat* to their regiment.

A staggering 1.5 million Indians served overseas in the First World War as soldiers and non-combatants. More than 74,000 of them died for the British Empire, and an almost equal number were wounded. They fought with distinction, earning 9200 gallantry awards, including eleven Victoria Crosses.

Their experiences were pieced together through the letters they wrote to their families and friends back home, in which they poured out their suffering and impressions of the strange lands in which they found themselves. Many were illiterate and required scribes to write for them in Urdu, Gurmukhi, Hindi, Marathi, or Nepali. These were translated by censors, which was fortunate because most of the original letters have been lost.

A wounded soldier wrote from hospital, 'Do not think that this is war. This is not war. It is the ending of the world. This is just such a war as was related in the Mahabharata about our forefathers'. Others wrote in despair as comrades died in battle, 'The corpses cover the country, like sheaves of harvested corn'. Some were anxious about the hardships of their families back home. Others wrote of the warmth of the French citizens, how kindly they were treated in hospitals, and of the beauty of European cities. They admired the discipline of everyday life and many observed that it was time that Indian women were allowed an education like their European counterparts.

The war ended in triumph for the Allies. For their service of men, money, and materials, the British had promised the nationalist leaders of India self-government at the end of the war. Instead, early in 1919, they imposed the notorious Rowlatt Act, silencing the press and stamping out opposition to the empire by arresting critics without warrant or trial. For the British, it was convenient to forget the courage and sacrifice of the Indian soldiers who had fought on their side in such large numbers. On the other hand, many Indians regarded the soldiers as having served in a colonial army and, hence, not deserving of recognition. Thus, the sacrifices of Indian soldiers like Daya Ram and the 74,000 others who lost their lives lay forgotten.

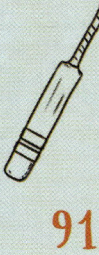

91

Batting for Freedom

Willow cricket bat used by C.K. Nayudu at Lord's, England, 1932 CE

They say that every ball that was hit off this cricket bat, the one you see in the illustration, was as good as a blow against the British Empire. The simple-looking willow with its black rubber grip belonged to C.K. Nayudu, the legendary cricketer and captain of the first ever Indian Test team.

How did a cricket bat come to be seen as a weapon against colonialism? This is a question that can perhaps be answered if we look at the history of the game of cricket in India.

There is no doubt that India is a cricket-crazy country. Every Test match, One-Day International, Ranji Trophy match, or Indian Premier League match is followed by legions of frenzied fans, with news headlines and television coverage of their cricketing superheroes often overshadowing all other national news. So, it is hard to imagine that the game came to India only recently with the British.

Cricket was invented in seventeenth-century England, slowly evolving from a popular rural game to one of the earliest sports in the world to have a code of written rules. By the nineteenth century, in Victorian England, the game came to be associated with values of fair play and discipline, qualities that the British believed to be part of their unique character. When they conquered colonies across the world in Australia, Africa, India, and the West Indies, British officials and administrators took the game with them. There, they set up cricket clubs and gymkhanas where they played for recreation and as a sort of nostalgic escape back to their faraway home. 'Natives' or the local people were excluded from these all-white clubs as they were considered inferior and unlikely to

C.K. Nayudu's Historic Bat

have the sporting talent or character required to play cricket successfully! It was a sign of British superiority, a game only the elite white rulers were able to play.

But the Indians decided otherwise. They took to the game enthusiastically, playing on street corners and town maidans, using makeshift bats and wickets. Tired of being excluded from the English clubs, in 1848, the prosperous Parsi community set up the Oriental Cricket Club in Bombay, now Mumbai, which shut down two years later. Eventually, they established another dedicated cricket ground known as the Parsi Gymkhana for their exclusive use. It was a pioneering effort because soon the Hindu and Muslim communities decided to follow, each gathering funds to make their own cricket gymkhana grounds.

In those days, it was common for people to come together on the basis of religion. Colonial rulers encouraged each community to see themselves as separate nationalities rather than as part of one nation. That is how the first cricket tournament in India, known as the Quadrangular, featured four teams—the Europeans, the Parsis, the Hindus, and the Muslims. Later, they were joined by a fifth team called the Rest, made up of all the other communities, such as the Christians and Dalits, in what was called Pentagular.

At first, cricketers were mainly from the elite and royalty. In 1886, the Parsi team played a series of matches in England and in 1911, an All-India team toured England. The British did not really consider these teams from their colony as serious competition. They considered themselves unbeatable. After all, they had invented the game!

Soon, things began to change. Against the backdrop of the rapidly spreading independence movement, Indians from all backgrounds began to play the game. Large crowds came out to watch the matches and cheer. As the popularity of the game spread, leaders of the independence movement and commentators questioned the divisive nature of the Pentangular teams. India should be united, they said. India's growing political confidence was now reflected on the cricket pitch.

In December 1926, when the Marylebone Cricket Club from England toured India, they expected to win easily. But they were in for a shock. Playing against the Hindus at the Bombay Gymkhana, they encountered Cottari Kanakaiya Nayudu, or C.K. as he was known, the formidable Quadrangular player of the Hindu team from the state of Nagpur. In front of delirious crowds, the big built batsman annihilated the English team with 153 runs in 116 minutes with eleven sixes and thirteen fours! Each of C.K.'s cracking shots was madly cheered by patriotic crowds. Indian cricket had arrived.

In 1932, C.K. was appointed the captain of the first Indian Test cricket team, leading their tour of England. In his first appearance at Lord's, C.K. used this bat at an All-India vs MCC match, putting in his usual scorching performance with a 118 not out. The team went on to play a historic first official test match against England on the same tour, a turning point for Indian cricket where the Indians were playing England on equal terms for the first time. Throughout the tour, it was as if C.K.'s bat was the voice of the Indian people, indicating to the colonial government that their days were numbered and telling the world that the emerging nation of India was confident and ready to meet them on its own terms. The game of cricket had become a symbol of Indian resolve and unity.

CHARGES OF MURDER AND
WAGING WAR AGAINST KING

92

Azad Hind Fauj

Newspaper cutting dated 6 November 1945, New Delhi

The illustration on the facing page is of a newspaper cutting from 6 November 1945 announcing the first of the 'Red Fort Trials', which began the day before. It was an event that was to mesmerize the nation and send the strongest message to the British colonial government that it was time for them to leave India. The first trial was the military court martial of three former officers of the Indian National Army—Major General Shah Nawaz Khan, Colonel Prem K. Sahgal, and Colonel Gurbaksh S. Dhillon. The charges against them were murder and 'waging war against the king', also known as treason. The tribunal hearing the case consisted of senior British army officers. Appearing on behalf of the defendants was a team of India's most prominent jurists including Tej Bahadur Sapru, K.N. Katju, and Jawaharlal Nehru himself, led by the veteran Congressman and ace counsel, Bhulabhai Desai.

The Indian National Army, or INA, was first formed not in India but in the Malayan peninsula, present-day Malaysia. As World War II raged across much of the world, Japan jumped into the fray in 1941, joining the Axis powers, Germany and Italy. They fought against the Allies which

Newspaper Cutting of the Announcement of the 'Red Fort Trials'

included Britain, France, Russia, and the USA. As part of their overall plan for the Southeast Asian region, Japan decided to support the cause of Indian nationalists fighting for freedom against the British. This decision happened in a rather unusual way.

When the Malayan peninsula and Singapore fell to Japanese control, more than 45,000 Indian soldiers were taken prisoner. Indian nationalists in the region, including the revolutionary leader Rash Behari Bose, urged the prisoners to desert the British and fight for India's independence instead. The Japanese offered to assist this armed force with training, logistics, and equipment. The idea was that while the Japanese advanced into Asia, this army could fight alongside, defeat the British, and gain independence. Local Indian civilians were called upon as well to support the cause. The Indian National Army was formed in mid-1942. It was based in Singapore and commanded by Captain Mohan Singh, an officer of the British Indian Army, himself a former prisoner of war.

However, later the same year, things soured between Captain Mohan Singh and the Japanese Army Command, leading to the disbandment of the first INA. At this time, a nationalist named Subhas Chandra Bose was in Europe trying to get military support for the cause of Indian independence. Although Bose admired and respected Mahatma Gandhi, he did not agree with his belief of a purely non-violent struggle for independence. According to Bose, an armed uprising was the only way to get rid of British colonial rule.

Due to his militant activities, he was imprisoned by the British authorities but managed to escape, making his way to Germany. Then, on Japanese invitation, Bose decided to travel to Tokyo. To escape detection, he travelled underwater for over three months making him possibly India's first submariner! The first leg of his journey, which began in February 1943, was in a German U-boat, a long-range submarine. Midway, he switched vessels, emerging rather dramatically from the innards of a Japanese submarine in Tokyo in June 1943.

On 21 October 1943, he proclaimed a provisional independent government for India in Singapore called Azad Hind, with the INA as its military arm. He called the INA the Azad Hind Fauj, or the Army of Free India. Bose reorganized what remained of the old INA with vigour, training the demoralized soldiers, even recruiting a women's fighting brigade known as the Rani Jhansi Regiment. His aim was for the INA to accompany the Japanese army in their planned military operations into India through the Manipur and Naga hills, defeat the British, and gain independence for India. 'Give me blood, and I will give you freedom!' was his call to the troops.

But soon things began to go wrong. The Japanese were defeated by the Allied forces in Burma. The INA were decimated. When Japan surrendered in 1945, the INA was disbanded. More than 16,000 soldiers were taken prisoner. Bose disappeared and is said to have been killed in an air crash over Taiwan.

Meanwhile, back in India, the British had been running a propaganda campaign. Worried about the activities of the INA and its effect on the morale of the Indian troops under their command, they had censored all news of the INA, painting a picture of the soldiers as a misguided lot, deserters and traitors who had broken their oath of loyalty to the king.

Much to their surprise, the public Red Fort Trials backfired. For the first time, Indians began to hear of the brave deeds of the men and women of the INA. Despite being poorly armed and woefully under supplied, they had been prepared to die for India's freedom. There was a great swell of sympathy. Protests and riots erupted across the country. Nationalist leaders rallied together, demanding the release of the officers.

For the first time since 1857, even the armed forces showed signs of resentment and rebellion, with a major unrest in the Royal Indian Air Force and a full scale naval mutiny in 1946. Eventually, the tribunal was forced to free the three officers. These were all signs that Indian troops could no longer to relied upon to maintain Britain's hold over India. The Red Fort Trials served notice to the British that their days in India were numbered.

93

Dividing a Country

Map appearing in the *Daily Herald* newspaper, England, June 1947 CE

Towards the end of the Second World War, the British finally understood that they would have to leave India for good. The intense pressure of the Indian independence movement combined with the war had taken a toll on the colonial rulers. While plans were afoot for their departure from India, in June 1947, the map in the illustration appeared in the British newspaper *Daily Herald*. Entitled 'How India May Be Split Up', it pointed readers to the various provinces of India and speculated on how they might be divided between two countries named Hindustan and Pakistan. So, while India was preparing for independence, there was also talk of a spilt in the country—a partition!

The suggestion of a partition had come about because, after years of fighting a common foe, the united front of the Indian freedom struggle now stood divided. The Muslim League and the Indian National Congress, the two main parties on the political scene at the time, simply could not agree on sharing power in the new India. While the Congress insisted that they should all live together in a secular nation, the Muslim League believed

HOW INDIA MAY BE SPLIT UP

TO DECIDE BETWEEN HINDUSTAN & PAKISTAN IF PUNJAB DECIDES FOR PARTITION

TO DECIDE ON PARTITION

BRITISH BALUCHISTAN AND SIND TO DECIDE BETWEEN HINDUSTAN AND PAKISTAN

PRINCES' STATES ABOUT 500 IN ALL UNAFFECTED

HINDUSTAN

TO DECIDE HINDUSTAN IF BENGA FOR PA

0   Miles   500

KASHMIR

N.W. FRONTIER PROV. 3,038,000

PUNJAB 28,419,000

BALUCHISTAN

SIND 4,537,000

RAJPUTANA 15,670,000

UNITED PROVINCES 55,021,000

NEPAL

SIKKIM

BHUTAN

ASSAM 10,206,000

SYLH

INDIA

BIHAR 36,340,000

BENGAL 60,314,000

Calcutta

CENTRAL INDIA 7,504,000

BOMBAY 20,850,000

CENTRAL PROVS. 16,822,000

ORISSA 8,729,000

Bombay

HYDERABAD 16,339,000

MADRAS

MYSORE 7,329,000

Madras

Bay of B

AND

NWR

UI

III

the only way Muslims would have justice was within a separate land of their own to be called Pakistan.

As the leaders wrangled and bargained, Hindus and Muslims who had lived in harmony for centuries, sharing common languages, music, food, and culture, began to get restive. Insecure about their future and provoked by inflammatory political speeches, there were outbreaks of communal violence and rioting particularly in the provinces of Bengal and Punjab. The British, afraid that a civil war might break out, started to speed up their exit from India. Based on information given by the Viceroy, Lord Louis Mountbatten, they suddenly declared they wanted to leave by August 1947, a whole year earlier than they had originally planned. In July, British Parliament hurriedly passed the Indian Independence Act declaring India and Pakistan as two independent but separate countries with no defined borders.

A Boundary Commission was appointed to plan the physical separation of Muslim majority provinces from the rest of India. A large number of independent princely states were left to make their own choice. Into this precarious mix in early July 1947 came Sir Cyril Radcliffe, a lawyer from England. A man who had never set foot in India before and, as he admitted, knew nothing about the place, was appointed chairman of the Boundary Commission. His job was to redraw the borders of India, making sure Hindu and Sikh majority areas remained in India and Muslim majority districts formed Pakistan. For this, almost impossible task, he was given just five weeks. The deadline was 15 August 1947.

With no knowledge of the people, no reliable geographical information or updated census figures, working with outdated maps, and guided purely by the directive of religious division, Radcliffe locked himself in a bungalow in Delhi and set to work. As he wielded his pencil across the borders, drawing a dividing line across two ends of a subcontinent, eighty-eight million people waited anxiously for their fate to be decided.

On the afternoon of 16 August 1947, a day after India's independence, Lord Mountbatten revealed the new borders to the leaders of India and Pakistan. The Radcliffe Line, as it came to be called, had carved out a wavy path across the map. The two provinces of Punjab and Bengal were cut roughly in half, with the Punjab line marking out the new country of West Pakistan and the Bengal line defining East Pakistan, which later became Bangladesh.

The news trickled out slowly. Millions of terrified men, women, and children suddenly found themselves cut off from neighbours and family members as the line sliced through ancestral homes, fields, pastures, and villages. Hindus rushed to the Indian side. Muslims went the other way. However, many Muslims decided to stay put in India, and so did many Hindus and Sikhs decide to remain in Pakistan. No one was quite sure where they belonged, triggering the largest forced mass migration in history. Fifteen million people fled their homes on foot, in carts, and on trains, abandoning their land and livestock, carrying whatever little they could.

Desperate, displaced people suddenly found themselves refugees in their own country. Brutality overcame all sides. Hindus, Sikhs, and Muslims attacked and killed each other. Gangs of criminals roamed unfettered, looting, assaulting, kidnapping, and murdering. In the unprecedented violence, more than two million people were killed.

Partition divided assets too. The armed forces, government offices, museums and even libraries shared money and materials, right down to tables, chairs, books, pens, and paper clips. Sports teams were split, and even ancient artefacts, including one famous Harappan necklace that was broken and shared between two museums!

Radcliffe left India the day after he submitted his report, never to return. Back in England, he burnt all his documents and, it is said, refused the payment due to him as chairman of the Boundary Commission.

To this day, the effects of the Radcliffe line echo in the hostility between the two nations, spilling over into four full-fledged wars, insurgencies, and conflicts. A huge cost was inflicted on a nation, based on the winding squiggle of a pencil across a paper map.

94

We, the People

Calligraphed and painted parchment manuscript of the Indian Constitution, New Delhi, 1949 CE

The illustration on the next page is perhaps the most important document in the country. It is a handcrafted, finely calligraphed manuscript that sits in a special, temperature controlled, helium-filled case in the Parliament House Library. Written on the first page are the words of the preamble, or introduction, to the Constitution of India.

A constitution is a set of values of a nation, accepted by all the people who live in it. It describes the powers and limitations of the political organization that runs the country and also, importantly, the rights and duties of its citizens.

In 1946, after a long, hard struggle, freedom from colonial rule was finally at hand. The courageous leaders who had spearheaded the movement were now faced with a new dilemma. What path should the new nation take after independence? What political system should they follow? How should they choose leaders? How should they ensure justice for all citizens?

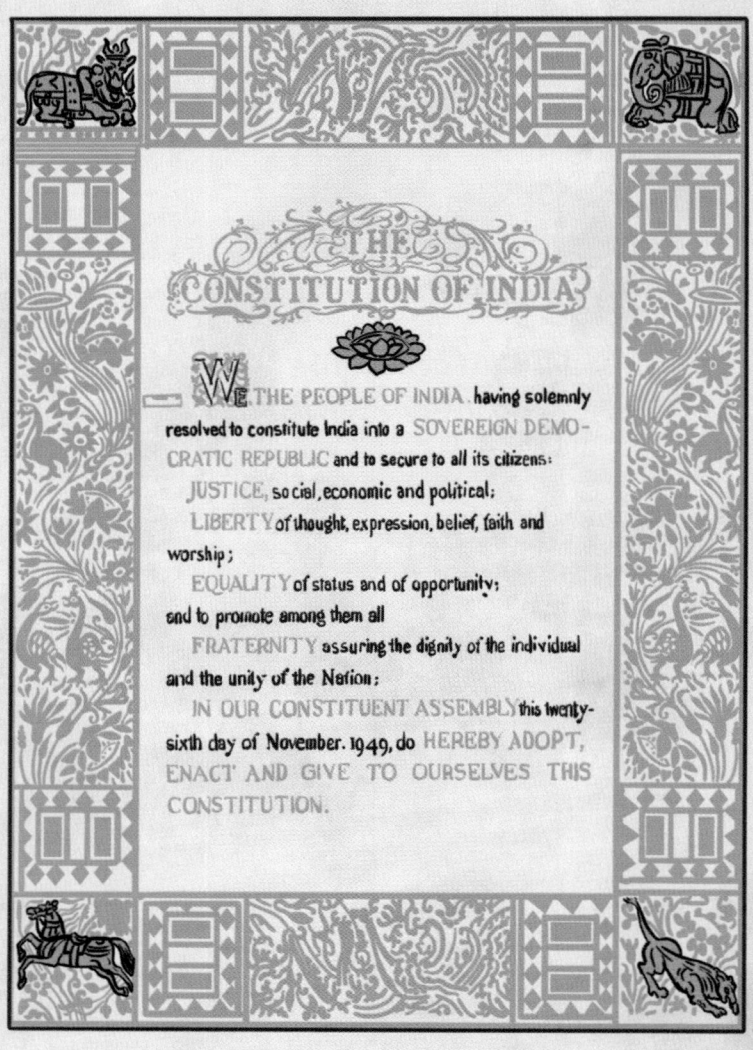

THE CONSTITUTION OF INDIA

WE THE PEOPLE OF INDIA, having solemnly resolved to constitute India into a SOVEREIGN DEMOCRATIC REPUBLIC and to secure to all its citizens:

JUSTICE, social, economic and political;

LIBERTY of thought, expression, belief, faith and worship;

EQUALITY of status and of opportunity; and to promote among them all

FRATERNITY assuring the dignity of the individual and the unity of the Nation;

IN OUR CONSTITUENT ASSEMBLY this twenty-sixth day of November, 1949, do HEREBY ADOPT, ENACT AND GIVE TO OURSELVES THIS CONSTITUTION.

The First Page of the First Hand-Written Constitution of India

In a country as vast and diverse as India, with all its cultural, social, and economic differences, these questions were hard to answer. There had been debates on these issues long before independence, with often sharp differences of opinion among the leaders. But they all agreed that there was a need to make sure that all the different people who lived in India were able to trust each other, that there should be democratically elected governments, and that there should be equal rights and opportunities for all, regardless of caste, creed, or gender.

India needed a constitution.

In July of the same year, 299 eminent members, of which fifteen were women, were elected to form the Constituent Assembly, a body that would be responsible for drafting a constitution for India. These members came from various parts of the country, from different castes, classes, and religions, spoke different languages, and followed varied occupations. They were to work under the guidance of B.R. Ambedkar, an eminent lawyer and economist.

The Assembly worked for three years against the backdrop of tumultuous events. The joy of gaining freedom was muted by the communal violence and massacres during Partition. Millions were refugees in their own country. There was also the challenge of integrating over 500 independent princely states and the upliftment of a largely illiterate and poor population.

The Constituent Assembly spent days in intense discussion and debate on what the Indian Constitution should look like. The constitutions of other countries that had fought for their freedom were carefully studied for inspiration. However, those ideas had to be tailored to fit India's own ideas and unique problems. Members were outspoken in their opinions, often disagreeing vehemently, discussing topics as wide ranging as social security, poverty alleviation, gender equality, and right to employment. But they managed to negotiate their differences. Even the public was drawn in, as they avidly followed newspaper reports on the Assembly debates.

Finally, on 26 November 1949, India had a brand-new Constitution, reflecting the principles and core values of a new nation.

The Constitution proclaimed that India was to be a sovereign, or independent republic with an elected head of state. Leaders were to be elected through a democratic system where every adult man or woman was granted a vote. For the first time, Indians could choose their own leaders. Moreover, the Constitution guaranteed all citizens justice, equality before law regardless of their social class or religion, and freedom of thought and action. There were special provisions to protect the rights of those who had been oppressed throughout history, like the backward classes, tribals, and Dalits. Details were drafted on how to implement these ideas. The framers even left room for later amendments to the Constitution which they felt sure would be needed with changing times.

With twenty-two parts, 395 articles and eight schedules, making a total of 117,369 words, it was the longest written constitution in the world. A skilled calligrapher named Prem Behari Narain Raizada was tasked with writing the original document in beautiful calligraphy on hand-made parchment paper. The 251 pages of the English version were then embellished with delicate artwork executed by a team of artists from Vishwa Bharati, Shantiniketan, supervised by the renowned artist Nandalal Bose. Delicately coloured scenes from Indian history appear on the main pages, ranging from Harappan seals, the lives of Buddha and Mahavira, rulers like Akbar, Shivaji, and Lakshmi Bai, to events from the freedom struggle.

The artist who embellished this first page visited monuments as far away as Sanchi, Ajanta, and Mahabalipuram to find motifs that expressed the spirit of India. The very first words of the preamble, 'We, the People of India . . .' are a message to the citizens of India that the Constitution truly belongs to each one of them.

India adopted the new Constitution on 26 January 1950, which is celebrated as Republic Day.

95

Gold Rush

Olympic gold medal for hockey, London Summer Olympics, 1948 CE

When India won the hockey gold medal at the London Summer Olympics in 1948, it was hardly a surprise. After all, the Indian team had achieved a hat-trick by winning gold at the previous three Summer Olympics in 1928, 1932, and 1936. After a break due to the outbreak of the Second World War, when this medal, the fourth consecutive Olympic gold medal for field hockey, depicted in the illustration, was won in 1948, India was declared the undisputed hockey champion of the world. What made this win in particular resonate with Indians?

Field hockey had been a common man's game in India for well over a century and a half. The game was introduced by the British army as far back as the 1850s, when it became a popular cantonment game. The pace and skills involved suited the Indian physique and, since it required just an open field and rudimentary equipment, it was easy to play anywhere. Soon, hockey clubs were formed in Kolkata, Mumbai, and Punjab and, in 1925, an Indian Hockey Federation was established.

The British Indian Army Hockey Team in New Zealand, 1926

In 1926, a British Indian army hockey team undertook the first tour abroad by any Indian sporting team. It was during this tour of New Zealand that the legend of Indian hockey was born. The team won eighteen of the twenty-one matches played, drawing huge crowds to see their dazzling stick work, lightning-fast movement, and clever field strategy. On the team was Sepoy Dhyan Chand of the 4/1 Punjab Regiment, who scored 100 of the 192 Indian goals on the tour. He was already being described by the foreign press as a 'hockey wizard', a 'magician', and 'possibly the best hockey player the world had ever seen'.

Soon afterwards, Dhyan Chand was selected for the Indian national team. His skills propelled India to three consecutive Olympic golds in Amsterdam 1928, Los Angeles 1932, and, most famously, as captain of the team, in Berlin 1936. In Berlin, the team was playing under the banner of British India. However, their deputy manager had managed

The 1948 Olympic Gold Medal for Hockey

to secretly smuggle in an Indian tricolour. So before each match, the team assembled in the dressing room to salute the flag. They went on to dominate the games, scoring thirty-eight goals in all and conceding only one in the entire tournament!

In the finals, they faced the strong German team who were the favourites to win. Adolf Hitler, Germany's leader, was convinced of the German victory before the match. He was out to prove the superiority of the German state to the world. Much to Hitler's fury, the Indians, playing in cold, soggy conditions, defeated the hosts 8–1 to take the gold. The 1936 Olympic field hockey final became the stuff of legend. Over the years, it accumulated myths around its retelling, including one in which it was said that Hitler grudgingly acknowledged the magical skills of the Indian captain, even offering him a job in the German army!

With this brilliant legacy, the Indian team at the London Summer Olympics 1948, had big shoes to fill. It was a year after independence. The formidable Dhyan Chand had retired. On all previous Olympic outings, the hockey team had played under the banner of the British Star of India flag. This was the first time they marched into a stadium and proudly unfurled the Indian tricolour. Coming out of the tumultuous events of the freedom struggle and the bitterness and trauma of Partition, they were determined not to let their new country down.

The team looked solid, captained by Kishan Lal, with stalwarts like K.D. Singh Babu, Balbir Singh Sr, Keshav Dutt, R.S. Gentle, Leslie Claudius, and Ranganathan Francis forming the core. Not many were aware that this was a team of Olympic debutantes. And that some of their strongest players and colleagues, like Niaz Khan and Aziz Malik, had been separated from them by Partition and were now playing for the new country of Pakistan.

After a series of group matches where they conceded only two goals, they reached the finals. Their opponents were none other than their former colonial masters, the British! Although already considered unbeatable, the Indians had everything to prove. On 12 August 1948, when they took the field at Wembley Stadium, it was filled to capacity with a noisily cheering, partisan home crowd. Focused, skilled, and speedy, playing to a deadly plan, the Indians blanked the British 4–0 to pick up independent India's first Olympic gold. It was a sporting triumph. But also, a message to Britain and to the world that India had arrived on the world stage.

The brilliant centre-forward Balbir Singh Sr scored two goals that day. Later, he described the feeling as the Indian tricolour went up and the 25,000-strong crowd stood to attention. 'As a child, I used to ask my father (freedom fighter, Dalip Singh), what independence meant and what we would get out of it. He'd reply that independence would give us our own identity, flag, and pride forever. I finally understood what he meant.' Indian hockey continued to dominate for three more decades, winning many more Olympic golds for the country.

96

Utterly Butterly

Amul Butter, Anand, Gujarat, 1955 CE

The packet of butter depicted in the illustration will be familiar fare in millions of kitchens across India. Generations of Indians have grown up seeing the little blue-haired Amul girl who advertises this butter. She appears regularly on outdoor billboards and print advertisements wearing her trademark red polka-dotted dress and cheeky smile. She has been the 'utterly butterly' girl for over fifty years, with her topical puns on everything from sports, politics, and films to controversial events, amusing the Indian public with their light-hearted humour.

The history of Amul butter goes back a long way, to pre-independence days. In the Kaira district of Gujarat, dairy farmers were having a hard time selling their milk for a decent price. Middlemen and contractors would pay the farmers poorly and sell it at a high profit in faraway Mumbai. In despair, the poor, mostly illiterate, dairy farmers complained to Sardar Vallabhbhai Patel. On his advice, they set up a co-operative, a business in which they were all equal partners and could jointly bargain for better prices and marketing, refusing to sell unless a fair price was paid to all members.

Under the leadership of Tribhuvandas Patel, a freedom fighter and activist farmer, the Kaira District Co-operative Milk Producers' Union Limited, headquartered at Anand, was established in 1946. Soon, thousands of villages wanted to join the successful co-operative. They produced such large quantities of milk that nine years later, H.M. Dalaya and Verghese Kurien, both dairy technologists, with the assistance of the Gujarat government, opened a processing plant for the Union to make butter and powdered milk out of the excess milk. They chose the brand name, Amul, from the Sanskrit word *amulya*, or precious. It was also an acronym for another name for the Union, Anand Milk Union Limited. It was here that Amul butter was born.

The dairy farmers directly participated in the process of manufacturing and marketing, making profits for themselves, transforming their lives, and turning the remote town of Anand into the milk capital of India.

There was more to come. In 1964, India's then Prime Minister Lal Bahadur Shastri visited Anand. At this time, despite having the largest number of cattle in the world, milk production across the country was still dismally low. India was forced to import most of its dairy needs. Shastri suggested that the rest of the country should follow the Amul model. Thus, a National Dairy Development Board (NDDB) helmed by Verghese Kurien was set up. Operation Flood, as it was called, was put into action in 1970.

Across the country, 1.8 million farmers were put on a vast grid that had direct contact with consumers. The result was that the dairy farmers not only got fair prices for their milk, but they also had a say in all decisions regarding their future. It was called the White Revolution. By the mid-1990s, over ten million rural families had joined the movement, including more than a million women. India stopped importing milk, instead becoming, the largest producer of milk and milk products in the world.

Something similar took place in the field of agriculture. Post-independence, the food situation in India looked grim. A disorganized farming sector, the use of outdated techniques, and natural disasters like floods and drought meant that large sections of the population were looking at impending famine. At this time, India imported up to ten million tonnes of wheat per year from the United States of America, projecting the image of a poor country that could not be truly independent. In 1965, it was said that India had just two weeks' worth of grain left in storage before emergency foreign aid was sent in. A drastic, long-term solution was needed.

M.S. Swaminathan, an agricultural scientist, had an idea. He identified a hybrid, high-yielding, disease- and pest-resistant wheat plant developed by American agronomist Norman Borlaug as ideal for India. Many were doubtful about this idea. However, Swaminathan convinced the agriculture minister at the time to grow the wheat on the lawns of his residence in Delhi! The successful output stunned everyone. Borlaug was invited to India. After a study of Indian farms, he suggested certain hybrid varieties of wheat seeds for the best results.

Eventually, these were planted in fields across Punjab, Haryana, and Uttar Pradesh, and high-yielding rice varieties were planted in Andhra Pradesh. Along with modern methods of irrigation, pest control, fertilizers, and mechanized tools, yields almost quadrupled in a few short years! A green revolution was under way. By 1971, India had produced an incredible 104 million tonnes of grain, turning it into a food surplus country. Imports were immediately stopped. Although recent research has found that the environmental impact of these new techniques has been damaging, at the time, the Green Revolution saved millions from starvation.

The 'utterly butterly girl' was born in 1966, created by Slyvester da Cunha, the head of an advertising agency tasked by Amul to create their marketing campaign.

Amul butter is now sold with the tag line, 'The Taste of India', nudging the country into thinking about food security. It is a reminder of the collective hard work of scientists, farmers, and leaders who worked with a will to change a poor, struggling country into a self-sufficient nation with economic freedom.

97

Timekeeper to the Nation

HMT Janata watch, Bangalore, Karnataka, 1963 CE

In the early 1960s, the HMT Janata appeared in the Indian market with a hand-wound, mechanical watch, made with cutting-edge design and technology of the time. It was made entirely in India, just over a decade after independence. This was an amazing feat!

It is well known that years of colonial rule had left India with virtually nothing after independence. There were problems of poverty, hunger, unemployment, a lack of housing and education, and a total lack of manufacturing industries. How, then, had India produced such a watch?

Long before independence, leaders like Jawaharlal Nehru and Sardar Patel had envisioned a modern, self-reliant India with its own industries backed by strong research and development. Once the euphoria of freedom was over, it was time to get down to the hard work of building a new nation. With the help of brilliant scientists like Homi J. Bhabha, M. Visvesvaraya, P.C. Mahalanobis, and Vikram Sarabhai, India began to take small steps in this direction.

A Planning Commission was set up to design suitable plans for the country's economic future. Development was split between the government and private companies, with heavy industries and infrastructure like dams, steel plants, and industrial machinery under government control and other, 'lighter' manufacturing plants to be run by private companies. This was called a mixed economy. These industries, along with scientific institutes, were meant to jumpstart the industrial progress of the country. Nehru called them the 'Temples of Modern India'. In 1953, Hindustan Machine Tools, or HMT as it came to be known, was set up to produce 'mother machines', that is, machines that would fabricate metal parts for a wide range of machinery, from tractors to aircraft.

Not long afterwards, it was noticed that there was a growing demand for watches in the country. So far, watches had been imported from Switzerland and sold at rather high prices in India. To meet the need of the common person for an inexpensive watch, HMT was asked to come up with ideas. Now confident of their manufacturing processes, HMT collaborated with Citizen, the well-known Japanese watch manufacturer. A factory was set up in Bangalore, and the first design, called the Janata (meaning the 'public' in Hindi), emerged in 1963. The stylish, reliable, and affordable watches met with an overwhelming response.

With names like Sona, Rajat, Vijay, Rohit, Sujata, and Rakhee, HMT watches immediately endeared themselves to the Indian public. From politicians to students, everyone wanted one. Ladies liked the delicate-looking Sujata. The Jawan and Pilot had a more rugged association and were often worn by their namesakes. Doctors and nurses wore them, and there was even a braille watch for the visually impaired. Indira Gandhi was often seen sporting a favourite Janata watch.

Soon, the demand was so high that there were queues outside HMT outlets, and it was rumoured that a recommendation letter from someone in authority would help you skip the wait list! It was even said that people would plan wedding dates based on the availability of the gold-plated Kanchan model, an essential gift to the groom! Companies ordered special watches in bulk with their logos on them. Retired employees and graduating students received them as special rewards. They became family heirlooms, passed down from one generation to another. By the 1970s, almost everyone had an HMT story.

New factories opened in Kashmir and present-day Uttarakhand to meet the growing demand. A combination of state-of-the-art technology, appealing design, and a good servicing network meant HMT watches were wildly successful. Employees of the company took pride in their modern manufacturing process and work ethic. HMT watches soon came to be known as 'timekeepers to the nation'.

After selling nearly 100 million watches in five decades and becoming one of the world's biggest watch manufacturers, time finally caught up with HMT watches. In the late 1980s, the introduction of quartz watches and later, liberalization of the market that allowed the import of parts to competitors, sounded a warning to HMT. However, it was a warning that they did not heed. Unable to keep up with competitors and new demands in the market, HMT went into decline. Losses piled up until finally, the last

Two Models of the HMT Janata Watch

factory was shut down in 2014. It was the end of an era, but not the end of the HMT watch story.

Collectors have since revived interest bringing back the demand for HMT watches. They scour the antique markets and websites, hoping to acquire one of the iconic pieces. Many collectors see them as symbols of the vision and hard work of our early leaders, engineers, and scientists, and of the spirit of a young nation determined to be modern and self-reliant.

98

Votes for All

Steel boxes manufactured by Godrej and Boyce, Mumbai, Maharashtra, 1951 CE

Sometime in the middle of 1951, the Godrej & Boyce Manufacturing Company, known for its production of high-quality metal safes, cupboards, cabinets, and locks, was given an urgent order by the Government of India. The new republic was bound for the polls in October of that year. For the first time, the people of India were going to vote for their own leaders. The government needed specially designed, secure and tamper-proof ballot boxes.

An estimated two million ballot boxes were needed for the whole country of which Godrej was ordered to produce more than one million of them. And they had just four months in which to do so! It was a daunting task. There was a steel shortage in the country and not enough money in the state coffers to import the required amount for this project. Also, the company could not afford to allow their normal manufacturing work to slacken during this time.

The employees of Godrej, however, rose to the occasion. Working in three shifts, many doing overtime that extended beyond midnight, they worked at an unbelievable rate of almost 15,000 boxes per day. They met the production deadline with a total of 1.28 million steel ballot boxes, like the one in the illustration. They managed to keep costs low at Rs 5 per box. When it appeared that adding an external lock for security would increase the cost substantially, a worker came forward with a clever internal locking device that was incorporated into the lid of the box itself. From their workshops at Vikhroli, a suburb of Mumbai, the boxes were loaded on to waiting trains called 'election specials' to be sent out across the country.

Meanwhile, the colossal task of conducting India's first elections got under way under the guidance of the first election commissioner, Sukumar Sen, who was a highly qualified member of the Indian Civil Service. The newly minted Constitution of India had guaranteed universal adult franchise. This meant that every man and woman over the age of twenty-one, regardless of caste, religion, educational, or economic status, was eligible to vote. Later in 1989, the voting age was lowered to eighteen. Universal franchise was a progressive step since in most democracies across the world, including in the West, women, the uneducated, and minorities had been allowed the vote only many years after the introduction of elections.

The election commissioner was faced with multiple challenges. The first and most important one was to prepare a list of voters or electoral rolls. In a painstaking countrywide household-to-household operation, eligible voters were identified and registered. Nothing on this scale had ever been attempted before. It finally emerged that of the population of 360 million, 170 million were eligible to vote.

There was another major problem. More than 85 per cent of these eligible voters were illiterate. How would they read the names of the candidates or the party they wished to vote for? It was decided that each political party would be represented by a symbol. The symbols were taken from everyday life, such as a lamp, a banyan tree, a lion, a rising

sun. The Congress Party was represented by two yoked bullocks and the Scheduled Caste Federation by an elephant, while the Kisan Mazdoor Praja Party had a hut. To avoid further confusion for the voters, each party had its own ballot box labelled with the party symbol. This way, the voter simply had to put their ballot paper in the right box.

There was also the matter of the logistics of this enormous operation. Ballot paper had to be printed. A special indelible ink to mark a voter's status was devised in a factory in Mysore. Over 200,000 polling booths had to be established and manned in even the remotest corners of the country. Often, these were hard-to-access places in the hills or on islands where government officials had seldom visited. In many places, bridges had to be built or staff had to carry the ballot boxes across on boats or on camelback.

Since this was the first voting experience for the public, there was a stream of radio and newsreel broadcasts, educating them on how to go about exercising their democratic rights. Women had been included in the voting list. However, in many areas, conservative women were reluctant to disclose their names. They merely described their status, such as 'so-and-so's wife' or 'so-and-so's mother'! This caused a huge problem and led to more than two million women being struck off the rolls. Although it caused a huge uproar at the time, it eventually led to further empowerment for women, as more of them registered in their own names in the next elections.

In the final counting, 45 per cent of registered voters turned out to vote. As expected, the Congress Party won the elections with a good margin.

The steel Godrej ballot boxes were used in elections until well into the 1960s. Today, electronic voting machines (EVMs) have replaced steel boxes. But the elections in the world's largest democracy is still based on the processes put in place when India voted for the very first time.

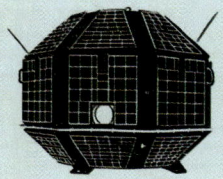

99

Launching into Outer Space

Satellite, Bangalore, Karnataka, 1975 CE

On 19 April 1975, this large polyhedron object that you see illustrated on the next page, was launched into space from the Kapustin Yar rocket launch complex, not far from the city of Volgograd, present-day Russia. The object was a 358 kilogram, blue and violet satellite, powered by the solar cells covering twenty-four of its twenty-six faces.

Curiously, it was called Aryabhata, after the famed fifth century CE Indian astronomer and mathematician. Why did it have an Indian name?

Aryabhata had been entirely developed and built in faraway India! Due to a space co-operation agreement between India and erstwhile Soviet Union, it was launched from the Soviet Union by a Russian Kosmos-3M rocket. Within minutes of its launch, the satellite started orbiting the Earth at a height of 600 kilometres, monitored closely by ground tracking stations near Moscow, Sriharikota, and Bangalore.

India's 'laboratory in space' was designed to operate for six months, sending information on outer space, the Sun, and the Earth's atmosphere. The launch of Aryabhata was a momentous event, making India the world's eleventh nation and only the second developing country after China to orbit a satellite of its own. A feat that astonished the world as India was a country recently freed from colonial rule and still struggling with challenges such as poverty, hunger, illiteracy, and a lack of resources.

It all began in 1957. Inspired by the launch of Soviet Union's Sputnik-1, the first man-made object in space, a young, dynamic physicist and astronomer named Vikram Sarabhai convinced the government of the day, led by Jawaharlal Nehru, of the importance of a space programme for India. To those who asked why India should waste precious resources on space research when people did not have enough to eat, Sarabhai had this to say:

'There are some who question the relevance of space activities in a developing nation. To us, there is no ambiguity of purpose . . . if we are

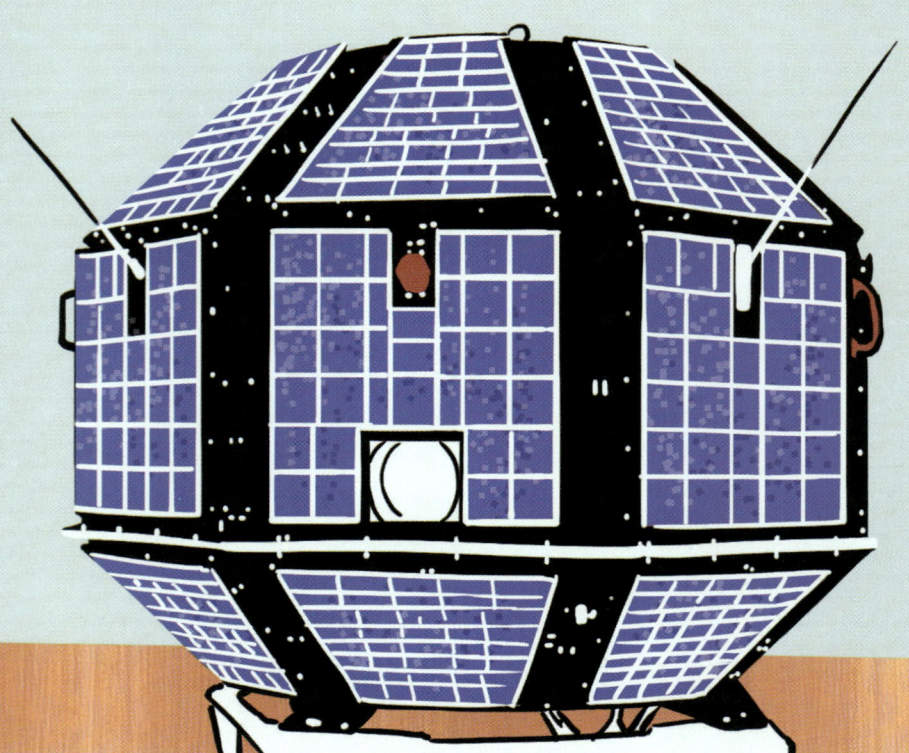

The Aryabhata Satellite

to play a meaningful role nationally, and in the community of nations, we must be second to none in the application of advanced technologies to the real problems of man and society.'

What Sarabhai had in mind was the application of modern satellite technology to predict weather patterns, flood warnings, communications, and the use of satellite television in remote rural areas to inform and educate people on subjects such as schooling, modern farming and health practices.

In 1962, the government set up the Indian National Committee for Space Research under the Department of Atomic Energy helmed by another legend in the scientific world and the father of the Indian nuclear programme, Homi J. Bhabha. In 1963, a team of young, NASA-trained scientists, working under basic conditions in the premises of an old church in the village of Thumba near present-day Thiruvananthapuram, Kerala, launched India's first sounding rocket. The rocket was intended to probe space to collect data and conduct tests on the atmospheric conditions during a short flight. It was the first of many such rockets and the launch of India's space programme.

In the early 1970s, Sarabhai, as head of what is now called Indian Space Research Organization, or ISRO, directed a team of scientists to develop satellites for India. That is how the scientist U.R. Rao and his team came to be building a satellite under four tin sheds in a dusty industrial zone outside the city of Bangalore. Many of them young scientists had never seen a satellite.

They built from scratch, working from outdated books and research papers since import of scientific information was restricted in those days. With their dedication and superb problem-solving skills, Aryabhata was built and ready for launch in record time. Five days into orbit, a failure of the satellite's electrical system meant the scientific instruments had to be switched off. But the scientists were not too disappointed because, by then, useful information had already been collected.

Since the Aryabhata, India has gone on to launch hundreds of indigenous satellites with its own launch capacity. In fact, now India even launches satellites for other countries. The satellites have yielded vital information to India's planners on everything from predicting crop pestilence, snow melt volumes, deforestation, and city planning. They have established television communications across the country even in the remotest regions, ushering in long-distance education and telemedicine, boosting ocean studies, monitoring weather patterns, and helping with rapid disaster response.

Today, ISRO is an icon and the work of India's space scientists has the respect of the world's scientific community. There is a slew of upcoming programmes including missions to probe the moon and Mars, study the Sun and send Indian astronauts into space. The vision of India's pioneering scientists has led to a self-reliance and confidence that Indians are capable of conceiving and producing cutting-edge technology in the field of space research.

100

The Talking Revolution

Nokia 2110 handsets, Kolkata, West Bengal, 1995 CE

On 31 July 1995, when the chief minister of West Bengal, Jyoti Basu, picked up a phone and called the union minister for communications and information technology, Sukh Ram, they made history. The call, made from present-day Kolkata's Writers' Building to Sanchar Bhawan in Delhi, was India's first mobile phone conversation. They used Nokia 2110 handsets, one of the earliest mobile phone models from the Finnish company. The call was carried over the recently inaugurated MobileNet network.

Soon after the call, mobile phone services were launched in India. Initially things moved slowly because handsets were expensive, costing the equivalent of Rs 200,000 each in today's money! This was way beyond the budget of most people. And the call rates were high, starting at Rs 8.4 per minute and going up to Rs 16.8 per minute during peak times.

Today, thanks to major changes in telecom policy and technology, there are more than 1.2 billion mobile connections in India, making it one of the fastest growing mobile markets in the world. Most Indians today probably could not imagine life without a phone! But this was not always the case.

India has come a long way since the introduction of the first telephone service in 1881 when the British Indian government granted a licence to the Oriental Telephone Company of England to set up telephone exchanges at Calcutta, Bombay, Madras, and Ahmedabad. The utility of these were essentially for the purpose of governing the country. Apart from important officials and certain strategic offices, very few people were allowed to have telephones.

At the time of independence, there were only 84,000 phones in a country with 350 million people. As late as the 1980s, things did not change much as telecommunications remained a government monopoly. A private landline telephone was considered a luxury, with waiting lists that went on for years. Some even used influence from higher authorities to speed the process along. For those whose patience was finally rewarded, the bulky Bakelite telephone with a rotary dial would usually occupy a place of honour in the house. Often the fortunate owners would magnanimously share the privilege of making calls with the entire building or neighbourhood. Manually operated switch connections meant that for an outstation call, merely dialling a number was not enough. It required booking a 'trunk' call with an operator, a process that could take hours or sometimes days.

In the early 1990s, the scenario began to change rapidly. With the liberalization of the Indian economy, there was a growing realization that telecommunications lay at the heart of progress. Information technology was given a strong push and communicated through a network of various devices including computers, televisions, satellites, and radios. Telephones were key to facilitating this outreach.

There was a focus on developing indigenous electronics with digital telephone exchanges suited to Indian conditions to take the place of expensive and often outdated foreign imports. Digital telecommunications spread to every corner of the country. A decade later, there were more than twenty-five million telephone lines covering 300 cities, over 4500 towns and, most importantly, over 300,000 villages. In an inspired innovation, phones with meters were installed in public call offices or PCOs with distinctive yellow signages. Often these were just tables on street corners or inside small grocery or tea shops where the public could walk in and pay in cash for a quick call.

By the turn of the century, over 600,000 PCOs had come up all over India including in the most remote areas. The social and economic benefits were unprecedented, particularly in rural areas. Rapid communication meant that information and knowledge spread quickly.

Soon afterwards, with improved network connectivity and drastically reduced taxes and tariffs, cheaper mobile phones entered the market. They were no longer seen as a luxury. Cheaper phones and inexpensive calls meant that the common people now had access to targeted information, data, business opportunities, education, healthcare, mobile payments, and banking.

The changes it brought were dramatic. News of community ceremonies and functions like marriages and funerals which would have earlier taken weeks to broadcast, were now easily announced, even to distant relatives, through a phone call. Emergency medical services were on call. Farmers could order fodder and fertilizers at competitive prices. Fishermen could check rates in neighbouring towns to better sell their catch. Daily wage earners could seek employment in distant places and small businesses could order supplies with ease.

Information technology through mobile phones enhanced business, generated employment, and improved the standard of living. They revolutionized the social, economic, and political landscape of India. By allowing even the most underprivileged users access to information, they enabled them to make their own choices, empowering them and driving forward both the economy and democracy.

❧ Select Bibliography ❧

Behl, Benoy K. *The Art of India: Sculpture and Mural Painting (Ancient and Medieval Period) Vol. 1 and 2*. Chennai: THG Publishing Private Limited, 2019.

Dalrymple, William. *The Anarchy: The Relentless Rise of the East India Company*. London: Bloomsbury Publishing, 2019.

Dalrymple, William and Anita Anand. *Kohinoor: The Story of the World's Most Infamous Diamond*. New Delhi: Juggernaut, 2016

Habib, Irfan. *Prehistory*. New Delhi: Tulika Books, 2004.

Habib, Irfan and Vivekanand Jha. *Mauryan India*. New Delhi: Tulika Books, 2004.

Keay, John. *The Great Arc: The Dramatic Tale of How India Was Mapped and Everest Was Named*. London: HarperCollins Publishers, 2001.

Lahiri, Nayanjot. *Ashoka in Ancient India*. Ranikhet: Permanent Black, 2015.

Liddle, Swapna. *Chandni Chowk: The Mughal City of Old Delhi*. New Delhi: Speaking Tiger Publishing Private Limited, 2017.

Peck, Lucy. *Delhi: A Thousand Years of Building*. New Delhi: Roli Books, 2005.

Sastri, K.A. Nilakanta. *The Illustrated History of South India: From Prehistoric Times to the Fall of Vijayanagar*. New Delhi: Oxford University Press, 2009.

Singh, Upinder. *A History of Ancient and Early Medieval India: From the Stone Age to the Twelfth Century*. New Delhi: Pearson Longman, 2008.

Sivaramamurti, C. *South Indian Bronzes*. New Delhi: Lalit Kala Akademi, 2006.

Thapar, Romila. *The Penguin History of Early India: From the Origins to AD 1300*. New Delhi: Penguin Books India, 2002.

❧ See What You Can See! ❧

Check out some awesome objects from history for yourself when you visit these museums around the country:

- National Museum, New Delhi
- Indian Museum, Kolkata
- Government Museum, Chennai
- Chhatrapati Shivaji Maharaj Vastu Sangrahalaya, Mumbai
- Bhau Daji Lad Museum, Mumbai
- The Partition Museum, Amritsar and New Delhi
- The Calico Museum, Ahmedabad
- The Museum of Art and Photography, Bengaluru
- Salar Jung Museum, Hyderabad
- Maharaja Sawai Man Singh II Museum, Jaipur
- Patna Museum, Patna
- Indira Gandhi Rashtriya Manav Sangrahalaya, Bhopal

And if you can't travel to the museums, never fear. There are online collections of very cool objects to be viewed on these websites:

- Sarmaya: The Museum without Boundaries (https://sarmaya.in)
- MAP Academy Encyclopaedia of Art (https://mapacademy.io)
- The British Museum (https://www.britishmuseum.org/)
- Victoria and Albert Museum (https://www.vam.ac.uk/)
- The Metropolitan Museum of Art (https://www.metmuseum.org/)

❧ Acknowledgements ❧

The sheer diversity and wealth of Indian history meant choosing a hundred objects was a formidable task, entailing tonnes of research and one very sleep deprived author!

This book is a labour of love for which I owe gratitude to many.

To my editor, Sohini Mitra, for her vision in choosing to undertake the project and her constant support throughout the process. To the very talented and hardworking team at Puffin, editors Sushmita Chatterjee and Yasmin Rahman, and designer Isha Nagar for their creativity in condensing complex material and creating a structure and design for the book.

To Priyanka Tampi for bringing the words to life with her wonderfully imaginative illustrations.

To Dr Swapna Liddle for very graciously taking the time to read the final drafts and sharing generous advice and valuable insights.

To my family, Chit, Vallari, and Chengis, for their constant and unstinting support.

And finally, to scholars, museologists, and archivists across India who continue the arduous, complex task of preserving our history for the benefit of future generations.

Scan QR code to access the
Penguin Random House India website